Anarchism

The term anarchism derives from the Greek word άναρχία meaning 'without ruler or leader, and without law'. Although the roots of the word can be traced back to Ancient Greece, anarchism as a political ideology is relatively new. Anarchism developed as a political ideology at the end of the eighteenth century at the time of the emergence of the modern State. And, as is well known, anarchism developed both a politics and a way of life that did not include the State as its compass, support and structure.

In contrast to the extensive contemporary literature about anarchist politics and ideas, this book focuses on the practices and attitudes that constitute what the author refers to as an anarchist 'art of life'. The book draws on archival material that records the life and actions of the anarchist Emma Goldman and her associates, legal documents and writings by classical (Pierre Joseph Proudhon, Peter Krotopkin) and contemporary anarchists (David Graeber, Saul Newman, Ciarra Bottici), as well as contemporary groups such as the Clandestine Insurgent Rebel Clown Army and Occupy Wall Street. By studying the idiosyncrasies of this art of life, it argues, we are better able to appreciate how anarchism is not some future utopian oriented project, waiting to come into existence after a revolution, but rather exists in parallel to the life and politics offered by the State.

Anarchism: An Art of Living Without Law will be of interest to graduate students and academics working on critical legal theory, political theory, sociology and cultural studies.

Elena Loizidou is Reader in Law and Political Theory at the School of Law, Birkbeck, University of London.

Anarchism

An Art of Living Without Law

Elena Loizidou

a GlassHouse Book

First published 2023
by Routledge
4 Park Square, Milton Park, Abingdon, Oxon OX14 4RN

and by Routledge
605 Third Avenue, New York, NY 10158

A GlassHouse book

Routledge is an imprint of the Taylor & Francis Group, an informa business

© 2023 Elena Loizidou

The right of Elena Loizidou to be identified as author of this work has been asserted in accordance with sections 77 and 78 of the Copyright, Designs and Patents Act 1988.

All rights reserved. No part of this book may be reprinted or reproduced or utilised in any form or by any electronic, mechanical, or other means, now known or hereafter invented, including photocopying and recording, or in any information storage or retrieval system, without permission in writing from the publishers.

Trademark notice: Product or corporate names may be trademarks or registered trademarks, and are used only for identification and explanation without intent to infringe.

British Library Cataloguing-in-Publication Data
A catalogue record for this book is available from the British Library

Library of Congress Cataloging-in-Publication Data
A catalog record has been requested for this book

ISBN: 978-1-138-59300-8 (hbk)
ISBN: 978-1-032-32609-2 (pbk)
ISBN: 978-0-429-95269-2 (ebk)

DOI: 10.4324/9780429952692

Typeset in Bembo
by Taylor & Francis Books

In memory of my brother Christos Loizides, who left far too young. Missing you and your laughter all the time.

Contents

Acknowledgements ix

1 Introduction 1

The violence of foundations and the creative force of anarchism 2
Art of living 14

2 Without law? 19

Introduction 19
Law as an aid to anarchism 25
Without law: hurtful, useless, wooden law 33
Why law? Contemporary anarchist thinkers and law 44

3 Disentangling the psyche: from disobedience to *parrhesia* 53

Obedience, embodied habits and psychic entanglements 55
Disobedience and its limits 61
Parrhesia as a way of life 74
Parrhesia, an anarchist techne of living 77

4 Anarchism and love 87

Figure One: love in a fragment 92
Figure Two: law and love 95
Figure Three: love and anarchism 100
Conclusion 111

5 Humour and the uncommon of laughter 113

Humour, wit, comedy, laughter 122

Exodus and jokes 135
The wit not to will 139

6   Mutual aid instead of conclusion   148

Why doesn't mutual aid work? 150
Mutual aid revisited 160

Bibliography   170
Index   182

Acknowledgements

'Go down to the Bluestockings Cooperative bookshop. You may find something that enables you to think about violence, Emma Goldman perhaps?', said my dear friend Marike van Harskamp when I was on sabbatical in New York, undertaking research on political violence. I am of course paraphrasing Marike's suggestion; it's been a while, and my memory is faltering. The direction to this gem of a bookshop, the only bookshop in New York that is run by a queer, trans and sex worker community, began the journey to this book. I recall buying three items on my first visit: Emma Goldman's two-volume biography, *Living My Life*, and a pamphlet about a Black Panther project in New Orleans. All three have been steady companions through this journey. My research on violence turned into research on Anarchism, the only way of life and politics I have encountered so far that comes close to challenging the violence unleashed by capitalism, neoliberalism and beliefs in Sovereign authority. So, first my gratitude goes to Marike van Harskamp who suggested Bluestockings and Emma Goldman to me. Thank you, Marike, for this and your friendship through the long process of writing this book and all the personal difficulties this period has thrown at me. I also would like to extent my gratitude to Emma Goldman. Her words, her feisty spirit and her perception of the world has been an inspiration. When the chips were down, Goldman's voice kept lifting me up. Whilst this is not a book about, or just about, Emma Goldman, I think it is Goldman's and Peter Kropotkin's anarchism that is re-lived and re-imagined in *Anarchism: An Art of Living Without Law*.

My gratitude to friends for encouraging me to finish this book: Brenna Bhandar, Chrysanthi Nigianni, Marinos Diamantides, Peter Goodrich, Les Moran, Maria Aristodemou, Piyel Haldar, Leticia Sabsay, James Martel, Andreas Philippopoulos-Mihalopoulos, Julia Chryssostalis, Fiona Macmillan, Sappho Xenakis, Evi Michalaki, Marty Slaughter, Morris Kaplan and Jean Morris. Thank you also to the anonymous referees that provided insightful comments and the School of Law, Birkbeck College, for financially supporting the proofreading of the book. Thank you also to Carrie Hamilton for her impeccable proofing.

My immense gratitude goes to Lina Dzuverovic, whose care and support and insightful comments at the last stages of the book, as well as her humorous reservations about anarchism, contributed to the completion of this book. Thank you, Lina.

Chapter 1

Introduction

In a *New York Times* article 30 years ago, the cultural critic Anna Kisselgoff described the late modern dancer and choreographer Merce Cunningham as an anarchist (1992). I was positively surprised to see anarchism associated with the art of dancing, with creativity, and not as a type of politics associated with violence and destruction. Of course, anybody who either identifies with or writes/researches anarchism knows that anarchism is mostly a creative rather than a destructive political theory and practice. The question of the use of violence to either propagate anarchism or make visible the wretched grip of capitalism has always been a very important point of discussion within anarchism. For example, in her essay 'The Psychology of Political Violence' (Goldman, 1969c:79–108), the late-nineteenth-century anarchist Emma Goldman concludes that because anarchists value life above everything, they may resort to violence occasionally, as the social and economic conditions that engulf them become unbearable (107–8). Despite (the existence of) a rich history of reflections within anarchism on the question of violence and politics, anarchist thinkers and activists have to constantly reiterate anarchism's position on violence. In her wonderful book *The Government of No One* (2019), Ruth Kinna had to remind us at the very start of the book that anarchists are usually wrongly conceived as instigators of violence and destruction (1–2). She went on to debunk this idea by succinctly explaining that this 'cultural stereotyp[ing] of the anarchist … conceal[s] a history of critique and resistance' (2). In other words, the use of violence by anarchists – for example, the destruction and defacing of property belonging to oppressive institutions (banks, police stations, police vehicles) during anti-G8 gatherings are actions of *resistance* against capitalism and authority as well as a *critique*.

After all, *anarchy*, as the etymology of the word suggests, calls for a society without hierarchies (e.g., leaders), authority (e.g., law) and capitalism (e.g., private property). The destruction of property or use of violence against authority as a form of critique exposes the legitimacy of hierarchies, authority and capitalism as unfounded. All those familiar with French critical thought of the 1980s will be well aware that Derrida (1992) and Foucault (2003:81–107), amongst others, pointed through critique to the mythical foundation of authority. Kinna is doing

DOI: 10.4324/9780429952692-1

nothing but pointing out that anarchist acts of resistance and use of violence become the means by which the illegitimacy or myth of authority, foundations, etc. is exposed. Whilst it is important to be aware of the conditions that propel anarchists to use violence, as well as the critical theoretical effects of those same conditions, I will not engage with these issues in this book. I am interested, rather, in the creative or life-affirming aspect of anarchism. Whilst Kinna, for example, offers a good explanation of why violence, or destruction, is used by anarchists, she unfortunately conceals the creative aspect of anarchism that, as I noted at the start, Kisselgoff points to when she describes Merce Cunningham's choreographies as anarchic. Kinna, it could be said, provides us with a somewhat partial picture of anarchism. By choosing to explain anarchism's use of violence or destruction, she also offers us a defensive image of anarchism, one that can only be constituted by what it is not (violence) and not what it is (a creative force and an art of living).

Anarchism: An Art of Living without Law focuses instead on the *creative* aspect of anarchism. Moreover, as I explain in the forthcoming section, I will go as far as arguing that there is no destructive or violent aspect in anarchism. Anarchy, as any etymological dictionary will tell us, derives from the Greek word ἀναρχία, which means 'being leaderless'. Anarchism, in turn, refers to the principles and practice that bring to the fore a society that governs itself *without* relying on the State, *without* law, *without* authority and hierarchies, *without* exploitation and *with* mutual assistance. *Anarchism: An Art of Living without Law* aims simply to tell the story of what it takes to *build* a world that is not held together by the State, by the institution of law and order, by hierarchies and masters.

The following sections are devoted to disentangling anarchism from the stigma of violence and destruction, and revealing it as both an *art of living* and as a creative force.

The violence of foundations and the creative force of anarchism

How do we begin, then, to understand anarchism as an art of living, as creative rather than destructive? Moreover, how can we persuade anarchist thinkers such as Ruth Kinna to turn away from offering a defence of the use of violence by anarchists? We can do so by focusing on the creative aspect of anarchism, and the late philosopher Reiner Schürmann can assist us in spelling out anarchism's creative verve.

In *Heidegger on Being and Acting: From Principles to Anarchy* (1990) Schürmann explores Heidegger's move from *being* to *acting* in the world. I will not engage here fully with the thesis of the book but rather focus my attention on a particular aspect of it that enables us to understand *destruction* as a *creative* force. How can this be possible? As Schürmann explains, for Heidegger any form of thinking and action that has reason at its foundation, that, in other words, explains the world through the faculty of reason, is mythical. This is, however, not the end of Schürmann's thoughtful analysis. To say that reason is not the foundation of everything does not amount to much. We can contest it or agree with it. What is more prescient is to try and understand what happens if we stick with this mythical premise. What are its effects? According to Schürmann, by sticking with the premise that reason is the foundation of everything, we *obstruct* anything *new* from emerging into the world. Whilst Schürmann is not writing explicitly about anarchism, I would like to suggest that his interpretation of Heidegger – and ultimately his critique of foundations, specifically that 'the' idea of reason is the mythical foundation in philosophy – translates easily to anarchist political theory/practice and enables us to see anarchism as an art of living embedded with a creative force.

Schürmann writes, then, that for Heidegger the very idea that our thinking and action are founded upon reason is an *assault*. It is an assault because it stops *newness* emerging in the world. Forgive the circular explanation that will ensue, but it becomes necessary to understand Schürmann's thinking. What he is proposing is simple: anything (obstructions) that stops newness from emerging in the world becomes an assault. These obstructions, Schürmann advises, come in a lot of guises 'speech, grammar, logic and metaphysics …' (275) and have reason as their *arche*. Take grammar, for example. Grammar refers to a set of rules that guide the use of language in a standardised way to enable communication, especially in written form. These rules, the arche of grammar, consequently have reason as their arche. If we follow Schürmann, we can say that grammar rules, as long as they have reason as their arche, sometimes obstruct new ways of communicating, ways that undoubtedly emerge through years of usage to become recognised as new standardised ways of communicating. While, for example, emoticons are used widely in text messages and on social media platforms, they have not been recognised by the rules of grammar. I am not suggesting that they either should or should not be recognised; but their sheer global popularity as a way of transmitting a message, forming a sentence, tells us that a new norm in communication is emerging. Grammar rules *obstruct*, if we continue with the emoticon example, emoticons, stopping them from becoming part of standardised grammar. The rules obstruct newness. So, as Schürmann writes, '[t]he practical task for our age: [is] to remove everything that tends to place itself in front of the emergence of things into the world' (275). Therefore, removal – as the opposite of holding onto reason or any other foundational claim – is *not* violence as it takes away all that stops things from becoming or emerging in the world.

Consequently, we may ask: If the removal of objects that are obstructing newness from entering in the world is neither violence nor destruction, what might it be? How can we speak of acts that remove foundations, grammar, law, the State if we do not resort to describing such acts as being violent? Anarchism, after all, as a theory and practice, is intimately engaged in the removal of foundations, and it is this very act of removing foundations that earns it its badge of violence.

I would like to suggest that we can recognise such acts, i.e., acts of removing foundations (obstructions), as creative or δημιουργία. If an act allows something new to emerge, it means, by definition, that is not destructive but rather creative. The Greek word for creative is δημιουργία, and understanding this is helpful. Δημιουργία is a derivative of the Ancient Greek word δημιουργεω, which refers either simply to work or to fabrication. Most political acts that we may want to call non-violent, in the way that Kinna has defended anarchist acts as non-violent, tend to be acts that sustain ideals that have not yet come to full fruition, or have not yet exhausted their potential within the structure of the State or the law. In other words, they are acts that will bring to fruition the unfinished *work* of the State in delivering equality and justice. The actions of Extinction Rebellion (XR) or the *Indignados* in Spain and Greece are some contemporary example of getting this work done and pushing the State to address questions of economic inequality and environmental injustice through occupying spaces, performing, making demands and protesting. Through such actions these groups are not really calling for the removal of foundations. They merely demand that the State or the law recognise its failure to fulfill its promise of economic and environmental justice. Such groups work to try to bring to fruition ideals such as equality and environmental justice, ideals that they think have not yet exhausted their potential within the parameters of the State. But, and this is the difference, I want to stress, they do not do the work of inventing something new. If we follow Schürmann's thought, they participate in sustaining foundations. This can only change if the other part of the definition of the word, δημιουργέω meaning fabrication, is invoked. Δημιουργεω gestures towards a *different* way of doing things, it invokes the removal of foundations. How, after all, could something new emerge if the old is not uprooted? Δημιουργεω – *creativity* and not destructiveness – I then propose is what anarchism performs when it calls for worlds, communities, associations, art to be without law, without foundations, without authority, without capitalism. In short, anarchist.

It may be difficult to visualise this new world, a world without foundational concepts (reason, authority, law, State), a world in which the meaning of freedom or equality would be constantly invented without the guidance of the law and the State, but rather with the consent and collaboration of the members belonging to such associations. It might also be daunting. How could we navigate ourselves in the world without the solidity of foundations, without grounds to hold us, you may ask? The Taiwanese director Tsai Ming Liang, in his silent minimalist film *The Deserted* (2017), based on his own personal experience of retreating into the mountains, uses virtual reality (VR) technology to enable us to experience such a lack of foundations/groundlessness. The film follows the male protagonist through his everyday activities (cooking, working, resting). He has a goldfish as a companion and the visits of two ghostly female figures (a motherly woman and a young woman). The film is a meditation on loneliness, illness and recovery. Aesthetically, *The Deserted* is plain and stunning at the same time. The use of VR technology places us in the film, where we find ourselves accompanying the protagonist and his companions in the kitchen, forest, bathroom or wherever they move. We become voyeurs of their everyday activities. One particular moment in the film is disorientating. We suddenly find ourselves suspended in space with no ground to hold us. This, admittedly, is a dizzying experience. Unable to stand on anything, at first I found myself overtaken by anxiety, sweating profusely. After a few seconds, I noticed a sense of excitement overtaking me. I could, paradoxically, stand without the ground holding me. This cinematic experience gave me a taste of how it would be if our existence was not dependent on any foundations. This moment in the film enabled me to experience both the myth of foundations (reason, authority, the State and law as necessary indexes of navigating us in the world) – nothing really bad happens without them – and the ambit of possibilities that we may discover once we let them go. Our imagination livens up and enables us to visualise how things can be, or even could be done otherwise. We begin to see how we can actually be in the world without foundations. Fear can turn into possibilities by simply letting go of attachments. Any fear we may have acquired, over the years of obedience to norms about what the loss of grounds or foundations may bring, dissipates and a lightness takes its place. I offer this interlude here so as to make us aware that it is always possible to create worlds that do not rely on mythical foundations. If we perspire when we find ourselves without foundations, without law, it is a perspiration that allows us to face our fear of a future without foundations but also the very violence of such foundations. If we perspire it is because we are experiencing the creative potential of existing without *arche*.

Merce Cunningham was aware of the creative aspect of anarchism, of the innovative potentials that may arise if we do not use blueprints or, as he said, if we do not follow 'well thought objectives' (Kisselgoff, 1992). It is the antifoundational aspects of *anarche* that Cunningham embraced with his dancers at the Merce Cunningham Dance Company that earned him the badge of anarchist. Cunningham is known for inventing a type of dance called *chance* dance. In his dances he used props such as a large plastic bag (e.g., *Place*, 1966) and music (e.g., *Exchange*, 1978), and explored space in innovative and theatrical ways. In *Exchange*, for example, an industrial/city sounding score composed by David Tudor accompanies the choreography. Moreover, in *Exchange* we do not have dancers dancing to the tune of the score, but instead to the rhythm emanating from their own bodies. Music, on this occasion, is literally a backdrop to movement and not directing movement. As innovative and counterintuitive as this technique may be, this is not what prompted Kisselgoff to call Cunningham an anarchist. Rather, it was his use of *chance*. Cunningham did not compose his choreographies based on a 'well thought objective' (Kisselgoff, 1992). On the contrary, along with John Cage, the minimalist composer – his collaborator and life partner – he believed that structures are produced by random movements or events, in other words by *chance*. For this he drew his inspiration from the *I Ching*. The *I Ching*, or the *Book of Changes* as it is titled translated into English, is one of the oldest sacred Chinese books. It uses cleromancy to guide and predict the future and is consulted by numerous religions, including Taoism and Buddhism. Taoism and Buddhism are two of the earliest religious practices and philosophies that show 'clear expression of an anarchist sensibility' (Marshall 1993:53). The practice of *I Ching* is executed through the tossing of coins, sticks or whatever the practitioner decides to use to form six lines (hexagram), which in turn provide us with numbers that we can look up in the *I Ching* for advice and guidance.

Cunningham used unconventional methods to create very powerful choreographies. Whilst all this is pretty impressive, and whilst Cunningham's dance practice was created 'without a well thought objective', was it necessarily anarchist? Whilst it is paramount to undo the 'cultural stereotype' of the anarchist as a violent thug, to insist on violence as critique and resistance, like Kinna – or, even more importantly, to insist that anarchism is creative, a world building project – this does not mean that every creative project is anarchist, despite its anarchist tendencies. If Cunningham's work is anarchist, we need to see how he understands it as being such. We turn once more to the interview.

When Kissenlgoff suggests to Cunningham that the 'festive anarchy' (Kisselgoff, 1992) evident in his early choreographies is absent from his later work, Cunningham rebuffs her suggestion: 'I still work that way, by going at a dance without having an objective in mind' (Kisselgoff, 1992). What does this mean though? For Cunningham, anarchism appears to designate a way of doing things that is not based on blueprints or intentions. Consequently, the process of choreography, and not the choreographer, is deemed to be in the driver's seat, or the master of the dance creation. That this is what he understands as anarchy becomes clear in another interview he gave to Lesschaeve, where he explains his preparations for creating a choreography. He prepared, he states, 'the phrasing and the continuity, ahead of time before the dancers came to rehearsal' (Cunningham, 2009:20) by using the *I Ching*. Through the use of *I Ching*, he concocts the phrases of a choreography. In the case of *Torse* (1976), for example, the *I Ching* revealed the number 64. Cunningham then used this number to create a choreography consisting of eight phrases repeated eight times. Once in rehearsal, Cunningham informs us that he consults the *I Ching* again, this time to decide the number of dancers who will be performing in each phrase as well as their gender/age composition (Cunningham, 2009:20–1). Furthermore, decisions as to which dancer is to exit or stay on stage were also made randomly, through the toss of a coin (Cunningham, 2009:22). Cunningham's *chance* method, as you can see, subverts normative choreographical practices by putting chance and not intention at its centre.

Recall also that when we were discussing Schürmann we found out that the removal of foundations, especially normative ways of doing things, is undoubtedly anarchic. In introducing chance into choreography, Cunningham certainly challenges normative dance practices. Nevertheless, can we conclude that he is anarchist? We can certainly say that he had anarchist tendencies. For example, he did not rely on rules or conventions in creating his choreographies; he used coins and *I Ching* to decide and the names of dancers were listed alphabetically in the programmes of dance performances, symbolising a certain lack of hierarchy. All these are surely good ways of creating something new without following any predetermined rules. Nevertheless, perhaps something more is required to call Cunningham an anarchist. Despite all his good intentions to break all hierarchies, he remained the master choreographer and his method of dancing bears his signature – the Merce Cunningham Dance Company. The company could have been called the Chance Dance Company, for example, to exemplify the method used to decide the phrases that made up the choreography. If the Dance Company did not bear Cunningham's name we could have agreed with him and Kisselgoff that his choreographies are anarchic. The name of his company demonstrates a certain attachment to mastery, a certain investment in marking the company symbolically as his own.

It is becoming common for individuals, ensembles of activists, cultural practices, social enterprises and so on to demonstrate sufficient anarchist tendencies for them to be perceived as being anarchist. For example, we may have ensembles of activists involved in environmental activism, such as XR which are leaderless, that have horizontal decision-making practices and take direct action as a way of propagating the urgent need to do something in order to save our planet from climate catastrophe. They appear at first glance to be anarchist. But a closer inspection reveals that despite their anarchist practices they still see the State as the driver for change. Contemporary anarchist thinkers like Saul Newman even encourage us to think of groups like XR as anarchist. We may need to see anarchism, Newman suggests, not 'as a distinct project' but rather 'in terms of a certain mode of thought and action through which relations of domination, in their specificity, are interrogated, contested and, where possible, overturned' (Newman, 2016:13). If for Newman anarchism is not 'a distinct project', one that wishes to bring about freedom from rules and rulers and the total transformation of our social, political and economic spheres, then what exactly is it? He invites us to see anarchism as an idea that is typified by 'autonomous thinking and acting which transforms contemporary social spaces in the present sense, but which is at the same time contingent and indeterminate in the sense of not being subject to predetermined logics and goals' (13). For Newman, then, if universalist claims cannot be made any longer, nor can universalist ideology such as anarchism make universal claims any longer. Therefore, anarchism cannot be a 'distinct project' but it can be a practice or thinking that is played out in different moments in our everyday and political lives.

In Chapter 3 I will critically engage with Newman's proposition that today anarchism should be viewed as a mode of thinking as opposed to a distinct project (Newman, 2016). For the moment, it suffices to say that this mode of thinking allows Newman to identify as anarchist, or rather as postanarchist (the 'post' referring precisely to the end of anarchism as an ideology), those groups and entities that have anarchist tendencies. Occupy, Anonymous and the demonstrations against police brutality in the United States (33) are some of the examples Newman uses to demonstrate precisely this notion of anarchism as a mode of thinking. So although during the Occupy movement, for example, we witnessed a type of politics and organisation that is associated with anarchism (i.e., leaderless, horizontal decision-making, people's assembly, etc.) Occupiers were not just anarchist, they came from disparate ideological positions. What we witness, though, is an anarchist way of thinking or doing politics without an overarching drive to abolish the State. Whilst Newman is critical of recognition politics – that is, political practices that address their demands to the State (28–32) – he does not call for the abolition of the State (35–46) but instead for more anarchic modes of thinking that can lead to or provide us with a sense of freedom in the moments of action. In some respects, Newman's thinking is in alignment with Schürmann's understanding of anarchy. Nevertheless, if Newman still holds onto the State as delivering the demands of distinct anarchist formations, then we can say, if we follow Schürmann, that he holds onto the State as a foundational structure and therefore reproduces, in a different way, precisely that for which he criticises classical anarchism.

Nevertheless, Newman is not alone amongst contemporary anarchist thinkers in proposing that we should recognise as anarchist those struggles that are not invested in the undoing of the State. The political theorist and anthropologist James C. Scott, in his highly influential *Seeing Like a State* (1998), offers a similar argument. Scott sets out to explain that centralised political systems cannot govern well without taking account of local understandings and knowledge about such issues. In *Seeing Like a State*, he demonstrates how Brazil failed to transform Brasília into an economic and socially fair city precisely because the government ignored local knowledge regarding how to improve living conditions in Brasília. Scott understands this failure as a lesson; it can teach us that there is a potential for the State to be transformed, to deliver better conditions to its citizens, if it lets them participate in their planning projects. In his more recent book, *Two Cheers for Anarchism* (Scott, 2012), he goes as far as suggesting that if we are to create an equal and free society, the State must play a vital process in this endeavour. Anarchists need to collaborate with the State if their goals are to be reached. He sees the State as playing a vital role in protecting the interests and needs of the people. It is difficult to see how Scott's claim – that the State protects the interests of the people – can be sustained at a time when police brutality against Black people is notably on the rise in the US, when refugees and other destitute populations are welcomed on the shores of Australia and Europe by being put in detention camps or sent back to the very zones they were escaping from and left to die. It is difficult to see how Scott can sustain such a claim whilst also being critical of State brutality and oppression.[1]

Ruth Kinna, like Newman and Scott, does not think that we can have an anarchist society without the State. In *The Government of No One*, an astute

---

1 For a useful critique of Scott's work, see Çubukçu (2021:495–7).

presentation of anarchist history, culture and trends, she concludes that is quite impossible for anarchism to undo the State. Instead of anarchism pursuing an impossible project, she proposes that it would be better if it encouraged every facet of our lives, institutional or otherwise, to adopt anarchist practices (such as horizontal decision-making) and goals (such as egalitarianism). Kinna calls the process of occupying our lives, institutions, art ensembles and organisations with anarchist practices, 'anarchization'. As she writes:

> The chances of anarchizing our social relationships and institutions are a lot higher than the likelihood of replacing the state with anarchy. Building confidence is one of the essential ingredients and here anarchism excels. To borrow Paul Goodman's phrase, anarchism offers utopian visions and practical proposals in abundance. It has a host of inspiring role models, a toolbox stacked with ideas about how to act and why and, as Voltairine de Cleyre argued, bridled optimism about the prospects of change. Anarchism tells us that present injustice is the justice of the past, made plain by fearless denunciation and capable of redress through direct action.
>
> (Kinna, 2019:271)

It is, of course, important that we *anarchize* and give support to those that want to *anarchize* social and working spaces. And whilst this can bring changes it does not however guarantee that the changes achieved will be sustained within the framework of the State. Let's take once more the example of XR. XR use non-hierarchical techniques during people's assemblies (April 2019), civil disobedience and demonstrations to bring the global environmental crisis to the attention of the public and politicians. Their actions and practices can be identified as anarchist or as being used by anarchists. I talk more extensively about XR later on in the book. Here it suffices to note that whilst XR engage in direct action and they are non-hierarchical they still require the State to activate their demands. They exemplary of what Kinna calls 'anarchization' without being anarchists. Nevertheless, whilst Ruth Kinna may see the 'state … play[ing] a positive role in people's lives' (247) she has not provided us yet with a clear explanation of how they defend such a perspective at times where States actively keep refugees or asylum seekers in detention centres, where police brutality against minorities is on the rise and where the State is on the side of capitalism (Brown, 2015). Another way of putting this is that Kinna is good at describing how there are more and more examples of 'anarchization' but she stops short of problematising the existing limits and violence that are still perpetrated by States. The same can be said of Scott.

Kinna, Scott and Newman provide us with their own visions of anarchism and anarchist studies in the twenty-first century emanating from their long scholarship on anarchism. They are of course right to point to the proliferation of anarchist practices in society. During the Covid-19 pandemic, for example, we saw the creation of over 4,000 mutual aid groups (O'Dwyer, 2020) in the

UK, providing practical (food shopping, fetching prescriptions) and moral support (talking) to older and vulnerable individuals. Whilst their vision, studies and observations are welcome, *Anarchism: An Art of Living without Law* nevertheless diverges from the positions put forward by Kinna, Scott and Newman by suggesting that the State cannot be considered as the vehicle for an anarchist polity, even if it does champion some social justice goals (gender, sexuality, race, ability). This is because, paradoxically, the State in its neoliberal form is being strengthened at the expense of sections of the populations that are both economically and socially non-privileged. The Marxist geographer David Harvey's well-known mantra that the dominant practice of neoliberalism is 'accumulation by dispossession' (Harvey, 2004:63–87) aptly describes the way in which Western democratic States govern. There are ample examples – from welfare cuts to the privatisation of public services (e.g., prisons, detention centres, public transport, national health systems) – that demonstrate how the neoliberal State makes some sections of the populations destitute. Patrick Butler (2019) writes about how cuts in welfare funds, together with the increase in platform economies and zero-hour contracts, have put 22 per cent of the population into the poverty zone and caused the creation of 2,000 food banks in the UK. The neoliberal State is not therefore our friend, in the same way that we should not confuse the smile of a police officer with the idea that the officer is on the side of anarchists or non-anarchist activists.

In an interview he gave to Pablo Ortellando and André Ryoki in Brazil in 1996, Noam Chomsky discussed anarchism's call for the abolition of the State. Chomsky is of the belief that the problematic of the abolition of the State is anarchism's Achilles' heel. As he stated:

> in my view the libertarian movements have been very shortsighted in pursuing doctrine in a rigid fashion without being concerned about the human consequences. So it's perfectly proper … I mean, in my view, and that of a few others, the state is an illegitimate institution. But it does not follow from that that you should not support the state. Sometimes there is a more illegitimate institution which will take over if you do not support this illegitimate institution.
>
> (Chomsky, 2005:212)

He went on to suggest that anarchists who stick to the doctrine of insisting on being against the State jeopardise the small victories that have been achieved for the lower socio-economic classes:

> As a result of centuries of extensive popular struggle there is a minimal welfare system that provides support for poor mothers and children. That's under attack in an effort to minimise the state. Well, anarchists can't seem to understand that they are to support that. So they join with the ultra-right in saying: 'Yes we got to minimise the state,' meaning put more

power into the hands of private tyrannies which are completely unaccountable to the public and purely totalitarian.

(Chomsky, 2005:212–13)

Chomsky could be right about the danger that anarchists who insist on the abolition of the State may pose to underprivileged citizens, especially those who rely on State financial support for their survival. Indeed, by not dropping the idea of the abolition of the State, they may bolster ultra-right libertarians who think the abolition of the State will bring them profit maximisation and freedom. Moreover, the anarchist attachment to the withering of the State may risk undoing any social settlements (e.g., equality and difference-based justice projects) reached in the twentieth and twenty-first centuries. This is a danger for sure. Nevertheless, we know – and undoubtedly Chomsky does too – that anarchists hold onto the idea of State abolition not because they are advocating profit maximisation, nor because they want to rip apart any social settlements. On the contrary, any form of leftist anarchism does not advocate profit as its objective, but instead calls for stronger social settlements that will be agreed by members of anarchist polities and associations to ensure that needs are met before anything else. Indeed, the whole idea of mutual aid that Kropotkin proposed was based on co-operation and support, as well as rewarding each member of a polity according to their needs. So, when Chomsky claims that those anarchists who still hold onto the abolition of the State are rigidly and unwittingly collaborating with the ultra right he is misleading. First, he fails to account for the anarchist ideas of mutual aid, non-profit, no hierarchy and so on that accompany classical anarchism. Second, he gives the *impression*, in the same way that Scott and Kinna do, that the State is operating in ways that are still beneficial for us. Ortellando and Ryoki (Chomsky, 2005) reminded him that when reforming the country's health system the Brazilian government co-opted anarchist practices to their advantage. Healthcare is a right enshrined in the Brazilian Constitution and the healthcare system is run by a combination of the federal and local authorities. In 1995

the mayor of São Paulo proposed a reformation of the city health system that consisted of doctors, nurses and other health workers receiving their pay from the state, but running health centers on their own. However they are allowed to pass the management of the centers to private companies if they feel they are not able to run it properly.

(213)

Ortellando and Ryoki use this example to point out that anarchists' ideas of self-government can be used to privatise public systems such as the health system. In this instance the State was interested in divesting its responsibilities and maximising its profit using this method. The State divested its responsibilities by passing the management of healthcare spaces to the people who work in it – who are already overworked – and forcing them eventually to get private companies to run them, maximising in turn the management companies' profits. I would like to suggest that in this case the State is acting as more than just an 'illegitimate institution' (212). The State is acting in a way that could jeopardise the wellbeing of its citizens through the indirect privatisation of its healthcare system. Although it is meant to provide security for all, the State repeatedly demonstrates that security comes at a cost: a cost to the poor (when it comes to welfare issues), a cost to minorities (when it comes to social justice issues), a cost to minorities, especially Black communities in the US (when it comes to criminal legal-justice issues) and, most of the time, all these costs intersect. The *State* becomes, therefore, an apparatus for delivering social, political, legal and economic *insecurity*.

There is nothing new in what I have just said. If you had been a critical legal scholar for the past 25 years, this argument would have been your bread and butter. What is new, though, is that this message needs to be transmitted to fellow anarchists and anarchist studies travellers who see the State as a good collaborator with the anarchist project. 'Anarchization', to borrow Kinna's neologism once again, needs to continue but without forgetting that the structures in which it operates, the State and its apparatuses, do not host the conditions needed for anarchist polities. Of course, we should encourage our art, social, political and work worlds to become more anarchist, but nevertheless I would like to argue that if we really want to live in worlds and polities where there is *no* hierarchy, *no* distribution of wealth based on privilege and profit, and where self-government is its operating practice, we need to do so outside the claws of the State and without law. This is the central argument of this book: anarchism *cannot be* within the framework of the State, but, more importantly, it cannot be *within the claws of law*. As long as we see the State and its apparatuses – the law – as guarantors of our security, I argue in Chapter 3 along with Stirner (2006), we will never achieve self-government and all our thinking and deeds will be eternally colonised by the State.

However, Stirner was not the only one to remind us of the colonising effects of law. The anti-colonial writer and philosopher Frantz Fanon speaks of the colonising effects of law and order insightfully when he writes:

> [t]he colinized world is a world divided in two. The dividing line, the border, is represented by the barracks and the police stations. In the colonies, the official, legitimate agent, the spokesperson for the colonizer and regime oppression, is the police officer or the soldier
>
> (Fanon, 2004:3)

Law and its executors, the police, play an important role in keeping us hemmed in in our places, hindering our growth and ability to engage and create in the world. This image of law was forced upon colonised populations particularly. Nevertheless, Fanon reminds us that each time the police arrest, beat and kill us, because we demonstrate against capitalism (Anti-G8 demonstrations, Occupy), in favour of the environment (Earth First, XR), for racial equality/justice (Black Lives Matter (BLM)), law and order 'turn[s] the colonized into a kind of quintessence of evil' (6). Law and order is used to demonise those who do not share the colonisers' values, and by extension those of the law. We are reminded that demonisation turns the colonised into the 'enemy of values' (6). It is no coincidence that Emma Goldman was demonised in the US for acts that she did not commit. When a young man from Buffalo called Leon Czolgosz assassinated US President William Mckinley on 6 September 1901, citing Emma Goldman as the inspiration for the assassination (Goldman had nothing to do with it), Goldman was demonised. As she tells us in her biography, when she was held as a suspect for this assassination and until she was released with no charge, the only letters she received in prison (she was 'kept *incommunicado*' [Goldman, 1970a:301] from her friends) were anonymous letters from people that expressed their utter hatred for her. She gives a graphic description of the content of some of them below:

> 'You damn bitch of an anarchist,' ... 'I wish I could get at you. I would tear your heart out and feed it to my dog.' 'Murderous Emma Goldman, ... you will burn in hell-fire for your treachery to our country.' .... 'We will cut your tongue out, soak your carcass in oil, and burn you alive.'
> (Goldman, 1970a:301)

As the quotes from letters sent to Goldman reveal, anarchists are condemned for criminal actions that they may not have done but are connected to by mere association with the people who committed them. The existence of a penal system will always guarantee that those who are deemed enemies of the existing regime's values are demonised, criminalised and made to suffer. We cannot, in my opinion, imagine anarchist polities or talk of anarchy or 'anarchization' if we are not willing to remove the State and its apparatuses.

The State, even the neoliberal one, needs the law to prop it up. To talk about anarchism as a way of thinking, as Newman does, and to consider the State as an ally to anarchism, as Scott, Kinna and Chomsky do, detracts from one of the most important aims of anarchism: to build polities based on freedom, equality and redistribution according to needs, and instead invest in practices that continue the colonisation of thinking and life by the law. These thinkers continue to reinforce and unwittingly prolong existing State violence.

To sum up, the reconceptualisation of anarchism into 'anarchization' and its variations, as I outlined above, is sensible but it may have a few undesired effects: (a) it makes anarchism subservient to the State, by waiting for the State to implement whatever demands direct action groups are making; (b) consequently, it creates hierarchies (State above activist groups); (c) inevitably, if the State is another word for capitalism, it replicates the economic and social inequalities that are produced by capitalism; and (d) it ignores the creative aspect of anarchism and its ability to bring new things into the world.

Anarchism: An Art of Living without Law sets out to tell the *story* of how it is possible to have a world that can foster equality, freedom and justice as its compass if attachment to the State and law is abandoned. What does it take, therefore, to organise our lives without law and the State? It requires that we enter freely into associations that are self-governing, that decisions in such associations or polities are taken collectively, that mutual aid is practised and the redistribution of wealth is done according to one's needs. It also requires us to talk truth to power (parrhesia), humour and a type of love that constantly questions our doctrines and beliefs. To be able to live *without* law (and the State) we must immerse ourselves in an anarchist *art* of living.

It is important, though, to note here that anarchism is not a utopian project. The etymology of the word utopia, as is well known, derives from the Greek word ουτοπία and refers to 'no place' or nowhere. The sixteenth-century writer Sir Thomas Moore gave the title *Utopia* to a book in which he imagined an island whose inhabitants had the pleasure of enjoying perfect laws, politics and social relations. *Anarchism: An Art of Living without Law* does not lay the grounds for the creation of a polity or associations that are future oriented; nor is it about a place that is located nowhere. As we have seen so far through the cursory invocation of Newman, Kinna and Scott's writings on anarchism, anarchist practices exist in our contemporary society and we have witnessed their use to organising political movements during Occupy and, more recently, with XR. Mutual aid is practised daily by ordinary citizens when they risk their lives to save war-ravaged refugees. In 2020, during the Covid-19 pandemic, we witnessed more than 4,000 mutual aid groups in the UK and elsewhere. Anarchism is an art of living that exists parallel to the way of life that the modern State has carved for us. Anarchist polities, I argue in this book, are not, unlike Moore's utopian island, perfect societies; on the contrary, I suggest that anarchism is an experiment in living without masters, without laws, without authority, with equality and through mutual aid, and it does not have perfection as its goal, but rather to create the conditions for the best possible life. As such, it places questioning at the centre of its activities.

Art of living

To show how this is possible, I draw upon the work of Foucault, especially his work on the 'art of life', to present an anarchist art of life., Foucault wrote about the art of life in relation to Ancient Greek life. He informs us that the most prevalent ethic in Ancient Greece was that of an art of life (1991:348) which consisted of practices that enabled the Greeks to reach 'self-mastery' and live their lives at a distance from a juridical order or authority (348), in order to have the best possible life. These practices varied from regulating eating (dietetics) to physical exercises and note taking. Like the Greeks, we notice that anarchists, at least the anarchists that I am presenting here in this book, live their lives at a distance from juridical authority precisely because they can only have the *best* possible life at a distance from juridical institutions and authority. The practices and attitudes that make up an anarchist art of life sketch a life bereft of sclerotic ideological positions by constantly questioning anarchist ideology (see Chapter 4), talking truth to power (see Chapter 3), challenging juridical law (see Chapter 2), aiming for a large-scale mutual aid association (see Chapter 6).

To this effect, I identify a handful of practices and attitudes that are aligned with an anarchist art of life: (a) a life away from law; (b) fearless speech; (c) passionate love that questions anarchist ideology; (d) humour; and e) mutual aid. These are traced through: archival material that records the life and actions of the anarchist Emma Goldman and her associates; legal documents; writings by classical (e.g., Pierre Joseph Proudhon, Peter Krotopkin) and contemporary (e.g., David Graeber, Saul Newman, Ciarra Bottici) anarchists; and contemporary groups such as Clandestine Insurgent Rebel Clown Army (CIRCA), UK Uncut and Occupy Wall Street. The archive may be characterised as somewhat eclectic and incomplete. This is deliberate. I am of the belief that no archive can be other than eclectic, aligned with the interests and tastes of the researcher, and it can never be complete. Indeed, the hope is that this archive may inspire others who will, in turn, try and gather together new archives that can tell us how we can live our lives without law, and the type of artistry that accompanies such a possibility. If at times you find that the archive is speculative, I invite you to think of the possibilities that speculation may open up in forming a different world, and different stories. I have always felt that speculation, along with associative thinking to enhance our horizons (cognitive and sensual), as opposed to legal reasoning, which frames the way we see the world. Just remind yourselves of the criminal law judgments, guilty or not guilty, or, if you were ever in doubt, of the frame-making legal vocabulary and reasoning.

Therefore, at a time when the State formation is not living up to its image (to ensure the economic, political and social security of the people; see, for example, the Greek State after the austerity crisis or Britain after Brexit and during the Covid-19 pandemic), we need to explore different ways in which we can begin to rebuild better social, political and economic relations with each other. Most writings on anarchism, with some exceptions,[2] focus on the political efficacy of anarchism. Without discounting the political efficacy of anarchism, I invite us to think of anarchism as an artistry that constantly requires new tricks and practices to enable us to be together in ways that don't necessitate the wrath of authority, the aspiration of a hierarchy, prosperity based on profit, the solidity of law and individualism. Each chapter in the book provides us with either an insight into how anarchists carve a space to live their

---

2   For example, Christos Marneros' doctoral thesis, 'Human Rights After Deleuze: Towards an An-archic Jurisprudence' (University of Kent 2021), focuses not on the politics of anarchism but rather on the possibility of having an anarchist jurisprudence.

lives parallel to the one offered by the State and its laws, or an insight into some of the practices they engage in that enable such a life – or both.

Chapter 2 addresses anarchism's relationship with the law. While the etymology of the word anarchism refers to a polity that is without a ruler or without an authority, it is not always clear whether anarchists imagine such a polity being without law. This is true of classical as well as contemporary anarchist writings. Within classical anarchism, there is a strong desire and demand for the withering of the State and the establishment of self-governing polities; it is not, however, explicit whether or not classical anarchists anticipate any *withering* of the *law*. Pierre-Joseph Proudhon, for example, has an ambivalent relationship with the law. Whilst he criticises State law he simultaneously envisages that anarchist societies will have some type of law. State law for Proudhon is corrupt as it is a tool in the hands of the privileged, whilst the law that will emerge in an anarchist society is seen as capable of guaranteeing freedom, equality and justice for all. There is, we may say, hope in Proudhon's writings in the potentiality of law in an anarchist society. Anarchists like Emma Goldman and Peter Krotopkin are less optimistic about the institution of law and its rule. In this chapter, I align with the critiques of law emanating from Goldman and Krotopkin, and argue that an anarchist society needs to divest itself of the idea of the rule of law altogether, for even the smallest investment in alternative laws runs the risk of investing law with godly qualities, contrary to the anarchist principles.

Anarchists are often said to be disobedient subjects. In Chapter 3, I track down the various ways in which we find ourselves obeying either the juridical law or normative injunctions. The work of the psychoanalyst Adam Philips, the writings of the anthropologist James C Scott and the political theorist Etienne de la Boétie guide me through this diagnostic move. I also consider the critique offered by Max Stirner on disobedience. For Stirner, the concept and practice of disobedience locks subjects to the object which they revolt against, and he urges revolutionary subjects to distance themselves from disobedient actions if they want to achieve freedom and self-mastery. Stirner's critique is important in that it shows us that anarchist disobedience distances itself from the object of disobedience, whether that is the law or the State. Instead I argue, guided by the writings and actions of the anarchist Emma Goldman as well those of the activist group UK Uncut, that anarchists are not disobedient for the sake of being disobedient, but rather when they disobey it is because they want to question obedience and the fear of *diverging* from the well-walked path of life. Moreover, their 'disobedience', if we can call it that, takes the form of fearless speech, talking truth to power and exposing the deceptive character of institutions such as the law, the police or the State. *Parhessia* (fearless speech) is identified as the art required for an anarchist life to flourish.

Chapter 4 preoccupies itself with the question of love. Focussing on Emma Goldman's biographical experience of love, I sketch how erotic love *moves* Goldman politically and how it becomes her *compass*, enabling her to question core anarchist positions around the governance of intimate relations such as free love, marriage and possessiveness. Goldman's biography and writings enable us to see how the anarchist subject in love *differs* from the subject that has given themself to the State and law. The anarchist subject uses the turbulence that erotic love may bring to question themself – not to ask for a resolution, but to sit with this turbulence, to sit with the ambivalence that it creates. The anarchist's (or at least Goldman's) critical reflections on erotic love question anarchist ideology and enable anarchism to address limits and adjust to new circumstances and challenges. As we will see, when law engages with the problematic of intimate relations it fails to use the turbulences of love to question itself; instead, it tends to offer resolutions that enforce the authority of law.

Anarchists tend to critique the political status quo and diffuse tension through humor that breaks into laughter. CIRCA, for example, diffuse tensions at political demonstrations such as the Anti-G8/11 demonstrations by blowing kisses to heavily armed police officers and drawing flowers on officers' protective shields. Through humorous gestures they demonstrate that authority (symbolised in this example by the police) may not be as potent and powerful as it appears to be. Goldman also used humour to diffuse the tension created by her arrests, and deface police authority and the law. However, anarchist humour fails to provoke laughter from the State and its apparatuses. On the contrary, on the occasions when anarchists direct their jokes at officers of the law and other officers of the State, we witness their jokes falling flat on the ears of such officials. In Chapter 5 I suggest that this failure to join in the joke reveals that the State and its apparatuses tend to be humourless. More importantly, this failure brings to the surface the difference in values between an anarchist and a Statist life, and enables us to see that they co-exist in parallel to each other. We find through the various theories of laughter (incongruity, superiority, tension relief) that humour revels in unpredictability, ambivalence and difference. We find out that the State, on the other hand, reproduces itself through holding onto fictitious values such as those of security, normativity and sameness. The anarchists' embrace of humour in their acts, of literally not taking their failures – failure to invoke laughter – seriously, is an embrace of their belief that life is ever-changing and uncertain and therefore not normative. Chapter 5 suggests that if we are to have better lives our new polities need to ensure that humour, ambivalence and difference are a breathing part of them. In some respects, the embrace of humour by anarchist subjects is already evidence that they are living their lives parallel to the State, and in so far as this is the case we can say that anarchists have to some extent already exited the State formation.

The concluding chapter, Chapter 6, turns to the practice of mutual aid via the writings of Peter Kropotkin, and argues along with him that a possible way of bettering our lives and detangling ourselves from the claws of neoliberalism is to engage with the practice of mutual aid. Mutual aid, as Kropotkin noticed, is something we human beings tend to practise in our everyday lives. Mutual aid is often, for example, practiced at distressful moments. We have witnessed in the past 2–3 years how citizens in Europe have been saving refugees from their capsizing boats as well as the mutual aid groups that emerged in response to the Covid-19 pandemic. These are two examples of mutual aid being practised at times of distress. Whilst the mutual aid or support instinct, as Kropotkin argues, may be stronger than that of the survival of the fittest and there is wide evidence of it in the human and animal world, if we are to have polities run by mutual aid as he argues, they need to exist in conjunction with the abolition of private property and the remuneration of all according to needs. These two principles will make sure that the violence of profiteering that is the most common practice in our neoliberal worlds disappears. The chapter argues that if we are to have associations, polities or societies that operate without law, then mutual aid needs to be at the centre of the organisation of life. And for this we don't only need the abolition of private property and remuneration according to needs, we also need trust.

Anarchism: An Art of Living without Law is an experiment. It traces existing practices within anarchist political theory and invites you to see how anarchist life exists parallel to the neoliberal world that claims dominance over our everyday lives, proliferating economic, social and political injustices. Like any experiment, it will be ridden with flaws, with ellipsis, with things that need to be thought through further. But, like any experiment, it provides the opportunity to imagine a different way of organising our lives, a better way of living. Its materialisation is up to us, up to all of us. *Anarchism: An Art of Living without Law* invites you to entertain such a possibility and always remember that perfection is not the compass of anarchism. If you decide to take this leap of faith, I am certain that together we can learn along the way what is the best way of being and living together.

It may not be easy, but it will certainly be euphoric.

Chapter 2

Without law?

Introduction

It is no exaggeration, nor will it come as a surprise to anyone, if I say that Western democratic governments rely on law to help them carry out their everyday operations, protect themselves, discipline and control people, be these people citizens, denizens or aliens. Moreover, it is no surprise if I say that the law is the mechanism through which 'we' the people gain formal equality and justice. Equality and justice in lay terms, we may say, have become synonymous with law. Even when legal academics[1] are critical of law, pointing to its

1   Over the past 30 years the UK strand of critical legal studies has seen a number of important writings that address the limits of law and its failures to deliver justice. Such writings tackle law's failure to recognise, include and offer access to law and justice to marginalised subjects. Moran (1996) tracked the marginalisation and exclusion of the homosexual subject in law, Tuitt (2004) uses the deconstructive method to show how racialised subjects are constructed in law and Sharpe (2010) points to the legal construction of the transgender body as monstrous. More recently, Gearey (2018) offers an excellent account of the exclusion of the most vulnerable in our society, the poor, from poor laws. This is by no means an exhaustive list. Nevertheless, this rich oeuvre of writings has not just been engaged in attributing blame or addressing the limits of law. Critical legal writers have also pointed to the *mechanisms* by which marginalised groups are not addressed by the law. One of the things identified is that law privileges reason as the main medium of communicating grievances and in doing so it excludes any grievance that, albeit worthy of consideration, is transmitted and articulated through emotion. Peter Goodrich's *Languages of Law* (1990) was one of the first to address this point. Costas Douzinas, Ronnie Warrington and Shaun McVeigh also address this limit in *Post-Modern Jurisprudence* (1991). Aristodemou (2000) points to the exclusion of women from legal reasoning, and Haldar (2007) studies how Western law set up pleasure as a problem and used it as a mechanism to subjugate colonised subjects. This mode of critical legal thinking has been extended to various areas of law. Phillipopulos-Mihalopoulos (2015) highlights the way legal reasoning excludes consideration of space from its decision-making, Diamantides (2000) points to the exclusion of Levinisian ethics from medical law and Wall (2012) offers a damning critique of Human Rights and their failure to take the people as their grounds for acting. Others, like Fitzpatrick (2010), point to how modern law uses fictional grounds in excluding populations, such as colonial subjects, an idea that Motha (2018) explores

DOI: 10.4324/9780429952692-2

limitations, to law's failure to either protect or provide justice, as Goodrich aptly puts it in his essay 'The Critique Love of the Law: Intimate Observations on an Insular Jurisprudence' (1999), they still remain paradoxically *attached* to the law:

> The critics manifest a paradoxical or unwitting commitment to legality: the contradictory yet complementary stances of hate and love lead eventually in this analysis to a transcendence of legality, a beyond of law, a spirit world of eros or interiority, of proximity or alterity, in which law is reproduced in default of any relation between the domain of the spirit and the institutions of professional practice.
>
> (Goodrich 1999:344)

At the centre of critical legal scholars' writings, no matter how inadequate they consider law to be in attending to people's needs, demands and injuries, there is law. Put differently, whilst critical legal academics describe and criticise law for failing to deliver what it promises, they do not put forward or imagine Western democratic societies operating *without* the assistance of *law*. Problems of equality, freedom and justice remain for critical legal scholars problems that the law could fix by being more attentive to the marginalised and excluded (women, racialised and sexual minorities, the poor, refugees, etc.) and ensuring their legal recognition or inclusion within law. This usually happens as a result of demands for the expansion of rights, reforming legislation and access to justice for all excluded and marginalised peoples. As Goodrich points out, even when critical legal scholars appeal for something *beyond the law* – whether it is ethics or aesthetics (Douzinas and Warrington, 1996), postcolonial narratives (Haldar, 2007; Motha, 2018) or politics (Douzinas, 2013; Bhandar, 2018; Wall, 2021) to name but a few – as the horizon for justice or equality, 'the law is reproduced in default' (Goodrich, 1999:344). We can say that whenever the law is the subject of critique, critical legal scholars end up by default writing about law – or rather how law can be fixed if it adopts different political and ethical frameworks.

Let's take a recent example of critical legal scholarship that offers a critical legal and political analysis of law's investment in the colonial project. Brenna Bhandar in *Colonial Lives of Property* (2018) addresses in nuanced ways the limits of critical legal and political scholarship when critiquing and attempting to rectify inequalities. Focusing primarily on the ways in which property law and property interests (i.e., possession and ownership) were used by colonisers to subjugate native populations – through the appropriation and use of land – she aptly demonstrates how property law became 'the primary means' (Bhandar, 2018:3) through which colonial powers realised their plans to rule colonies to

> further, showing the ways that law as a state apparatus uses fiction to deliver violence in colonial and postcolonial settings.

the detriment of racialised and Indigenous populations. In this respect, Bhandar argues that law, and in particular property law, was the main instrument used to shape racial capitalism (6). Property law became an ally to capitalism, Bhandar tells us, working with it to categorise subjects as *proper* (land and capital owners) and *improper* (racialised, colonised and disposed) (4). Property law, therefore, turned into a political weapon. By identifying the legal role that property law played in colonisation, its contribution to creating *proper* (property owners) and *improper* (racialised dispossessed) subjectivities, Bhandar goes beyond the habitual response of redressing injustices through adjusting, listening or including subjugated knowledges and people within law. Merely adjusting the law or including subjugated knowledge and people within the ambit of law does not guarantee justice for *improper* racialised subjects. If we are to address racial inequality, Bhandar argues, the ways in which we relate to things and peoples must be reconfigured, and then a three-pronged method should be offered that can get us to this:

> The first is to understand, study, and revive the ontologies of property relations that have been suppressed by colonial techniques of dispossession and appropriation. The second is to imagine what radically alternate ways of holding and relating to land might look like. The third is to consider the kinds of transformation of the self and our relations with one another that are a precondition for wider social and political transformations.
> (Bhandar, 2018:193)

This three-pronged method, by drawing on existing Indigenous practices – such as those of the Bedouins in the unrecognised village of Al-Sira (116–48) – that have the social and not-for-profit use of property as their organising principles, demonstrate how we can change our relationship to property and free ourselves from the shackles of private ownership and possession that create and sustain racial inequality (197–200). Nevertheless, as Bandar points out, most of the time the Indigenous understanding of property that has cultivation as its basis gets subjugated to Western ideas of cultivation that are based on the appropriation of land (116–48). If, however, we were to disentangle ourselves from the Western understanding of property that creates racial inequalities, Bhandar argues we would need to embrace alternative models of ownership, such as that of cultivation practised by the Bedouins.

Bhandar differs from other critical legal scholars, as she does not merely gesture towards alternative ways of doing justice but also provide us with examples of how to decolonialise our ideas of property law; however, her analysis still recognises law as a significant instrument in this process. Her argument for an expansion of forms of property (a shift from ownership to social usage) is significant and it goes a long way towards attending to the need to decolonise property law. Nevertheless, it does not *recognise* the institution of law as a colonising tool that hinders change or our ability to think of solutions to social (access to justice) and economic (redistribution of property), as well as political (freedom), questions *without* the law. Bhandar retains law in the process of socialising law and decolonisation. This is a paradoxical position, not only because some classical anarchists such as Kropotkin and Goldman point to the limits and colonial character of law, as we will soon see, but also because this was the understanding that the decolonial philosopher and psychoanalyst Franz Fanon highlighted in *The Wretched of the Earth* (2004), the complicity of law in the process of colonisation (3–6). In this chapter, I argue and show that we can *only* decolonise our world and achieve both freedom and justice if we get rid not just of the State but also of the institution of law. Not every anarchist, of course, thought it was necessary to have societies without law. Indeed, the anarchist Proudhon, as we will see below, thought that a reformed law would not jeopardise the anarchist project. The contemporary anarchist political thinker Saul Newman is of the same opinion, as this chapter will show. I remain antithetical to these positions and argue as you will see, that if law continues to organise our lives it retains its position as *master* of our lives, colonising our imagination, which in turn obstructs free and equal living.

What, though, is anarchism's relationship to law? Do anarchist writers see law as the vehicle for delivering justice, equality and freedom? Anarchism may mean *without* an *arche*, which means, as we know, to be governed without a ruler or without an authority. But does it mean governing without law? Classical nineteenth-century anarchists have clear messages regarding the dissolution of the State (they advocate it) and the establishment of self-governed associations, but they remain ambivalent as to whether these new status quo Stateless societies should be without law. As we will see in this chapter, there are conflicting ideas among classical anarchist and contemporary anarchist writers regarding law's role in an anarchist polity. It is also important to note at the start that not only do those anarchists have conflicting views about the role of law in anarchist societies but some classical anarchists like Proudhon altered their views regarding the need for law to run anarchist societies during their lifetime. At one point Proudhon was critical of the legal order: 'Laws! We know what they are and what they are worth. Gossamer for the mighty and the rich, fetters that no steel could smash for the little people and the poor, fishing nets in the hand of government' (Proudhon, 2005:90).

He considered law to be an instrument that protects the most privileged in society and consequently is differential towards the unprivileged members of society. The law, he argues, is an instrument, a 'fishing net' (Proudhon, 2005:90) that governments use to maintain poverty and inequality, and expand the needs and desires of the rich. In other writings, such as his influential essay 'Property is Theft' (48–54), we find Proudhon not only being less antagonistic towards law, but rather envisaging law playing a significant role in 'end[ing] … privilege, the abolition of slavery, the equality of rights, the rule of law' (49). We therefore witness an attachment to law. I will explore later in the chapter how he imagines law can deliver all the things mentioned above. For the moment, I want to suggest that these pictures of law that Proudhon draws are not that contradictory; in the first place, he critiques Statist law – law in the hands of privilege – and in the second he presents an alternative type of law, a desired law, a law that will ensure freedom, equality and justice, a law that will come after a revolution, that will uproot the political regime that produces inequality, poverty and injustice.

Whilst Proudhon proposes that some types of law can play a constructive role in anarchist societies, other anarchists, like Emma Goldman and Peter Krotopkin are less optimistic about the institution of law and its usefulness to anarchist societies. Nevertheless, even if we go along with Proudhon's sympathetic view of law, law as an ally of the anarchist project, it is somewhat curious that he does not worry that law could colonise the way in which anarchist societies organise and jeopardise the anarchist emancipatory imaginary. Put differently, he does not worry that law may gain an *authority over* people and jeopardise core anarchist principles, such as those of self-mastery and mutualism. I will return to this observation later in the chapter. The aim in introducing Proudhon's contradictory statements on law was to point out the ambivalent relationship that certain anarchism(s) have with law.[2]

I need to clarify here that when I refer to law, I refer specifically to what is generally recognised as institutional law, such as cases, statutes and treaties vested with a branch of officials (e.g., the judiciary, court clerks, lawyers, police officers, prison officers) and institutions (e.g., courts, prisons, detention centres, etc.). I am aware, and I have argued elsewhere (Loizidou, 2007), following the work of Judith Butler, that norms may be as powerful as formal law in ordering life. For example, The Gender Recognition Act 2004 allows transgender people to apply and gain a Gender Recognition Certificate (GRC) and have

---

2 Newman, (2012: 307–29) offers a nuanced critique of anarchism's ambivalent relationship with law. Newman first traces the rejection of law as authority in the writings of Bakunin and Godwin, amongst others. He then points out that the anarchist rejection of juridical law reproduces unwittingly other forms of authority – those of science and the moral authority of society. He concludes that the only way of avoiding such reproductions is to remain constantly antagonistic to juridical law and thus cultivate an ethic of disobedience. A similar position is taken by Angus McDonald (2012:349–68). McDonald focuses on Bakunin's 1872 'programmatic statement for the Slavic Section of Zurich of the International' (350) to point out the limits of his rejection of juridical law, especially its naive conception of the nature of human beings and its limited understanding of the inventiveness of law, to call for an anarchism that disguises its anarchism. Stone (2011: 89–105) looks at the relationship between anarchy and law through the philosophy of Levinas. Like Newman, he concludes that an outright rejection of law is not advisable; law should remain, but we should embrace a 'perpetual ethical resistance' (89) towards it. Others, like Griedje Baars (2011:415–31), warns us that if the economy remains subjugated to the juridical it we will never reach the withering of the State. For Gelderloos (2010), an anarchist and ex-prisoner, any invocations of justice made by anarchists and social movement activists are doomed to reproduce injustice and, moreover, dehumanise all those who become victims of the juridical and police State.

their preferred gender recognised if certain conditions are fulfilled.[3] Despite attempts to change this part of the formal law,[4] we see that normative views about transgender people have not altered, with Nick Duffy reporting in the *Pink Paper* an increase of 81 per cent in hate crimes against transgender/sexual people (Duffy, 2019).[5] Norms can be forceful, violent and unjust, ordering lives and making people feel insecure despite the existence of formal laws that aspire to protect them. Nevertheless, I am focusing on formal law and its institutions for two reasons. First, formal laws, as I suggested at the start of the chapter, are not free[6] of prejudice and nor do they guarantee justice and equality, so it is important to see how we can demolish our reliance on them. Second, when classical anarchist thinkers invoke the law, they tend to refer to formal laws or the institutions of law.[7]

In the ensuing pages, I will elaborate on the complex relationship that anarchism has with law. Nevertheless, it is important to bear in mind that anarchism is a diverse project – we cannot talk of anarchism in the singular – and that while anarchists may be anti-authoritarian and believe in self-mastery, they also disagree on what form or shape an anarchist society should take. For example, some, like Max Stirner, foresee an anarchist society as 'a Union of Egoists drawn together by respect for each other's ruthlessness' (Woodcock, 1983:17) and others, like Proudhon, aspire to a more mutual society, organised by a combination of 'a federation of communes and worker's cooperatives' (17). Given the variation in and plethora of anarchist writings, especially by classical anarchists, I have chosen to look at the perspectives on law in classical anarchist writings and speeches that reflect individualist (Goldman) and mutualist (Proudhon, Kropotkin)

---

3   Nevertheless, it is important to note that a request for a GRC is not granted automatically. Applicants need to prove and have evidence from a GP (medical doctor) and a gender specialist (s. 3(1) of The Gender Recognition Act 2004) that they were genuinely suffering from gender dysphoria (s.1(a) The Gender Recognition Act 2004), they need to have transitioned into their acquired gender for two years (s.1 (b) The Gender Recognition Act 2004) and intend to live as their acquired gender until death (s.1 (c) The Gender Recognition Act 2004).
4   In 2016 the Women's and Equalities Committee recommended a reform of the 2004 Act. In particular, it recommended that applicants for a GRC do not require medical evidence of their wish to transition. There was a public consultation that ended on the 22 October 2018, but we have not yet seen a reform of The Gender Recognition Act 2004. See Fairbairn, Gheera, Pyper and Loft (2020).
5   See Duffy (2019). For an academic discussion of violence on transgender people, see Sharpe (2002: 2010).
6   For a caustic critique of formal liberal law's guilt of injustice, see Fitzpatrick's (1987) assessment of The Race Relations Act 1976 and Connaghan and Chudleigh's feminist critique of labour law (1987). For more recent critique of liberal legal racism, see Tuitt (2004) and El-Enany (2020).
7   There are exceptions to this generalisation, of course. The Russian anarchist Alexei Borovoy is conscious of social norms, and he briefly talks about conventions being an unavoidable part of every society, showing an awareness of the need for some kind of regulatory framework. See Borovoy (2011).

perspectives. The section that follows focuses on Proudhon's understanding of law and its aiding role for anarchism, whilst the second section reveals why Goldman and Kropotkin are sceptical of law's role in anarchist societies. The final section tracks contemporary debates on anarchism and views expressed in them on law's role in anarchism. It is important to forefront from the start that, to my mind, questioning the role of law as one of the ideological apparatuses of the State, as Louis Althusser (2001:85–126) has pointed out amongst others,[8] is paramount to anarchist life. Put differently, a life organised around the formality of law cannot adhere to the anarchist idea of living without masters or authority.

Law as an aid to anarchism

There are many signifiers that accompany institutional law, such as equality and justice. One of the more important aims of anarchism, as we have seen earlier in reference to Proudhon, is to secure equality for all by creating a society that has as its core the principle of equality. Equality is an objective to be attained, but is also an integral part of the process and practices that work towards achieving equality. Generally speaking, for anarchists an equal society can only be achieved if the State is dissolved, if masters, rulers or people who are stationed above others cease to exist, goods are distributed to all equally and decisions are taken without coercion and collectively. As I explain in Chapter 6, the practice of mutual aid or anarcho-communism becomes the anarchist vehicle through which I propose that this equal, free and just society can come to fruition. There is, therefore, an explicit critique by anarchist thinkers and

---

8   See Althusser, (2001), 85–126. Ideological State Apparatuses such as religion, family, communications, education and culture are realities. State Apparatuses are the other part of the Superstructure: the police, courts, prisons, army, head of state, government and administration. Law is part of both the State Apparatuses and the Ideological State Apparatuses. In this essay, Althusser explains how the subject is a product of ideology. 'Ideology …' he writes, '… interpellates [or, hails] individuals into subjects' (115). He uses an example of a police officer shouting at a passer-by, 'Hey, you there!' (118). The passer-by turns around. Althusser argues that '[by] this mere one hundred-and-eighty-degree physical conversion, he becomes a subject' (118). The turning around is a moment of recognition, a moment whereby the passer-by 'has recognised that the hail was "really" addressed to him, and that "it was really he who was hailed" (and not someone else)' (118). By turning around (an act of recognition), the passer-by (the concrete individual) takes his position in the world as a subject (abstraction). For Althusser, this 'concrete' example, this 'little theoretical theatre' (118), is merely a demonstration of his wider point that 'ideology has always already interpellated individuals as subjects … that individuals are always already subjects' (119). Interpellation or the process of subjectification (the turning of individuals into subjects) plays a central role in Althussser's understanding of how the relations within production are reproduced, the very problematic entertained in the essay cited. Interpellation, to recap, is both the process whereby the individual turns into a subject and simultaneously explicates that 'we are always already subjects'.

activists of claims made by the State in delivering equality, freedom and justice. In short, anarchists consider equality as championed by the State to be defunct. As I mentioned at the start of the chapter, it is common in our Western liberal and capitalist world to use the law as the medium for distributing equality. And, as I pointed out, this position has been successfully critiqued by critical legal writers in the twentieth and twenty-first centuries. It is, however, important to reiterate that liberal perspectives on law see the State as able to deliver equality through an array of rights – social rights (e.g., universal suffrage and gay marriage) and freedoms (e.g., freedom from discrimination) – or through economic adjustments (e.g., unemployment and housing benefits, as well as taxation). These are rights and freedoms that we find enshrined in law, as well as distributed and protected by law. The perception that liberal law can deliver equality was championed by the liberal political philosopher John Locke as early as 1689 in his *Two Treatises of Government* (1988). The social contractarian philosophers (Locke, Hobbes and Rousseau) created a fictional world which they called the 'state of nature', and attributed to it and people inhabiting it certain characteristics, identified problems that plagued the state of nature and proposed that these problems could be fixed if we had a government and a legal framework. Each had a slightly different version of the state of nature. For Hobbes, as he writes for example in the *Leviathan*, individuals in a state of nature, whilst equal to each other in mind and body (Hobbes, 1985: 183), are governed by self-interest that puts them at war against each other, and they therefore require a government or a Sovereign to protect them from each other and external enemies. For Locke, on the other hand, people are not governed by self-interest in the state of nature, but rather by some kind of moral equality (Locke, 1988: 269).[9] Moreover, this very moral equality ensures not only that we are all equal but also that nobody has the right to subject or harm another's liberty, property or health (271). For Locke, there is no entity, theological or political, that transcends man. Nevertheless, Locke admits that even in this peaceful state of nature, conflict may arise over how justice will be administered, over the meaning of justice and over the scarcity of material goods, and therefore a civil society – one that requires a government and laws – is necessary to adjudicate property and social conflicts, as well as war. As individual freedom, autonomy and equality were cornerstone principles in Locke's thinking, he considered that these could best be maintained in civil society, as individuals would have to *consent* to their governments and laws, making them equal to the laws and governments that they found themselves in. Locke, like classical anarchists, saw the state of nature as a space where equality and freedom thrived but, unlike anarchists, he could not see how this equality could be sustained without the aid of a government. My aim here is not to compare John Locke's concept of equality to that of anarchism, but to point out that he

---

9 Graeber and Wengrow (2021) point explicitly to the speculative aspect of the social contractarians, including Locke.

too envisages that equality is present in the state of nature, and that it can only endure if it is legalised.

It is nevertheless this very legal equality that Proudhon criticises – and differentiates anarchist thinking from liberal thinking – in the quote on page 22. The State, or any hierarchical form of government, he argues, makes equality impossible, capturing it within fishing nets and rendering it unable to *be* and *breathe*. Put in less metaphorical language, legal equality is not equality as it caters for the interests of those more privileged in society, those in government, the rich, men and white people. If equality is captured within the framework of the State, and if anarchists foresee and desire equality as an organising principle in an anarchist polity, we must expect them to be critical of the legal form of this equality. And, as I have argued earlier, it is not enough to be critical of liberal law, as critical legal scholars are, unless the possibility of having a society *without* law is entertained. I will turn to Proudhon first and his ideas of equality and law which, as I indicated earlier, are somewhat ambiguous, as he both wants and doesn't want the law to be a feature in an anarchist society.

So how does Proudhon move from considering laws as 'fishing nets in the hand of government' to proposing law should be an integral part of an anarchist society? How, in Proudhon's view, can an anarchist society hold onto equality and simultaneously be governed by the rule of law? How does he not see his stance being in contradiction with the anti-Statist and anti-authoritarian stand that anarchism holds? Could it be, we might ask, that he sees the emergence of some kind of different 'rule of law' than the one propagated by liberal philosophers such a Locke, in a non-Statist political system? Alex Prichard, in his essay 'Justice, Order and Anarchy: The International Political Theory of Pierre-Joseph Proudhon (1809–1865)',[10] reflects on Proudhon's International Relations Theory and his understanding of justice. I will engage here mostly with Prichard's lucid understanding of Proudhon's conceptualisation of justice in an anarchist society, which will in turn help us understand how it is connected to Proudhon's concept of equality and the rule of law. Proudhon, Prichard writes, understood justice as emerging out of our social relationships, *not* as transcendent, not owing therefore its existence to a god or, a god-like figure such as that of the Sovereign (Prichard, 2007:629). Justice, for this classical anarchist, is in other words immanent (Harbold, 1969:724; Prichard, 2007:629):

> Justice is not a commandment ordered by a superior authority to a lesser being, as the majority of authors who write on the rights of man teach;

---

10 See Prichard (2007). I am relying on secondary sources like Prichard's essay to present Proudhon's relationship to law and his understanding of justice primarily because Proudhon's essays 'La Guerre et la Paix' and 'De La Justice', where he explicitly talks of justice are in French and there are no translations of them yet in English. Other articles that engage with justice in Proudhon include Harbold (1969).

> Justice is immanent to the human soul ... [and] it constitutes its highest power and supreme dignity.
>
> (from Proudhon's *La Guerrer et la Paix*, quoted in Prichard, 2007:629)

As justice does not descend upon individuals and society as a gift from a god, Sovereign or god-like figure or body, we can conclude that justice is *created*. It is important to note that Proudhon's concept of justice is also present in the so-called state of nature. How, then, is justice created? Who creates it and how? Prichard writes that justice for Proudhon is the outcome of antagonism 'driven by our ideals, our passions and our needs, no less than by the internal conflict between our emotional and rational faculties' (629). Proudhon, as the above quote suggests, has his own understanding of how we function as individuals – as individuals we are imagined as having conflicts internally (emotions vs reason) and externally (desire vs need). As members of a society, Proudhon suggests we also replicate some of these antagonisms, as when our individual conscience comes into conflict with others in the communities we are part of. How does this conflict between individual and community get resolved? For Proudhon, the individual gradually acquires a 'collective conscience' (629) which transforms individual subjectivity into a collective one. As a result, a new idea of justice is achieved, one that attunes our self-interests with collective interests.[11] Put differently, individual conscience is no longer different from the collective conscience, because individuals work together to produce a sense of collective conscience. As the subject has a 'collective conscience' (629), the subject can produce norms arising out of collective interest that consequently produce a sense of communal justice. In this way Proudhon produces a 'theory' of justice based on the idea of 'collective conscience' and, as a result, of a three-layered process:

> The individual is the primary source of justice; the communities and groups individuals build or join become the second layer of justice, are irreducible to the individuals comprising them, and have a moral autonomy which Proudhon derives from the reality of their 'collective conscience'; and finally, the norms of these collectives or associations feed back on to individual rationalisations of justice, and both help and hinder the subsequent development of the moral capacity in humans and in society.
>
> (Prichard, 2007:630)

The sequence of Proudhon's understanding of justice flows, as you can see, from an individual justice reconciled with a collective sense of justice that in turn transforms what the initial individual justice held onto. This tripartite

---

11 For Proudhon, we are 'savage' in the state of nature, but we are also able to shed our self-interest over time as we constantly improve ourselves to become collective subjects (Prichard, 2007:630).

operation of justice also has at the basis of its operation individual freedom, dignity and equality. For Proudhon, it is paramount that individual justice is meaningless, or null and void, if it is not on a par with that held by a community, or association (Harbold, 1969; Prichard, 2007). We can see more clearly now, unlike my initial suspicion to the contrary, that Proudhon's concept of justice has nothing to do with legal justice. Proudhon's concept of justice is the *outcome* of a struggle that individuals have first with themselves, then with their communities. The outcome of the latter struggle informs and affects individual understandings of justice. In addition, Proudhon's concept of justice does not have individuals being subordinated to law – as they are in effect law-makers – nor does it function within the framework of the State. We can *contrast* this to any liberal understanding of justice that merely *balances* norms between individuals and society and functions within the parameters of the State, with individuals subordinated to the law. Proudhon's understanding of justice is different, as you may have guessed, from Locke's understanding of legal justice and equality. Locke, as we have already seen, anticipates that equality and justice cannot be sustained in the state of nature and therefore the State and law need to be created to give a fair judgement on conflicts that arise over the scarcity of goods. Consequently, we as individuals will not lose our individuality and equality because we will have to *consent* to the State's or a government's management of common affairs. Locke envisages that individuals will have equal bargaining powers to those that govern in civil society, because they will have the right to dissent to anything they do not agree with. Even if Locke does not anticipate the individual being subordinate to government, his proposition of justice and equality is very different from that of Proudhon. Proudhon first transforms the individual into a being that, through struggle between the individual and collective sense of justice, acquires a 'collective conscience'. Second, in his vision of justice, individuals are not subordinated to the norms or laws of their community, because they are not only part of their very making but also their *embodiment*. Justice is immanent, and is therefore always in the process of being made by individuals and associations.

As you may have guessed by now, Proudhon's concept of justice is inextricably linked to the production of equality. As Harbold tells us, quoting from Proudhon's *First Memoire*, "'[t]he practice of justice is to share equally in the good produced, subject to the condition of work'", and Proudhon recognised "'equality of conditions [as] the principle of social life and universal solidarity [as]its sanction'" (Harbold, 1969:728). A failure to run a society based on principles of equality, he predicted, will give rise to revolutions (728). Moreover, his understanding of equality addressed both social (e.g., education) and personal (e.g., equality between men and women) matters. Whilst he was aware that interests exist that may put individuals into conflict with one another, Proudhon also believed that

> [interests] ... are "crude facts" that, in all their diversity, point to a law that will render them comprehensible, and with our discovery of that law can

be ordered, coordinated and harmonized, and the human good and liberty they have imperfectly represented can be fully realized.

(cited in Harbold, 1969:726)

Here we can see that Proudhon anticipated that self-interest can be diluted by a type or a kind of law that would ensure equality *as* justice. The question that remains to be answered is how can law, a 'fishing net', a tool in the hands of government, bring *equality as justice*, or the harmonisation of interests, to fruition without jeopardising anarchism's anti-authority stance?

The answer to this question can be found in Proudhon's 'General Idea of the Revolution in the Nineteenth Century' (2011a:543–99), published in 1851. Here Proudhon envisages two stages in the making of *equality as justice*. The first is a *distributive* stage, where privileged members of society give social, political and economic 'goods' to those who do not have them. The second stage of reaching equality he calls *commutative* justice, or the rule of contracts (Harbold, 1969:729). Proudhon understands the distributive stage of justice as being governed by 'the *reign of law*, or in more concrete terms, *feudal, governmental*, or *military* rule' (Proudhon 2011a:562). Distributive justice is the type of justice that political systems, whether democratic nation-states or kingdoms, use to appease the people by providing them with rights, albeit restrictive, as we have witnessed, for example, in the case of The Gender Recognition Act 2004. The equality that distributive justice creates is somewhat inadequate according to Proudhon. Distributive justice is inadequate because it is given to people by government and, therefore, it does not correspond to the interests of those who may be affected by it, as is the case with The Gender Recognition Act 2004. As I explain in footnote 3, a person cannot have their acquired gender recognised automatically. An acquired gender can only be recognised if it fulfils an array of conditions, including being certified by two professionals (a medical doctor and a gender professional) about the physical and psychological status of the applicant. Although The Gender Recognition Act 2004 superficially recognises that transgender people should acquire equal rights, it is inadequate as it does not in its current guise correspond to the interests of transgender people who demand the abolition of medical certification, for example. It is not just that governing through a form of distributive justice does not adequately address demands for equality, it simultaneously puts government above the people, sustaining in this way a system of authority. Having sovereignty or authority over people's lives, as I have already suggested, is antithetical to anarchist principles. Put differently, we can say that distributive justice privileges, under the guise of democracy, the interests of the few and gives them power over the many (Proudhon, 2011a:567–73). It is important to remember that in Proudhon's understanding, justice and equality are constantly interlinked to each other and to the 'form' of polity that they are supposed to be operating with. There is no justice if, for example, equality is absent, furthermore, if there is no equality there is *no* anarchic polity. It is not surprising, then, that Proudhon suggests that the future of equality as justice relies on another form of justice, *commutative justice* (Harbold, 1969:729).

Commutative justice, as Proudhon explains in 'General Idea of the Revolution in the Nineteenth Century', operates through contracts (Harbold, 1969:729; Proudhon, 2011a:562). These contracts are, he says, social in their form (Proudhon, 2011a:562–6). If communicative justice operates through the idea of the social contract, then how does Proudhon's account of the social contract differ from those given by other social contractarians (Locke, Hobbes, Rousseau)? In the 'General Idea of the Revolution in the Nineteenth Century', Proudhon elaborates on his idea of the social contract, and consequently on communicative justice, by critiquing Rousseau's *Social Contract* (Proudhon, 2011a:562). Proudhon considers Rousseau's thesis to be limited for two important reasons: (a) it champions the subordination of people to a representative form of government, for it fails to consider whether people have the freedom to contract (564); and (b) it is inadequate, because whilst it articulates the political rights of people, it consistently remains silent or 'supresses' any discussion about their social, economic, etc. rights (564). Rousseau's *Social Contract*, according to Proudhon, is nothing but a political contract that wants to secure in this way the rights of the already privileged in this way. To this effect, in the eyes of Proudhon, Rousseau's idea of the social contract becomes a *war contract* and consequently has very little connection to any idea of the social: 'It is a contract of hatred, this monument of incurable misanthropy, this coalition of the barons of property, commerce and industry against the disinherited lower class, this oath of social war indeed, which Rousseau calls Social Contract …' (Proudhon, 2011a:566). How, then does Proudhon come to the conclusion that Rousseau's *Social Contract* is a *war contract* that does not secure the rights and liberty of people? He does so by exploring the legal definition of a contract, following the definition of a French nineteenth-century politician and lawyer, and a significant figure in French jurisprudence, Alexandre August Ledru-Rollin. Ledru-Rollin, Proudhon explains, describes a contract as an 'agreement for equal exchange; it is by virtue of this agreement that liberty and well being increase; while by the establishment of authority, both of these necessarily diminish' (Proudhon, 2011a:562–3). At the centre of the legal definition of a contract, Proudhon writes, lay two fundamental principles: (a) the principle of freedom, i.e., the idea that parties enter into a contract freely; and (b) the principle of exchange (563). According to Proudhon, Rousseau fails to address the horizontal aspect of the contract, the ways in which individuals freely agree to undertake a contract, and instead focuses primarily on a vertical political contract, where – and this is the important part of Proudhon's critique – there is *no* exchange or reciprocity between the parties. At first, this might sound strange. For all of us who are familiar with the social contractarian philosophers are very much aware that part of their narrative consists of an exchange: individuals give up their freedom *for* security or *to* gain rights, the right to vote, etc. We may say that exchange or a form of reciprocity is very much part of this 'transaction'. For Proudhon, this is *not* an exchange and this is because Rousseau does not consider as part of the concept of the contract: (a) the freedom of the party that contracts; (b) the personal direct engagement of the party in the contract; (c) the party's signature, which demonstrates their understanding of the exchange that it is to be undertaken; and finally (d) the 'share of liberty and prosperity which he should experience' (564). Instead, what we witness in Rousseau's *Social Contract* is a:

> [s]ocial contract [that] is neither an act of reciprocity, nor an act of association. Rousseau takes care not to enter into such considerations. It is an act of appointment of arbiters, chosen by the citizens, without any preliminary agreement, for all cases of contest, quarrel, fraud or violence, which can happen in the relations which they may subsequently form among themselves, the said arbiters being clothed with sufficient force to put their decisions into execution, and to collect their salaries.
>
> (Proudhon, 2011a:564)

We may agree with Proudhon that the failure of Rousseau's *Social Contract* lays in considering that people can be directly involved in the managing of the polity, as well as the social and economic aspects of their everyday lives. Rousseau gives such governing matters to functionaries who, in turn, in their representative capacities, tend to ignore the very people who have entrusted such a task to them; moreover, they subtract from the people the possibility of being 'free' to act. Put differently, for Proudhon, Rousseau's *Social Contract* in its entirety takes away from us the freedom to exchange with others according to our conscience.

A proper social contract, for Proudhon, should be made between parties that share an interest and 'it implies that a man bargains with the aim of securing his liberty and his revenue at the same time, without any possible loss' (Proudhon, 2011a:563); it is reciprocal because 'it imposes no obligation upon the parties' apart from fulfilling the agreement, and is not answerable to any governing body or authority (563). Such a contract could be made between people exchanging labour, products, education or political rights. Most importantly, it is a contract that vests the whole of the person in the exchange: '[it] should include all citizens with their interests and relations' (563). In Proudhon's words:

> The Social Contract is the supreme act by which each citizen pledges to the association his love, his intelligence, his work, his services, his goods, in return for the affection, ideas, labor, products, services, and goods of his fellows; the measure of the right of each being determined by the importance of his contributions, and the recovery that be demanded in proportion to his deliveries.
>
> (563)

Proudhon anticipates that such a contract is an inclusive contract. Any sign indicating that citizens are being prohibited from contracting will render a contract null and void or, as he writes, 'it will be a fraud, against which annulment might at any time be invoked justly' (563).

Proudhon's 'social contract' or *commutative justice* is a very different social contract from the one proposed by Rousseau. It is a contract that has at its heart equality and justice, as well as exchange and freedom. It is a contract that will be void if it becomes the instrument by means of which citizens can be excluded. It is this reason, bearing in mind that democracy was built on the bones of slavery, that urges Proudhon to reject slavery in the 'General Idea of the Revolution in the Nineteenth Century' (567). Historically democracy was practised through exclusion; no women or slaves were to participate in the everyday affairs of the Greek polis. But despite the fact that Proudhon's concept of *justice as equality* differs from those offered by liberal and contractarian political theorists like Rousseau, we may want to be sceptical of Proudhon's transplantation of a legal term, that of a contract, as the 'tool' that will ensure justice and a concept of justice (*commutative justice*). The concept of commutative justice as discussed by Proudhon recognises that there can only be equality in a political system that recognises that we have property in our human beingness, that we hold property within ourselves (and thus we are not the property of the State or any authority) and as such we can freely contract in our political, social and economic interests. However, the history of the idea of commutative justice that he promotes demonstrates that it excluded certain people from having such a right in themselves. The concept of *commutative justice* that has its roots in Roman law which excluded slaves from having resort to it (Beever, 2013:288–9) as slaves were not recognised as having property within their being. It is true that Proudhon foresees this possibility when he writes that once a contract becomes exclusionary it is not a contract. But this does not detract from the fact that what he is proposing be considered the vehicle for justice and equality is a legal instrument that, once ossified into rules of operation, runs the danger of exercising mastery *over* the freedom that individuals have to reach agreements. In other words, what Proudhon proposes runs the risk of becoming the very thing that can take freedom away from individuals, vesting it in the law. So the problematic of justice and equality may remain unresolved, or reproduce in a different way the problems of distributive justice. Other anarchists, like Kropotkin and Goldman, were aware and critical of the limits that law imposed on anarchism and its possibilities. I follow their criticisms below.

Without law: hurtful, useless, wooden law

In his essay 'Law and Authority' (2002:195–218) Kropotkin explains why law is both *useless* and *hurtful* to society (212). His characterisations of law as such follow his summary of a brief history of modern law. Kropotkin believed that in pre-modern societies people did not need laws because everyday affairs were arranged through 'customs, habits and usages' (201). Pre-modern people, he observes, were, like animals, social by nature and managed their everyday affairs through customs, habits and usages because they recognised that these practices were *useful* to their preservation (202). Moreover, Kropotkin considers such practices as 'anterior to all law' and religion (202) because they are not derived from either law or God. Such practices, he writes, 'are found amongst all animals living in society' and 'are spontaneously developed by the very nature of things, like those habits in animals which men call instinct' (202). Like Proudhon and the social contractarians, Kropotkin draws his own image of the 'state of nature' or pre-modern society. It is a society, where everybody is imagined as working harmoniously, a point that he reiterates, as we will see in Chapter 6, in his book *Mutual Aid* (2009). Is his vision of a harmonious state of nature valid? It is as valid as that of any of the other political theorists who engaged with it and, to a large extent, even if we accept the scientific validity of Kropotkin's understanding of the state of nature, it does not interest me. As somebody writing in the twenty-first century, I am aware of the criticisms that any theory that provides us with the proposition that nature describes who we are or how we do things is essentialist. We may, though, imagine some readers objecting to the emphasis that Kropotkin puts on nature, or the natural way in which 'things are done'. Indeed, we can imagine a critique emanating from post-structuralist feminist philosophy, such as Judith Butler's critique of biological or natural concepts. As early as *Gender Trouble* (1990) and *Bodies that Matter* (1993) Butler questioned philosophical and feminist accounts that present gender as the cultural construction of sex, creating in this way two genders – men and women – that leave un-problematised the idea that sex is a 'natural' category. Moreover, through the theory of performativity Butler has shown that claims to natural categories do not pre-exist the very utterance that makes such claims (Butler 1993; Loizidou 2007:35–42). Following Butler, we may therefore say that Kropotkin's reference to a natural state of life is a performative speech act that by its very enunciation creates or brings into being a 'natural' state of life. Such a criticism, however, would be short-sighted. It would not take into account the fact that Kropotkin's nature – or rather state of nature – is not 'natural', but rather is presented as an amalgamation of *techne* and nature (*physis*). It is not dissimilar to Heraclitus's aphorism about nature: 'Nature loves to hide'. Heraclitus's aphorism has been interpreted to mean that nature is not bereft of technology, and, more precisely, that nature holds within itself a technology of appearance (growth) and disappearance (decay or destruction) (Hadot, 2006). Similarly, Kropotkin thinks of nature *as* technology. It is noticeable that when Kropotkin talks of 'customs, habits and usages', which for him are practices that both cement and preserve the social, these are presented as practices that develop over time; they grow (appear) and decay (disappear) depending on the role they play in social preservation. They are not therefore static practices but rather an ever-altering process towards accommodating changes in communities or society. Indeed, when Kropotkin refers to humans developing these practices (customs, habits, usages) out of instinct, as animals do out of habit (Kropotkin 2002:202), he brings to our attention firstly that human instincts are *not* a given but rather they are 'cultivated' over time to 'keep society together in the struggle it is forced to maintain for existence' (202). Secondly, human instinct is unlike animal habit. Whereas animals preserve themselves through habitual or automatic practices (we know, for example, that bears hibernate over the winter period in order to preserve heat), human instincts, which develop spontaneously and contribute to human preservation, require a struggle, thinking or a mastery over how we are to live together. It is not coincidental, I propose, that Kropotkin puts the word instinct in proximity to the problematic of co-existence and in relation to animal habits. I want to suggest that his understanding of the state of nature is one that requires different techniques – in animals a technique of automatic preservation and in human animals contemplation or reasoning. Let's not forget that the word spontaneous, the attribute that Kropotkin gives to human instincts, comes from the Latin *sponte*. As Sara Ahmed reminds us in *Wilful Subjects* (2014), the etymology of the word *sponte* refers us to 'willing' or 'of one's free will'; this, in turn, directs us to the process of thinking, of reflecting and understanding, attributes that we have designated to the will since Kant. I will return to specific defences of Kropotkin's use of nature and the non-essentialist element when I address his concept of mutual aid in Chapter 6. I hope that for the moment I have convinced you, even temporarily, that his concept of nature is not so essentialist, and is more complex than it first appears.

Even if we do not engage in this debate on whether or not Kropotkin's state of nature is an amalgamation of both nature and culture, it suffices to note that his understanding of the state of nature is very different from that of Hobbes. As Saul Newman (2012) points out, Kropotkin's understanding of the state of nature is diametrically opposed to the one offered by Hobbes. Kropotkin did not see the state of nature as a threat to humanity. On the contrary, he and other 'anarchists see [it] as the basis of ethical community …' (Newman, 2012:313). Indeed, Kropotkin suggests that the state of nature sustains and maintains sociality. However, Kropotkin sees the introduction of law – institutional law – as a disruption to social cohesion. In his opinion laws become useless and hurtful because they serve not society but rather 'the ruling class' (Kropotkin, 2002:203). For Kropotkin, State laws are divided 'into three principal categories: protection of property, protection of persons, protection of government' (212) and have the effect of stabilising and petrifying (through inscription) customs that accommodate the ruling class, inevitably at the expense of society (Kropotkin, 2002:205–6) or those they oppress. If we briefly look into some of the categories of law that Kropotkin refers us to, we may see more clearly how law is injurious. Let us take first the category of law, the category that protects the government. He writes that all administrative laws, from tax laws to the 'organisation of ministerial departments and their offices' (Kropotkin 2002:214) serve to create and sustain agencies of the State which, in turn, will be invested in protecting the 'privileges of the possessing classes' (212). Moreover, if we focus upon laws protecting the person, such as criminal laws that appeal to the whole social body or cater for the security of the whole social realm, we will notice that he writes that the breach of such laws does not reveal a harm to society. Most crimes are the result of economic inequality or are property-related offences, affecting private property owners (215). Indeed, even if we look at contemporary statistics from the Office of National Statistics for England and Wales for the year ending June 2021, these show that over 72 per cent of crimes were property related (robbery, theft, criminal damage, fraud and misuse of data).[12] For Kropotkin, the answer to the disappearance of crime does not lie in better laws or in more severe forms of punishment, but rather in the abolition of private property (which he considers to be the root of most crimes against the person) and the abolition of punishment (215–16). He considers punishment useless in addressing the economic inequalities that are at the root of every crime. This is very different from the argument made by utilitarians like Bentham, who saw prison in the shape of panopticon as a better way of reforming prisoners and causing them to modify their behaviour because of constant surveillance. Kropotkin did not desire better punishment but rather no punishment. Why? His starting point was that law cannot protect the whole of the social body, but instead sustains and expands upon the power of the ruling class: for Kropotkin any laws and any form of punishment injurious. Law removes from the social body the equality that exists in the state of nature and, moreover, it denigrates individuals and ignores the welfare of the governed. Kropotkin describes law as being useless or without value precisely because it fails to deliver justice and equality to society. And as law cannot deliver what it promises, Kropotkin proposes, 'No more law! No more judges!' (2002: 315)

Similarly, the Russian-born anarchist Emma Goldman was critical of the law. We find her criticism of law in essays such as 'Anarchism: What It Really Stands For' (1969a:47–68) and 'Prisons: A Social Crime and Failure' (1969b:109–26). We can, however, find the most instructive criticisms of law – where she describes law as being wooden and a repressive machine that kills any form of individuality (Berkman and Goldman 2005:62–3) – when we study her personal encounters with law (arrest and trial). As we will see below, Goldman's acts in encountering the law reveal an unsavoury image of law; they show that law is an apparatus for sustaining inequality and inflicting torture. Moreover, she also demystifies law's authority. I will turn to these instances later on in this chapter, but first I will navigate us through Goldman's essays that critically engage with law.

---

12 See link for Year Ending June 2021 edition of this data set at Office of National Statistics, Crime in England and Wales at: https://www.ons.gov.uk/peoplepopulationandcommunity/crimeandjustice/datasets/crimeinenglandandwalesappendixtables. Accessed 1 December 2021.

Most anarchist definitions describe anarchism as a politics without authority or leadership. Any references to law that seek to demonstrate its role in sustaining authority and any critiques of law raised in connection with critiques of non-anarchic forms of governing are usually secondary, as we have seen with Proudhon. This is a moot point, and we if we follow the etymological definition of the word anarchism we notice that it gives us both possibilities: the possibility of anarchism understood as a way of life bereft of rulers, and anarchism as a way of life bereft of law. Emma Goldman is one of the very few anarchists who embedded in her definition of anarchism the idea that anarchist society is one *without* man-made law:

> Anarchism: The philosophy of a new social order based on liberty unrestricted by man-made law; the theory that all forms of government rest on violence, and are therefore wrong and harmful, as well as unnecessary.
> (Goldman, 1969a:50)

For Goldman, anarchist philosophy explains how anarchist society will be organised. An anarchist society is one that has freedom from *man-made* law, what I call institutional law, as its bedrock. In the same essay, Goldman recognises and offers an analysis of how organised religion, property and the State are harmful to and violent towards society and are foes of anarchism (Goldman, 1969a:53–6). So, if anarchism is a society without *man-made* law, how does Goldman imagine such a society will organise its everyday affairs without disputes and violence? In explaining how anarchism aims to build a society that is free from man-made law, without any centralised hierarchical authorities governing, Goldman turns to natural law. Natural law becomes the guiding tool for an anarchist society. We have already noticed from the above that her critique of law is somewhat precise; it is *man-made* law that she denounces. It is the very commanding (to act or be in certain ways) and regulatory (regulating whether we act or are in certain ways) aspect of man-made law that presents itself as being *above* all of us that she finds unsatisfactory, even violent, as the earlier quotation reveals. Man-made law, law as authority or master of our lives, is understood to be against the core idea of anarchism, freedom. Goldman does not view natural law as an imposing law. On the contrary, she understands it as being in synchrony or comradeship with us. It is important to note that her natural law is not sophisticated. It does not draw on Thomas Aquinas or any other renowned natural lawyer. By natural law Goldman simply means the natural behaviour of humans, unrestricted by institutional law. Consider her words:

> A natural law is that factor in man which asserts itself freely and spontaneously without any external force, in harmony with the requirements of nature. For instance, the demand for nutrition, sex gratification, for light, air, and exercise, is a natural law.
> (Goldman, 1969a:58)

This natural law is a flow that passes through each one of us, letting us know when it is time for food, light or exercise, or to satisfy our sexual needs. We may agree that natural law can alert us to these needs, but we may want to ask how would or could such needs be satisfied without jeopardising someone else's freedom or needs? Goldman does not provide an answer to this question, but she is adamant that such needs cannot be satisfied within the parameters of institutional law:

> But this expression needs not the law, the gun, the handcuff, or the prison. To obey such law, if we may call it obedience, requires only spontaneity and free opportunity. That governments do not maintain such harmonious factors is proven by the terrible array of violence, force and coercion all governments use in order to live.
>
> (Goldman, 1969a:58)

Undoubtedly, institutional law and its enforcement branch, the police, have proved over the centuries to be violent, forceful and coercive, and have been used, as well as capitalism, to protect those who are already privileged, rather than produce an equal and just society. Nevertheless, while the critique of institutional or man-made law is valid, Goldman does not provide, unlike Kropotkin, an in-depth detailed analysis of how natural law may be better or how it will operate. She just lets us know, somewhat rhetorically, that harmony amongst us will be achieved if we follow natural law because it 'grows naturally out of solidarity of interests' (1969a:59). As I have nothing more to go on to explicate Goldman's understanding of natural law, we can suppose – drawing on her critique of institutional law and its mechanisms, such as punishment and the institution of prison (109–26) – that like Kropotkin (whom she cites), she could see that there was a flow in life. This flow could attend to individual and group needs without needing to regulate them, as long as there were opportunities for work for everybody, equality and a spirit of solidarity in the management of life. She says as much when she criticises governments for destroying opportunities for economic and social equality and sustaining this destruction through the law (59). In her essay 'Prisons: A Social Crime and Failure' (1969b:109–26) Goldman blames crime on the lack of work opportunities, precarious and harsh working conditions, long working hours and lack of affordable housing, and sees institutional law, punishment and prisons as artificial and false mechanisms for addressing the root of criminality. She argues more security will not be achieved through draconian law and heavy punishments but rather through the amelioration of the conditions that enslave us and direct us to property crime or violence as a way of redressing the unjust conditions that exist in our society. And, like Kropotkin, Goldman points to property ownership as creating and sustaining inequality (1969a:53–5). We may conclude, therefore, with the little we have in terms of a sustained exposition of natural law, that for Goldman natural law creates better conditions for a social life because it is not vested with the divisive and forceful dimensions of man-made law. We can speculate then that what Goldman aspires to is a society that, once free (from oppression) and equal (social, economic, political), requires no other law than the flow of interactions between people or associations to organise it and sustain it.

We shall see next how Goldman demystifies the authority of man-made law through her own encounters with the law. She points both to the oppressive, unequal and deceptive character of institutional law and its executors, such as the police. There is no better explication of the failure of law than her conspiracy charges against the draft that I engage with below.

In 1917 Emma Goldman and her fellow anarchist Alexander Berkman were tried for conspiracy against the Selective Draft Act 1917. The Act authorised the US federal government to conscript young men between the ages of 21 and 30 into the army in preparation for the US entry into World War I. Goldman and Berkman, along with other anarchists, lawyers and academics, organised various events including a debate at the Harlem Casino on the evening of 18 May 1917, the same day the draft bill was going through Congress. The event was attended by around 10,000 people and it aimed to inform citizens of the perils of war, the devastation that World War I was already spreading across Europe and why the organisers were against conscription. On 1 June 1917 they also published in their magazines *The Blast* and *Mother Earth* an essay written by Goldman against conscription.[13] Both Goldman and Berkman insisted during the trial that the aim of their gathering at Harlem Casino and of Goldman's essay 'The No Conscription League' (Goldman 2000:398–9) was not to influence young men or discourage them from registering. Rather, they wanted to create a space where they could disseminate information about the perils of World War I and conscription, as well as to enable young men to make an informed decision regarding the draft.[14] In his closing speech to the jury, for example, Berkman categorically denied that he would encourage anyone not to register, on the grounds that because he was not of conscription age and thus not put in the position of facing punishment if he decided not to register, it would be irresponsible of him to make others do what he did not have to do:

> I would never advise anyone to do a thing which does not endanger me. I am willing to resist tyranny. If I were willing and ready to resist tyranny, I might advise others to do so, because I myself would do it. I would be

---

13 See Goldman (2000), 398–9.
14 The prosecution's case rested upon Berkman and Goldman conspiring against the draft, and specifically conspiring to influence young men not to register. Berkman and Goldman, in their closing speeches to the jury and during cross-examination, argued that they did not attempt to stop young men from registering. Instead, they wanted to inform them why compulsory conscription was against anarchist ideals. Anarchists considered themselves to be anti-militarists and anti-nationalists.

with them and take the responsibility. But I was excepted from that registration business. I did not have to register. I was beyond the age. I was not in danger. And would I advise anyone to do the thing which does not put me in danger?

(Berkman and Goldman, 2005:54)

More importantly, as Berkman pointed out, as an anarchist he would never try to force his position on any man, but rather encourage decisions to be made according to the conscience of each man (Berkman and Goldman, 2005:28). Similarly, in a letter sent to her secretary and associate Mary E. Fitzgerald, to be presented at the first non-conscription meeting that took place on the 23 March 1917, Goldman explains her position:

I do not advise or urge young men to refuse to register. As an anarchist, I could not do that, because that would be taking the same position as the Government, by telling someone to do this or that. I refuse to advise young men to register, it must be left to the individual.
(Goldman [&] Berkman v United States; Transcript of Record 1917 Sept. 25 Supreme Court of the United States: 241)

Goldman and Berkman were nevertheless found guilty as charged. They were sentenced to two years' imprisonment, each incurred a $10,000 fine and were subsequently exiled to Russia in 1919.

The trial transcript, along with statements surrounding the trial, offers an insight into Goldman's – and anarchism's more generally – relation to law. We witness Goldman not being afraid of law or of punishment. She never saw law as the author of her life. In other words, she did not seek legal recognition. Law was only useful to her as a theatrical stage, from which she could demonstrate her beliefs. Moreover, she always turned her appearances in court into opportunities to propagate anarchist beliefs. When, in 1916, she was convicted for breaching the Comstock Law of 1873[15] (by giving lectures on the topic of birth control), she used the trial to defend contraception and took a whole hour in court doing so. As Shulman writes:

On April 20 Emma's case went to trial. Emma defended herself. Three staid judges presided over an overflowing courtroom. Emma, as always, was expected to put on the best show in town.
After some witty exchanges with the prosecution, Emma turned her trial into an eloquent defence of birth control. Her closing speech to the court lasted for one rapturous hour. 'If it is a crime,' she concluded with passion,

---

15 See 'Birth Control Pioneer' at The Emma Goldman Papers at: https://www.lib.berkeley.edu/goldman/MeetEmmaGoldman/birthcontrolpioneer.html. Accessed 15 August 2013.

'to work for healthy motherhood and happy child-life, I am proud to be considered a criminal.'

(Shulman, 1971:170)

Goldman conceived of the law as 'something', a stage that she could stand on and over – not beside or before (unlike critical legal thinkers, as we have seen earlier) – and account for a way of life that was *not* grounded in law.

Moreover, Goldman's understanding of the operation and effects of law was further elaborated in the 1917 trial. Goldman foresaw 'that [they] could expect not justice' (Goldman, 1970b:613) from their trial for conspiracy to undermine the draft. She thus decided to turn the courtroom and trial into a space where anarchism could be propagated (614). Indeed, in this remarkable speech Goldman both explains to the jury what anarchism stands for and reveals the limits of man-made law. She focuses upon two characteristics that are prominent in law. In doing so, she also clearly points out that these two characteristics are limits in man-made law. What are these characteristics? The first is hypocrisy. So, let's see why Goldman calls the law hypocritical. She considers law to be hypocritical because she deems the charge against herself and Berkman to be a 'trumped-up charge' (Berkman and Goldman, 2005:61). I would like to suggest that by characterising law as hypocritical, Goldman demonstrates that law is grounded in deceit and illegal methods. How does she reach this conclusion?

For somebody to be charged with conspiracy, it must be proved that there is an agreement between two or more parties to commit an offence and at least one of the parties must have committed an act aimed at the achievement of an offence. Berkman and Goldman were charged, as I have already noted, with conspiring to encourage men of conscription age not to register for military service. They were charged with section 37 of the Criminal Code. For them to be found guilty of the charge, it had first to be proved that they had agreed between themselves to encourage men of conscription age not to register. This would have fulfilled one part of the *actus reus* or conduct of the charge that required evidence of an agreement to do as much. Furthermore, the charge required the proof of a breach of US law. They would be breaching US law because on 18 May 1917 Congress had passed the Selective Service Act 1917. The prosecution would have needed to prove at least one overt act that breached the law, or that one of them had done something (e.g., circulating pamphlets with explicit instructions) that demonstrated that they were encouraging young men not to register. The Prosecutor, Mr Content, addressed the charge to the jury precisely in the way I described above (Berkman and Goldman, 2005:23). In making his case, Content presented as evidence of Goldman and Berkman's 'overt acts' the gathering at the Harlem Casino of 18 May and the subsequent publication of the essay 'No Conscription League' in *Mother Earth* and *The Blast* in early June 1917.

Goldman considers the charge hypocritical. There are two main reasons that provoke her to characterise the law as such. First, it was a well-known fact that as anarchists both she and Berkman were against militarism, nationalism and war. As she aptly puts it:

> To charge people with having conspired to do something which they have been engaged in doing most of their lives, namely their campaign against war, militarism and conscription as contrary to the best interest of humanity, is an insult to human intelligence.
> (Berkman and Goldman, 2005:57)

In her eyes this proved that they did not have to come to an agreement about the dissemination of information against militarism. Recall that the charge of conspiracy against the draft requires the proof of an agreement. The second reason relates directly to whether Goldman and Berkman breached the Selective Draft Act itself. On 18 May, when they were talking at the Harlem Casino, the legislation had not yet been passed. The Act was passed while they were in 'conference'. So, on 18 May, at least, they could not have committed an offence against the Selective Draft Act. Even if we suppose that they did find out while in 'conference' that the draft had been passed, Goldman contended that they never suggested eligible drafters should object, but rather they repeatedly merely presented drafters with their views against conscription in order to enable them to make their own decisions about whether or not they would register (Goldman [&] Berkman v United States; Transcript of Record 1917 Sept. 25 Supreme Court of the United States:241). Even in her essay 'The No-Conscription League' (Goldman, 2000:398–9), which was presented as evidence against her, she explains that the No Conscription League was a platform whereby those who had already or were about to make the decision not to register could ask for and be offered support, as well as a space where opposition to militarism and the killing of fellow human beings could be debated (398). Furthermore, as she writes in the 'The No Conscription League' essay, this platform could additionally enable the democratic recognition of the conscientious objector in the US, aligning the US democratically with other European countries, such as England, which recognised the democratic right of citizens to object on grounds of conscience to be drafted (398).

General jurisprudence's method of critique is not dissimilar to that of Goldman. Like her, it points to the inconsistencies within law. For example, in an early essay Costas Douzinas and Ronnie Warrington point out the paradoxical and contradictory ways in which law delivers justice. In '"A Well-Founded Fear of Justice": Law and Ethics in Postmodernity' (1991:115–147) they focus on the figure of the asylum-seeker refugee and the legal asylum process. As they inform us, the law on such occasions demands that refugees prove that they were persecuted and, moreover, that their fear of persecution was 'well founded'. In other words, a 'well-founded' fear would need to be 'satisfied by showing (a) actual fear and (b) good reason for this fear' (121). Douzinas and Warrington argue that it is paradoxical that law demands that 'fear', an irrational feeling, be proved through reason by people who have just escaped persecution, wars, etc. In other words, law's formula for delivering justice to asylum seekers and refugees is inherently corrupted by the disparity between how it describes the ground for seeking asylum and how it asks for the ground to be proved. Inevitably, they argue, this legal inconsistency leads to injustice. In conclusion, they propose that for the balance to be redressed, for justice to be done, law would need to have the refugee asylum seeker be judged on their own terms. Law would need to understand that fear is irrational.

Pointing to the inconsistencies and paradoxes of law is also part of Goldman's way of critiquing it. Nevertheless, her critique can be distinguished from that offered by general jurisprudence. Unlike general jurisprudence, Goldman does not merely expose to us how law is inconsistent. She goes a step further and shows that law is based on untruth, that law is at its core deceitful. While general jurisprudence points to the exclusive practices of law, Goldman points to the illegalities with which law engages. There is a fundamental difference between these two critiques. The first, general jurisprudence, accuses law of being exclusionary and aspires to 'correct' the law by pointing to its exclusions. The second, the anarchist critique, does not aspire to correct the law. On the contrary, the inconsistent and illegal aspect of law becomes for anarchists a platform from which they can argue and show that an organisation of life bereft of law could create a better life.

It is not only the fictitious, deceitful aspects of law that make Goldman desire its destruction. The second characteristic that Goldman adorns the law with is that of being unable to catch the flow of change in life (Berkman and Goldman, 2005:62–3), demonstrating in this way the non-relationship between law and life. As she points out in her closing speech to the jury, 'Progress is ever renewing, ever becoming, ever changing—*never is it within the law*' (63; my emphasis). Law is not imagined as the space where radical ideas and practices can be accommodated, but rather as a space where the status quo is preserved. Why? Goldman eloquently suggests that '[t]he law is stationary, fixed, mechanical, "a chariot wheel" which grinds all alike without regard to time, place and condition, without ever taking into account cause and effect, without ever going into the complexity of the human soul' (62–3). The law, as Peter Goodrich has shown in *Languages of Law* (1990), is tradition, or rather it preserves tradition. Goldman points out that if the jury looks into all the significant social, scientific and cultural transformations that have taken place over time, they will note that all of them took place against the law. On the contrary, Goldman suggests, the law always considers new ideas and the figures propagating them to be criminals, in the same way that it considers anarchists to be outlaws:

> we are criminals even like Jesus, Socrates, Galileo, Bruno, John Brown and scores of others. We are in good company, among those whom Havelock Ellis, the greatest living psychologist, describes as the political criminals ...,

as men and women who out of deep love for humanity, out of a passionate reverence for liberty and an all-absorbing devotion to an ideal are ready to pay for their faith even with their blood.
(Berkman and Goldman, 2005:63)

Goldman is not alone amongst anarchists in pointing to law's deceit and unfairness, law's inability to flow with the changes in life, to accommodate renewed social norms and demands for the 'destruction' of law. So far, we have seen how early anarchists, like Proudhon, Kropotkin and Goldman, have been critical of institutional law. Some of these accounts, such as Proudhon's, are sophisticated. He engages with concepts of justice and equality, and imagines a different justice, a *commutative justice*. I have pointed out that this form of justice still holds onto a form of authority, a form of law, and it may run counter to the anti-authority idea of anarchism. To use Proudhon's own words, it may become another 'fishing net'. Kropotkin and Goldman, on the other hand, offer us an avid critique of what I call institutional law. Kropotkin sees such law as useless, stopping us from doing everyday things; the example of the blocked road that we have seen him give says it all. For Goldman the law is wooden, a machinery that grinds us to pieces, drawing our attention to law's inability to catch up with the times as well as its ability to grind out our individuality, which as we shall see in the next chapter is paramount to a lot of anarchist discourses.

What we can take from the classical anarchist engagement with law, despite their differences, is that law, man-made or institutional, is corrupt. It is corrupt because it protects the interests of the privileged and is a major collaborator of the State in distributing inequality. While there may be some good reasons to try and reform the law or think of law as a possible way of maintaining, distributing and operating justice, as Proudhon suggests, critical legal scholarship points to the limits of the law in transforming our social relations.

Why law? Contemporary anarchist thinkers and law

So far, I have discussed the views on law of anarchist theorists and activists who lived and wrote in the late nineteenth and early twentieth centuries. We have seen that whilst they all agree that to have an anarchist society it is paramount that the State is abolished, they are somewhat divided about the role and existence of law in such a society. Despite their division, they all have a particular understanding of the law in bourgeois capitalist societies. Law (institutional law) is a tool of oppression which reproduces the values, privileges and beliefs of the middle classes. Consequently, political power is thought to reside in the hands of the few, the middle class and the elite, and if any real transformation is to be reached, if an anarchist society is to come into being, the State – and, of course, all the apparatuses that enable its social reproduction, such as institutional law – must be dismantled. We have come a long way in understanding political power and the State in structural ways. Michel Foucault, for example, has shown how power is not just an object to overcome or acquire but rather a relation that permeates all and can be possessed by anyone (Foucault, 1994:348). This means that neither the State nor the law have the monopoly on power but rather power can be located in a plethora of settings (Foucault, 1991:51–75). Our bodies, knowledge and discourses are presented as important locations where we can witness the relational aspect of power; we are not just passive recipients of power. Power, according to Foucault, is no longer oppressive but productive. This understanding of power, of power as generative, enabled critical legal theorists to view law not as an oppressive instrument in the hands of the middle classes but rather as being productive (Moran, 1996; Golder and Fitzpatrick, 2009). Ben Golder and Peter Fitzpatrick even went even so far as to say that law is responsive and open to societal demands (2009:101). Contemporary anarchist writings, as we shall see, have been influenced either directly or indirectly by the Foucauldian reading of power, and have used it to adjust and critique classical anarchism. In doing so, they all share one characteristic: they view the State and its instruments (law) as not inhibiting social struggles, and moreover enabling groups that are engaged in social struggles and share anarchic principles (i.e., anti-authoritarian horizontal decision-making structures) without necessarily being anarchist, to exist and contest State limitations. Such writers come from a variety of academic disciplines: anthropology (James C. Scott), politics (Saul Newman, Ruth Kinna) and philosophy (Todd May, Simon Critchley, Ciara Bottici). This list is not exhaustive. Taking the writings of James C. Scott and Saul Newman as representative of the academic trend of decoupling anarchism from its struggle against the State and consequently law, I hope to show the limits of this position.

In *Two Cheers for Anarchism* (2012) James. C. Scott tries to persuade us that neither the State nor the law are barriers to our freedom and equality. For Scott, the law is an instrument that can be used in the pursuit of freedom and the modern State is a better political iteration than the political entities that pre-existed it, such as the 'state of nature' (iv–xxvi). How, then, did Scott come to these conclusions? He draws on particular historical examples, to show his support of the modern State and its apparatuses. Here is what he says:

> Unlike many anarchist thinkers, I do not believe that the state is everywhere and the enemy of freedom. Americans need only recall the scene of the federalized National Guard leading black children to school through a menacing crowd of angry whites in Little Rock, Arkansas in 1957 to realize that the state can, *in some circumstances*, play an emancipatory role. I believe that even this possibility has arisen only as a result of the establishment of democratic citizenship and suffrage by the French Revolution, subsequently extended to women, domestics, and minorities.
>
> (xiii–iv)

Scott sees the state and the law as having some 'emancipatory role' to play. He is aware that this role is not taken up consistently (note his emphasis in the quote above: '*in some circumstances*'); he is also very much aware that most change comes because of 'unruly defiance' identified by acts of civil unrest, rebellion and revolution or *infrapolitics* (e.g., sabotage, foot-dragging, poaching, flight) (xx), and for the most part he is aware that the State has been eroded by capitalism (xv–xvi). But he still insists that it better to hold onto the State. We may wonder why, despite the fact that he identifies that law does not play that significant a role in our emancipation, he insists on its importance? His answer is simple. The economic and social differences that exist in our society reveal that 'democracy is a cruel hoax without *relative* equality' (xvi, emphasis in original). Nevertheless, as anarchists we believe that 'relative equality is a necessary condition of mutuality and freedom' (xvi) and therefore Scott suggests that he sees no way of trying to achieve relative equality in democracy without the State, and consequently without the law. It is unclear why Scott thinks that democracy and relative equality cannot be achieved without the State. It could possibly be because he is afraid that if we dissolve the State then there is a possibility the dominant neoliberal trends in society that have already eroded the State will dominate even more, bringing forward more individualism and social and economic inequality. He may be right; this is a possibility. But then again it is equally uncertain how our fragmented and occasional infrapolitics, our actions of mutual aid or our protests in recognition of civil rights can ensure that the State will transform in a way that will sustain relative equality. If the modern State and the law have only occasionally managed to 'play an emancipatory role' in the past 200 years, and if this neoliberal State has acculturated and abandoned 'the habits of mutuality' (xxii), I wonder whether there is any reason to hope for a democracy where relative equality, freedom and mutuality are possible within the structure of the State. After all, before we begin thinking about a democracy with all the anarchist characteristics that Scott puts forward, it may be necessary to question, as Wendy Brown does, the efficacy of democracy itself (Brown, 2015). Years of reforming laws to give minoritarian communities equality have not stopped police officers in New York from abusing their powers when arresting Eric Garnier. We know that George Floyd was not treated equally when the Minneapolis police officer Derek Chauvin knelt on his neck, deprived him of air and killed him.

Scott also argues, as I noted earlier, that the modern State (and consequently the law as an apparatus of the State) is not the worst perpetrator in curbing our freedom (Scott, 2013:xiv). How does Scott reach such a conclusion? He does so by briefly turning to the Hobbesian 'state of nature'. He points out that things in the state of nature were much worse than they are in the modern State. Whilst this observation contains an element of truth, it is simultaneously reductive and disorienting. Unlike the modern State, the Hobbesian state of nature does not have freedom, equality and justice at its centre. In contrast, modern States – recall, for example, France's adoption of the revolutionary motto *liberté, égalité, fraternité* as a symbol of the modern French State – have at least got freedom and equality as the basis of their government. To put it simply, Scott's observation regarding the lack of freedom in political regimes prior to the emergence of the modern State compares entities that are not comparable, as they had different objectives or governing principles. If anarchists are suggesting that freedom is jeopardised by State formation, it is not only because they want to do away with centralised and dominating governance; which is of course a priority. But it is also because they know that the promise of freedom or equality within such a political entity, despite promises to the contrary, is chimerical. If the law could ensure everybody's equality, then we would not still be exposing its failures to protect us from racial, gender and other inequalities. I am not engaging more here with Scott's understanding of the law, I leave that to the next chapter; I engage rather with his concept of disobedience because, as I hope I have indicated, it is built upon shaky premises. It rests on his comparisons of disparate and utterly different political societies.

Scott is not alone amongst contemporary anarchist thinkers in having productive and positive ideas about law and the State. Postanarchists have also been critical of classical anarchist theoretical assumptions about the nature of human relations and their universalist discourses. Postanarchists' reflections shadow indirectly, as we will see, the critique of law offered by Goldman and Kropotkin. But let's briefly consider these writers and their criticism of classical anarchism now. Postanarchism has given rise to a collection of theoretical work coming from disciplinary areas as varied as art theory and law, and is best exemplified by the work of Todd May (2004, 2008), Saul Newman (2001) and a few other more recent theorists.[16] As Newman aptly puts it, this new direction in anarchist theory puts the traditional libertarian and egalitarian strand of classical anarchist theory in conversation with poststructuralist theory and aims 'to broaden the terms of anti-authoritarian thought to include critical analysis of language, discourse, culture and new modalities of power'(Newman, 2008:101). This pedagogic and academic endeavour takes place against the backdrop of a more recent entertainment of anarchist ideas and practices by global social movements and radical political groups (Newman, 2008:101–5).

In his book *Post Anarchism* (2016), Newman describes anarchism as being:

> a form of politics and ethics which takes the value of human freedom and self-government – inextricably linked to equality – as central and sees

16 See Franks, (2008:135–52); Call, (2008: 154–72). There are also some academic engagements with anarchism that do not necessarily call their research postanarchist. However, given their engagement with theories of power that are poststructuralist, such as Foucault's, I think it may be useful to include them within this category. The collection *The Anarchist Turn* (2013), edited by Jacob Blumemfeld, Chiara Bottici and Simon Critchley, contains a number of essays that engage with poststructuralist theorists, although they do not explicitly fall within the postanarchist category.

authoritarian and hierarchical relations – those enshrined not only in the state, but also in capitalism, organized religion, patriarchy, even certain forms of technology – as external limitation and encumbrances upon human freedom.

(3)

Although his definition of anarchism is more elaborate than those of classical anarchists, it is not entirely different from them. He too puts freedom, self-government and equality at the centre of anarchism's political and ethical definitions. There is, however, one fundamental difference between Newman's understanding of anarchism and that of the classical anarchists. Whilst classical anarchists held onto universal claims, postmodernist critiques of universality debunk the efficacy of universalism. As Newman elaborates:

[t]he universal discourses central to the experience of modernity, the category of a universal objective truth that is or ought to be apparent to everyone, or the idea that the world is becoming more rationally intelligible through advances in science – that anarchism also held onto – have been undergoing a profound process of dissolution.

(7)

Indeed, claims to universal truths have been criticised and shown not to produce truth. We know, for instance, that there is no such thing as universal justice. There are too many examples of differential treatments within the justice system, differential treatment of women, black and ethnic minorities, that make such a claim indefensible. As such, we can conclude that the anarchist classical project, which adheres to such claims, is something of a failure. Nevertheless, even if universal truths are not sustainable, Newman writes, '[t]his does not mean that the social bond is dissolving altogether – merely that there is no longer one dominant, coherent understanding of society but, rather, a plurality of different narratives or perspectives' (8) that enable us to think of the anarchist project somewhat differently. It enables us to think of anarchism not as an overreaching political project but rather as a polyphonic project with different and multiple narratives and political interests. Before I elaborate on Newman's powerful reconfiguration of anarchism, I would like to point out certain discrepancies in his critique of the universal, and the implications that this may have for classical anarchism.

Newman is correct to identify that postmodern and poststructuralist philosophy have argued that claims to universal truths, equality and justice (Douzinas, Warrington with McVeigh, 1991a) do not hold anymore; but it is equally correct to note that classical anarchists were very much aware of the existence of difference and inequality. When Goldman and Kropotkin, for example, invoke freedom – freedom from law and the State, freedom to associate at will and self-mastery – they are critiquing a certain universal narrative embodied by law as an instrument of the State, which arrests life. When they are critiquing the law, they do so because they are very much aware that the law cannot hold onto the myth of universal justice, because they recognise the differences that exist amongst us and call for equality *within* these differences. In other words, they want to see these universal principles attending to the specificities of each individual. If we take Goldman's denunciation of the law during her trial on charges of conspiracy, we notice that she is clearly pointing out the unequal treatment that certain individuals, such as anarchists, receive in the hands of the law. She is addressing the myth of the universality of law and defacing it. So, while Newman's critique of modernity is accurate at a general level, I do not consider it applicable to classical anarchism. As I have suggested, when we look at classical anarchist actions, writings or statements, like Goldman's court speech, it is very clear that they were already aware of the fallacy of the pronouncement of universalisms. How else can we interpret the anarchist 'slogan', 'No Gods. No Masters'?

If we ignore my critique above and assume that Newman is right, and his critique of modernity is equally valid for anarchism, we need to ask how he sees issues of equality, justice, etc. 'operating' from a poststructuralist perspective? In order to address the questions of equality, justice and freedom in postmodern times and within an anarchist framework, Newman first familiarises us with his understanding of the political terrain and the political subject in postmodern times. Politics, from a poststructuralist perspective, Newman suggests, are politics without a foundation or arche (2016:9), politics that *ontologically* provide us with an experience of freedom. There are also, as he explains, politics without a certain revolutionary aim that will see the end of State formation:

> [i]t is possible to think of anarchism no longer as a project in pursuit of, and determined by, certain ends – the social revolution that will bring about the stateless society – but rather as a form of autonomous action, a way of acting and thinking anarchistically in the here and now, seeking to transform the immediate situation and relationships that one finds oneself in, without necessarily seeing these actions and transformations as leading to up to the great Social Revolution, and without measuring their success or failure in these terms[.] Moreover, seeing anarchism in this way – as a form of action and thought in the present moment rather than a specific revolutionary project – would place less emphasis on achieving the traditional goal of a stateless society.
>
> (Newman, 2016:12)

Once Newman has debunked the idea of universality and universal politics, he moves on to identify a different type of politics in our society. This, as we have seen above, is politics carried by activist groups, or by social movements, that strive to transform the conditions of the present that make life unliveable, unequal and unjust. Such groups, whilst not anarchist in the classical sense, are *anarchic* because they share similar principles and practices to anarchism. They are anti-foundational, espouse autonomy and desire freedom. Unlike classical anarchism they do not desire or call for the abolition of the State. On the contrary, the addressees of their demands for social, political and economic transformation are the State and State law. The plethora of political actions that we have witnessed over the past 20 years, from anti-G8 demonstrations and Occupy to BLM, Sisters Uncut and XR, can be viewed as being *anarchic* in Newman's sense, despite not subscribing to an anarchist ideology.[17] But Newman pays little attention to the idea of equality, or more precisely how classical anarchists articulate equality. As we have seen, none of the classical anarchists that I discussed earlier imagine that the State could be the vehicle for equality. Newman even fails to question whether there are any limits to claims of justice and equality that anarchic groups may encounter when they resort to law. I have already outlined earlier in this chapter the conceptual problems with leaving questions of equality in the hands of law; I will not repeat the same criticisms here. But by not paying attention to how and to whom anarchic groups reach out for justice and equality, Newman fails to see that whilst the politics may be polyvocal and multiple, the addressee of their messages or demands remain in the hands of institutions/structures that still hold onto universality (law, the State).

Let's take BLM as our example. BLM are an important political entity that addresses the prejudicial and lethal effects of policing and state exclusion in the US or, as they describe themselves, they are 'a chapter-based national organization working for the validity of Black life'.[18] Their ten-point manifesto of what they want does not demand anything more radical than the implementation of existing rights that recognise, respect and protect Black lives.[19] The maintenance of the State and State apparatuses, or the implicit belief that a reformed, more representative institution of law and policing will deliver justice, not only gives authority to the very things that classical anarchism has devalued, it also seems to contradict Newman's presumption that we are living in a decentralised world. While political groups may be multiple, their demands are addressed to the State, e.g., BLM showing us that the State is a political entity that both symbolically and materially seems to hold in activists' minds the answer to questions of equality and justice. We may say that while the ways in

---

17 It is possible that fascist or racist groups could be accommodated within such a definition of anarchist politics. Questions of equality and justice need to be part of any definition of anarchism if we are to make sure that exclusionary political figurations or subjects are not compared to anarchist ones.
18 See 'About' at Black Lives Matter at http://blacklivesmatter.com/about. Accessed 7 August 2016.
19 See 'What We Believe' at https://uca.edu/training/files/2020/09/black-Lives-Matter-Handout.pdf. Accessed 2 December 2021. This manifesto is no longer found on the BLM website.

which such groups organise themselves are non-hierarchical and anti-foundational, recognising the equality of each of their members, they are not always anarchic in their actual politics, as they demand a reformed State (in the case of BLM) or a different type of State or central organisation (in the case of the *Indignados*). It is also important to note the dangers of superimposing our observations on groups or individuals that never called or wanted to call themselves anarchic. If we continue doing so, we are appropriating their names and possibly harming their political strategies for creating better and more just worlds for the communities they are representing. In writing this I do not intend in any way to debase the political actions and the quests for justice of such groups, but merely to highlight the fact that even though they may share anarchist practices (e.g., horizontality, non-authoritarian organising) and they function and operate at the margins of the liberal State, they do not desire a world without law or without the State. Their reasons and causes are valid and important, but they are not anarchist.

Newman is not alone amongst postanarchist anarchists in not integrating into his theory of postanarchism more radical, and I would say more anarchist, positions on justice and equality.[20] Todd May's writings equally subject to the same problem. May offers us a Foucauldian critique of classical anarchism's conception of power as oppressive in *The Political Philosophy of Poststructuralist Anarchism* (2004). At the same time, he does not address the question of equality and justice explicitly outside the realms of institutional man-made law. While postanarchist anarchism has been extremely useful in considering the nuanced philosophical perspectives that we have inherited from poststructuralism and rethinking anarchism through them, its silence on the problematic of institutions of law, and its relation to not transforming the world or maintaining the same relationship of subordination, mean that no matter how productive law can be it will remain the arbiter of our lives and for that reason any movement/action group that does not denounce man-made law along with State formation is not to my mind anarchist. The fact that autonomy is a fallacy, as Bottici (2013) argues, or that power is both oppressive and productive, as May argues, or that universal truths do not hold, as Newman argues, do not mean that sovereign/juridical power is not still powerful. As Foucault himself reminded us in *Society Must be Defended* (2004), all three forms of power that he identified – sovereign/juridical, disciplinary or bio- power – are operating at the same time. If we want an anarchist society, we must direct our critique to man-made law and its supporting institutions. Otherwise, what we end up supporting is something that is not very different from the society that we are critiquing.

The views of the role of law in an anarchist society are varied as we have witnessed. They tend to be addressed in conjunction with the question of the role of the State in an anarchist society or in connection with the meaning of

---

20 See also Bottici (2013:9–34).

equality. Goldman and Kropotkin have made numerous critiques of man-made law, whilst Proudhon offers some space for law in anarchist polity. What they all share is the belief that an anarchist society cannot exist within the framework of the State. Contemporary anarchist thinkers like Scott and Newman either see a well-challenged State and consequently law as a vehicle for the creation of relative equality or inadvertently ignore critiquing the limits of equality that may be sheltered in anarchic formations. As I have already indicated, law creates conditions of inequality and servitude. Like Kropotkin and Goldman, I too think that the law is one of those apparatuses that by its sheer existence takes away from individuals, groups and communities the freedom to manage their affairs for themselves. Consequently, inequality is introduced in the management of everyday affairs, as the *law* as an institution becomes the *master* of social relations. If some institutions have authority over our lives, it means that we are in an unequal position in relation to those institutions and ultimately towards each other. If an anarchist society is to be reached it must not be based on law. More importantly, what we need, and what is present in the practices of anarchists, is a different *ethos* that will enable u to relate to and operate with each other without resorting to law. This may not be easy, but it is not impossible. I will address the possibilities of living without law and some of the ingredients that make up an anarchist ethos in more detail in the forthcoming chapters.

Chapter 3

Disentangling the psyche
From disobedience to *parrhesia*

In *Two Cheers for Anarchism* (2012), the anthropologist James Scott narrates a story which shows that disentangling ourselves from the familiar or habitual ways of doing things, following the paths that the Sovereign, the State or the law has crafted for us, may prove to be more difficult that we think. It is not just a matter of making a svelte decision to exit these pathways. These crafted trails are not just images that exist outside us, showing us the right way to do things; they are deep rooted in our psyches and put pressure on us, automatically making us follow them without reflection, without allowing us space to ask the question: Is there another way of doing things?

Scott explains how difficult it is to *disentangle* ourselves from well-trodden paths by studying the way people in the city of Neubrandenburg in Germany used zebra crossings in the 1990s. Scott spent some time in the city and he had the chance to observe the residents' habits. Scott noticed that at the train station in Neubrandenburg there was an intersection that was very busy during the daytime. The traffic lights were adjusted in such a way that pedestrians had to wait quite a while to cross the intersection. Although the traffic was minimal in the evening and there were few pedestrians, the lights operated at the same tempo as in the daytime and pedestrians had to wait ages to cross the intersection (Scott 2012:3). Moreover, Scott twice witnessed a pedestrian crossing before the lights turned green and receiving 'a chorus of scolding tongues and fingers wagging in disapproval' (3). He too found it difficult to find the courage to cross the street 'against general disapproval' (3). Later on, when he had plucked up the courage to walk across when the lights were red, he rehearsed the following speech as a way of rationalising this minor violation:

> You know, you and especially your grandparents could have used more of a spirit of lawbreaking. One day you will be called on to break a big law in the name of justice and rationality. Everything will depend on it. You have to be ready. How are you going to prepare for that day when it really matters? You have to stay 'in shape' so that when the big day comes you will be ready. What you need is 'anarchist calisthenics'. Every day or so break some trivial law that makes no sense, even if it's only jaywalking.

DOI: 10.4324/9780429952692-3

> Use your own head to judge whether a law is just or reasonable. That way, you'll keep trim; and when the big day comes, you'll be ready.
>
> (Scott, 2012:4–5)

Scott's example and 'speech' are instructive. They inform us about how our psychic world responds to pre-formulated pathways, the difficulties involved in disentangling from them and what it may take to disentangle ourselves from them. Pre-formulated pathways are presented inscribed in our psyche; people are automatically ready to castigate those who diverge from them. The castigation or the witnessing of reprimand makes all of us conform to these pathways even if we know that in diverging from them we are not posing any risk to others. In order to undo our attachment to these pre-formulated pathways we need to muster courage and, if we are to be able to create very different worlds, anarchist worlds, we may need (at least this is the lesson we get from Scott) to practise our law breaking on a regular basis. Practising disobedience will enable us to disentangle ourselves from those norms, rules, regulations, structures, ideas and gestures that tie down our psyches and eventually get to an anarchist world.

Although Scott's take on anarchism differs from mine, his observations about the obstacles that bar us from disobeying (psychic attachments), the ethos that brings about disobedience (courage) and the pedagogy/strategy (practice) necessary to introduce an anarchist world are instructive and important. Questions surrounding the problem of unreserved and unquestioned obedience have always been at the forefront of classical anarchist thinking. We can, for example, recall that Kropotkin was perplexed as to why people continue to follow health and safety or municipal laws, or demand more laws when a conflict arises, as these do not make sense and, more importantly, do not serve the common good. He uses examples from everyday life to demonstrate our obedience and attachment to law and authority, such as peasants demanding more laws to deal with roadblocks between villages, farmers demanding better laws to deal with reductions in production, and so on (Kropotkin, 2002:197). The question of how and why we become attached to norms, values and ideas that do not serve us or serve the common good, the reasons why we do not question them and how we can begin to question them and the quest for practices that become vital in disentangling ourselves not only from laws but from normative expectations have been extensively discussed by political theorists, psychoanalysts, anarchists and critical theorists. In this chapter I focus on a handful of thinkers that have reflected on these questions. The aim is not just to identify how and why we remain obedient or what disobedient acts may not be as disobedient as they appear, but also to identify certain practices that enable us to disentangle ourselves from pre-ordained pathways and enable us to build an anarchist world. You may have guessed by now that like Scott, I think that following norms and ideas without questioning them is one of the factors that stop us from transforming the world. I am writing this in a century in which the world has seen some significant acts of disobedience – Occupy Wall Street, the *Indignados*, XR, BLM and many more. A lot of these movements demonstrate to us, as Kinna (2019) explained, that they do not identify ideologically with anarchism but borrow anarchist principles to serve their purpose, such as that of horizontal decision-making, and we can therefore identify a kind of 'anarchization' in their formations.

In trying to understand the problem of obedience and how anarchist and anarchist-like formations find the courage to become disobedient, I take us on a journey in the company of a number of fellow critics of the concept of disobedience. I first engage with the account of obedience offered by the political philosopher, anarchist and judge Etienne De la Boétie (2007), which primarily emphasises the embodied manifestation of obedience; then I proceed to consider the psychoanalyst Adam Philips' (2015) pertinent remarks about psychic obedience and its limits. Although disobedience is generally seen as a radical practice and necessary ingredient for the emergence of an anarchist society, Marx Stirner does not consider disobedience against structures, ideas and psychic constellations as a necessary catalyst for an anarchist society. On the contrary, disobedient acts, as I explore through Stirner can continue the ties with the very things that we contest, be that the State or the Church. Stirner's thinking is helpful in enabling us to see the pitfalls of disobedience, but it does not throw any light on what practices there could be that would disentangle us from the shackles of the norms that govern societies and pave the way to an anarchist society. The last part of the chapter focuses on *parrhesia*, fearless speech, as a practice that can and does rattle normative structures by questioning them. The overall aim is to attune us to the subtle ways in which anarchists and anarchist-like formations disentangle their psyches from all those norms, ideas and pathways that dull our souls and bodies and make us forget to challenge them, moreover they redirect us to ways that can enable us to live a free life and grow. As we shall see, *parrhesia*, rather than disobedience, opens a portal to a way of doing things and to an anarchist world that it is not attached to the very structures that weigh us down. The fact that one talks truth to power means that the utterer has already done away with an attachment to structures, ideas and values that are inscribed or go hand in hand with the figure of power, whether this figure is a person or an institution.

Obedience, embodied habits and psychic entanglements

Etienne De la Boétie's sixteenth-century speculative essay 'The Discourse of Voluntary Servitude' (2007) is, as the title suggests, a treatise on understanding political obedience. In it De la Boétie, an anarchist, French judge and the founder of modern political theory in France, offers an insightful account of why populations fail to disobey tyrannical government. In doing so he identifies three types of governments that are or can be tyrannical: (a) tyrannical governments elected by the people; (b) tyrannical governments that come to power through the use of arms; and (c) monarchical governments that are established through inheritance.

Irrespective of the way in which tyrants come to power, De la Boétie observes that such governments take people for granted, considering them subordinate and servile to them.

Once he has identified the type of governments that force people into obedience, De la Boétie proceeds to track how obedience is created. One of the first things he points out is that obedience is a learned practice. For example, parents tend to train their children from a young age to obey them, to follow household rules and to be obedient at school. However, parental disciplinary practice changes as children get older and parents reverse this advice and tell their children to 'become slaves to nobody' (119). This change in parental advice from early childhood to adulthood prompted De la Boétie to ask why and how people continue to obey tyrannical governments when advice regarding obedience is constantly changing. Put differently, De la Boétie was curious as to why people continue to obey such governments and enslave themselves even when the imperative of being an independent and free agent is also part of their pedagogy. De la Boétie discovers that obedience is a learned and embodied practice, and although it is usually within our nature to seek freedom, our experience of certain events, our reluctance to embrace an unknown future and, moreover, our character which 'instinctively follows the tendencies that [our] training gives [us]' (128) incline us towards obedience. Moreover, as he explains, we get accustomed to the way we live and develop habits and responses that accord with our way of life, and being ignorant of anything better, we end up being obedient to these customary or habitual ways of doing things. But obedience is not just the result of habit or customary ways of doing things, he argues. We are also obedient because we are cowardly and submissive (131). Cowardice arises as a result of fearing for our lives and we become submissive because we know that if our liberty is taken away from us by tyrants we will lose any form of enthusiasm 'for [our] hearts [will be] degraded, submissive, and incapable of any great deed' (131). Nevertheless, obedience does not just arise out of learned experiences, discipline and habit. As De la Boétie explains, there are other scenarios and factors that make us obedient. For example, on the rare occasions when cities rebel against tyrants, they return to obedience when tyrannical rulers resort to providing the populations of such cities with celebratory events, alcohol and other perks, and divert their attention and manipulate them into thinking that the tyrannical form of government is beneficial for all. Deceived and stupefied by such events, rebels stop rebelling and in this way rebellions get suppressed (133–4). People also become obedient out of self-interest, because they want to make personal (secure positions of eminence) or material (wealth, property, etc.) gains.

Etienne De la Boétie certainly draws a complex picture of the obedient subject. There is no one single reason that can turn any of us into an obedient subject. The obedient subject may be disciplined into obedience from a young age and retain that habit into adulthood, because discipline acts on the body of the obedient subject in such a way as to make it either incapable (because of lack of enthusiasm) or fearful of disobeying. Other subjects, as we have seen, obey because they value material wealth and status above freedom. De la Boétie's analysis provides us with a useful understanding of how the body yields to obedience. Indeed, his understanding of obedience is inextricably linked to the body: a well-disciplined body obeys, out of habit, out of fear of punishment (losing its life) and then becomes an embodied subject who becomes stupefied by celebrations put on by tyrants to suppress rebellions. It is our bodies, exhausted from servitude, that become incapable of raising our arms against oppressors, and what is more, it is our bodily desires for material comforts and status that render freedom secondary and obedience primary as a way of life. So, if we are to free ourselves from political servitude following De la Boétie's thinking we may need to shift the yokes that chain the body to the ground (fatigue, fear, avarice, deception). As Scott pointed out, we need to train our bodies through small acts of courage and disobedience if we are to uproot the forms of government that not only turn us into slaves of laws that are inefficient and non-functioning and norms that tie us to well-trodden pathways, foreclosing the possibility of imagining or building different – and in our case – anarchist worlds.

If political obedience is learned and embodied, then to disentangle oneself from it requires some practice. As we have seen, Scott has already advised that we need 'anarchist calisthenics' (2012:3–5) or everyday acts of disobedience. But it is not just our bodies that need to be retrained, or re-acculturated to disobey. To disentangle ourselves from obedience requires disentangling our psyches from the psychological reasons that tie us to rules, norms and authority. The psychoanalyst Adam Phillips offers incisive explanations of how we psychically find ourselves attached to these structures, but he also presents the benefits of disobedience. Phillips's understanding of obedience – how we end up following unforbidden pleasures and the cost of this pathway – is telling: it enables us to see that the struggle to disentangle ourselves (psychically and bodily) from the chains of authority, norms and laws may not be as easy as developing 'anarchist calisthenics'; it is not as simple as training our bodies to disobey. Rather, it requires a fundamental overhaul of our psychic structures. As I have argued elsewhere (Loizidou, 2013; 2016), disobedience that can transform the political terrain in a radical way requires transformation at the subjective level. Chris Rossdale (2019) argues that this is better achieved with the solidarity and support of a collective subjectivity (206–36). Phillips' obedient subject is a subject that is produced through cultural practices and norms, not necessarily a universal subject or a collective one, but rather a subject that carries general attributes that pertain to all. His work is useful to study if we individually and collectively need to find ways of un-doing our attachment to authority.

Phillips presents us with a psychic understanding of how obedience takes over our lives and how, in turn, it enslaves us. If De la Boétie articulates how our *bodies* come to obey authority, Phillips offers an equally convincing account of how we *psychically* end up following laws, rules or unforbidden pleasures to the detriment of enabling ourselves to be free and enjoy those desires that are forbidden. It is not that in *Unforbidden Pleasures* (2015) Phillips provides a causative link between our psychic subjugation and the things that bar us from truly enjoying ourselves, or at least discovering what we may truly enjoy. But he does provide us with a story or a way of understanding how we come to be obedient psychic subjects. As he explains, our societies are mostly obedient societies and the law plays a central role in organising our obedience, creating boundaries between what is forbidden and what is unforbidden. What is labelled as *good* is usually *unforbidden* and what is labelled as *bad* is *forbidden*. As he explains, Laws are linguistic and psychic traps that limit our horizons and our sense of freedom creating ex nihilo a series of desires that are to be prohibited (9). When we follow the law we are simultaneously – as Phillips, borrowing from Oscar Wilde, writes – 'living for others' (11). And 'living for others', following their rules and the law, creates prohibitions that become part of the fabric of our psychic world. Although some imagine that prohibitions enable us to have a just life, Phillips argues that '[t]he language of prohibition is the dream of a language of straightforward influence, not strange influence; a language of orders, not impressions. A language of rules, not suggestions. Language as effective propaganda' (24). For some anarchists. as you may have gathered from the preceding chapter, law is both *restrictive* of *freedom* and a *coloniser* of *thinking*. For anarchists, therefore, Phillips' insights make absolute sense. Laws and rules leave very little space for *impressions* or *suggestions* to surface; *laws* (whether laws produced by legislatures and formal State institutions or laws that are laid down by the family, schools or other institutions) are, as Phillip reminds us, prohibitive, creating boundaries between right and wrong, *disallowing* conversations and *ambivalence*. Phillips is inspired by Oscar Wilde and Frederick Nietzsche's proposals that if we are to free ourselves from the chains of law we need to:

> forget, or unlearn certain words and phrases; to forget a vocabulary – words like 'seriousness', 'duty', 'explanation', 'fact' and 'limitation', and phrases like 'living for others', and 'making oneself useful' ('The sure way of knowing nothing about life', Wilde wrote, 'is to make oneself useful') – and to use words like 'beauty', 'disobedience', 'development', 'pleasure' and 'perfection', and phrases like the 'beauty of life' and 'the joy of living' instead.
>
> (Phillips, 2015:25)

It is through *movement*, acting in ways that remove all those rules that chain us and restrict our worlds, using *language* in ways that undo commands, prohibitions, limitations, that we will be able to release our souls from the chains of authority. Language, a specific use of language, creates space for different psychic possibilities. If we are to retrain ourselves or discard the moralistic words that restrain our growth, as Phillips proposes, we will be able to open the way to those forbidden pleasures that the law or authority prohibit us from having access to. In doing so, he writes, we begin 'to foster a remembering of a different self – the enigmatic self, the only self we are going to have if we want to have a self and its plenitudes and pleasures' (26). And moreover, in achieving this rewriting of the self through the rewriting of our vocabulary, we 'lay [...] down ... a different kind of law' (26). Phillips' observations enable us to see how prohibitions stop us from growing and experiencing pleasures that are forbidden. To begin with Phillips identifies how language is inextricably linked to obedience, then by getting hold of language for ourselves, by owning language and not letting it be hostage to moralism we are going to be able to create our own laws. However, the question of why or how we follow these linguistic commands or follow a linguistic pathway that allows us only to enjoy unforbidden pleasures is not immediately explained by this identification.

The question of why we remain obedient is addressed in *Unforbidden Pleasures* when we are asked to consider 'what kind of pleasure obedience may be[?]' (Phillips 2015:48). This is a different insight into obedience than the one offered by De la Boétie, who saw obedience as the result of necessity, fatigue or interest. De la Boétie failed to consider that servitude may be a pleasurable event, though he did acknowledge that servitude wields and fulfils personal interest. Even so, we cannot conclude from this that the fulfilment of a personal interest may be pleasurable. Phillips is clear that whilst disobedience releases forbidden pleasures, obedience also holds some pleasures. In identifying that obedience and disobedience give rise to different types of pleasures, Phillips offers an incisive account of why we are attached to obedience, and more precisely why we may psychically find it difficult to shed obedience. We are attached to obedience not just because we may be afraid of the consequences of not obeying, or because we are mindful of our survival, but also because attachment to rules releases some enjoyment. As he explains, the pleasures that are released by obedience are 'pleasures of being agreeable' (50). But we may still be wondering why being agreeable could be more pleasurable than being free? Phillips does not address this question, but does offer an insight into why we may continue to obey our parents. Obedience, he explains via Winnicott, marks the giving up of a child's spontaneity in order 'to follow the needs of those who are caring' for him/her (51). We can conclude from this that infant/children are not self-sufficient and tend to comply with the needs of their parents as they depend on them for their survival. They may drop any desire for spontaneity – exploring, for example, the sand box at the local park – because it does not concur with their parents' needs to keep their clothes spotless. Compliance to such a need may of course have taken place because the command 'Don't play' is uttered in an authoritative manner. As the survival of children depends upon their parents, compliance results in 'the child surv[ing] at the cost of living her own life' (52). Simply put, our obedience to authority and laws is the result of our need to survive.

Nevertheless, this compliance provides short-term safety. The child may keep their parent happy by complying with their rules, but they will never test or find out whether the rules can be stretched. This simply means that the child may be safe whilst growing up, but their safety may be jeopardised in the future because of their inability to find their own way. Phillips explains this succinctly when he makes the distinction between the obedient and the disobedient child. As he writes, 'the compliant child runs the risk of becoming a rebel; the non-compliant child runs the risk of wanting a permanent state of revolution, of more or less continual self-overcoming' (56). In political terms, as we know from the political theorist Hannah Arendt, rebels and rebellious actions aspire to a change in political leadership without uprooting the structures that support them, revolutionaries aspire to the total transformation of the structures and the creation of something new (Arendt, 1990). The rebellious child, if we follow Phillips's thoughts, will never be able to create something new, but just alter their life within the confines of the normative structures that it is familiar with. A non-compliant child, on the other hand, by becoming a revolutionary will be able to create themselves anew and create new experiences. Like De la Boétie, Phillips tells us the limits of obedience – sustaining the status quo, and not enabling a radical transformation and freedom to reach the subject – but unlike De la Boétie, who draws our attention to the ways in which obedience acts on the body, Phillips points to the ways in which we are psychically restricted by obedience. To enable ourselves to discover those forbidden pleasures which seem to have been forbidden by a Judaeo-Christian morality, Phillips follows Wilde in proposing, as we have already seen, to undo that the attachment we have for certain words and ways of seeing is undone and that we embrace a different vocabulary, one that enable us to question and critique social values, particularly those that are usually presented as being unquestionable. Moreover, as obedience has disciplined us into living for others, we need, as we have also seen, to lay down our own law and consequently become *selfish*. Only through a radical transformation of our psychic world can we, Phillips suggests, begin to free ourselves from the shackles of laws or ways of life that ban questioning, 'argumentation' (60) and 'free association' (61).

Therefore, if obedience at best resembles rebellion – the desire to hold onto rituals and routine (Phillips, 2015) – and at worst servitude (De la Boétie, 2007), and if obedience penetrates our psyches and bodies, can anarchism teach us something about freeing ourselves from the shackles of obedience, command and law? How can we decolonise ourselves from obedience? In other words, what can anarchism teach us about disobedience and the freedom and pleasure we may gain from being disobedient? For some, like the thinker Max Stirner, as I explain in the next section, disobedience may not be the practice that can free us from the shackles of norms. Acts of disobedience respond to existing structures, norms, laws, authority, beliefs and effects. In their attempt to suppress them these acts inadvertently find themselves caught in the framework and contours that the existing collection of apparatuses provide, making it impossible to articulate a world without them and consequently with freedom.

In following Stirner's critique of disobedience closely, my aim is not to suggest that disobedient acts do not provide us with growth, as Phillips suggests, or freedom, as De la Boétie foresees, but to try and understand under what conditions and circumstances disobedience cannot give us transformation, growth and freedom. It is with these questions in mind that I now turn to Stirner.

Disobedience and its limits

The Ego and Its Own (2006) was originally published in 1844 and authored by Max Stirner, whose thinking influenced anarchists like Emma Goldman, Rudolph Rocker and Max Nettlau (Ferguson, 2011b:171) but was also criticised, as is well known, by Karl Marx and Frederick Engels in *The German Ideology* (1998).[1] In this book, often forgotten, especially within the field of critical legal studies, Stirner puts forward a forceful argument regarding the importance of disobedience for our personal growth as political and social beings. Like Oscar Wilde, who, is central for Phillips in developing an argument for forbidden pleasures, Stirner saw laws as restrictive to the development of one's inner and outer worlds. He recognised much earlier than Wilde and Nietzsche that religion, liberalism, law and the State are responsible for our enslavement. Like Wilde, who thought as we have seen above that if we are to liberate ourselves and live like artists[2] we need to be selfish and not live for others, Stirner argues in *The Ego and Its Own* that our growth as individuals relies on our ability to disobey the State, religion and liberalism. I will discuss later on in this chapter why individualism, present in Stirner, Wilde and Phillips, is detrimental to left radical politics. At the moment, though, let's see what Stirner has to say about the need for disobedience to have personal growth.

The first part of *The Ego and Its Own* is preoccupied with presenting a history of the human and 'the nature of the modern epoch of *idealism*' (Leopold, 2006: xv). As Leopold tells us in the introduction to the book, the historical account of the human regrettably provides a racist account of our development into modernity (xvii). Stirner presented this history from a Western perspective and saw humans overcoming three stages, their 'innate Negroidity' (xvii) akin to childhood, their 'Mongoloidity', akin to adolescence (xviii) and the 'really Caucasian' stage where, 'having thrown off the Negroid and Mongol

---

1 In this book Karl Marx and Friedrich Engels offer a sustained critique of German philosophers Feuerbach, B. Bauer and Stirner, and track their philosophical roots to Hegelian idealism. Moreover, in *The German Ideology* they develop their theory of historical materialism, offering a challenge to Hegelian ideology. While Hegel thought that ideas and thought shape us, Marx and Engel argued and demonstrated how our material conditions influence our social life.
2 Phillips informs us that Oscar Wilde presented the figure of the artist as exemplary in its ability to ignore public opinion. This ability to set aside public opinion enables artists to enjoy forbidden pleasures and grow outside the parameters of normativity (Phillips, 2015:12–13).

inheritance, the egoistic self can escape its dependence on both natural forces and ideas' (xviii). I acknowledge, along with Leopold, the racism that underpins Stirner's understanding of making oneself. It is incorrect, hateful and, of course, indefensible to make a correlation between infancy and so-called 'innate Negroidity'. Anybody working with Stirner's ideas cannot deny this. There are other nineteenth-century anarchists or thinkers, such as Goldman, who were aware of the injustices that African Americans faced.[3] I consciously decided to note the racist history of the making of the liberal individual and focus on Part II of *The Ego and Its Own* where Stirner talks about how self-making undoes normative ways of being in the world as well as the institutions that support it (the Church, law, the State). We see in his critique of norms, institutions and liberalism a negation of Western ways of doing things and an emphasis on the individual owning of oneself and not being enslaved by others. It is this direction of his thinking that attracts anarchist political theorists today. We have seen, for example, the publication by the post-anarchist Saul Newman of an edited collection on Max Stirner entitled *Max Stirner* (2011a).

In Part II of *The Ego and Its Own* Stirner sets out to show how we become servile to religion, the State, property, ideas (such as the idea of humanity) and passions (such as love), and then how we overcome these dominant structures and ideas to become unique individuals. It is clear that for Stirner the unique individual is, or can be, the only radical entity that can direct us away from servitude to the State, religion, ideas and passions. To this effect he writes:

3   In the first volume of her biography, *Living My Life* (1970a), Goldman talks about an article that she wrote in the *New York World* regarding the conditions and treatment of White women prisoners by the matron of the prison ward. She noticed that White women were not given smaller portions of food in prison than Black women prisoners. This point was followed by the qualification that she was not prejudiced against Black Americans, she noticed that they are still treated as slaves in the US; but she wanted to protest against favouritism and the effects of that that she had witnessed in women's prisons (138). Her abolitionist comrade John Swinton reprimanded her for her article and her stance (154–5). She maintained her position that she was protesting against favouritism, however whilst this shows us that she was aware of the treatment of Black Americans in the US, and she knew that they were still treated like slaves, she could not recognise her comments on prisoner rationing as holding an unconscious bias. My point here is that Goldman was aware of the conditions of inequality and injustice in the US. In 1917 *Mother Earth Bulletin*, a bulletin accompanying Goldman's magazine *Mother Earth*, published an article reporting the mysterious hanging of 13 Black soldiers on an army base in Texas, an event that was silenced by other media and the government (Falk, 1999: 165l). The US authorities banned the mailing of the bulletin. Goldman's solidarity, support and alliance with Black Americans is also present in publications in *Mother Earth* by other anarchists. For example, an article by Martha Gruening in *Mother Earth* records the St Louis Riots of August 1917 which cause the deaths of 39–200 Black Americans, and saw the destruction of the homes and the displacement of 6,000 Black Americans (Gruening, 2000:400–4).

As unique you have nothing in common with the other any longer, and therefore nothing divisive or hostile either; you are not seeking to be in the right against him before a *third* party, and are standing with him neither 'on the ground of right' nor on any other common ground. The opposition vanishes in complete-*severance* or singleness [*Einzigkeit*]. This might indeed be regarded as the new point in common or a new parity, but here the parity consists precisely in the disparity, and is itself nothing but disparity, a par of disparity, and that only for him who institutes a 'comparison'.

(Stirner, 2006:186; emphasis in original)

For those of us on the left who may find that Stirner's call to a unique individualism echoes liberalism's individualism, Newman (2011b) has convincingly explained why Stirner's unique individual it is *not* the same as a liberal individual. Newman argues that Stirner's unique individual is a critique of liberal individualism. Apart from being a critique of the State and religion, *The Ego and Its Own* also offers a critique of humanism. For Stirner the designation 'human' is a quality that signifies another layer of alienation from oneself (Newman, 2011b:191). By designating myself as human, I am not holding onto the ownership of myself but rather giving to it this idea of the human. The theological designation of the alienation of the self is this idea of the human, and the political is, for Stirner, liberalism (193). If we look at the aspirational unique egoist that Stirner proposes, we can clearly see that this unique individual is not the subject of liberalism and rights. Two unique individuals own themselves when they have discarded the skins (the State, being human, religion, love, property, etc.) that envelop them and make them servile. As Stirner suggests in the earlier quote I shared, they will no longer be opposing each other 'on the ground of right' (186), instead they will be engaging in disparity with each other. It is also clear that the Stirner's unique individual is not that of liberal rights. On the contrary, Stirner is critical of liberal individualism and sees it, as I already pointed out, as the source of all our perils. Moreover, Stirner points out that it is not just the idea of rights, the promise of equality through them, that is the problem with liberalism. Liberalism, for Stirner, as Newman astutely points out 'should be understood as a certain rationality of government; a technology of normalization which relies, in large part, on the individual's self-subjection' (193). Therefore, according to Stirner, liberalism replaces religion as an ideology and governs us with its promise of equality through rights. For this reason it is one of the most powerful weapons of the State. So, if we are to be truly free, we need to detach ourselves from these layers of domination. But how are we to own ourselves? Can we begin to gain ownership of ourselves by resisting or disobeying those structures, passions and ideas that prefigure us, according to Stirner, whether they come in the form of the State or property or love?

Stirner's understanding of disobedience is not one that takes the form of resistance but rather requires each individual to create a self that does *not* relate at all to predetermined structures, passions or ideas. For Stirner, disobedience or critique becomes a vehicle for making us servile to the fantasy of the commonwealth. Most of Part II of the book is a record of how this commonwealth privileges or serves mostly those that have ordered it for the most part. So criticism, or disobedience, is another way of supporting the fantasy of the commonwealth. As he writes:

> If I criticize under the presupposition of a supreme being, my criticism *serves* the being and is carried on for its sake: if I am possessed by the belief in a 'free state', then everything that has a bearing on it I criticize from the standpoint of whether it is suitable to this state, for I *love* this state ... All servile criticism is a product of love, a possessedness, and proceeds according to that New Testament precept, 'test everything and hold fast the good'. 'The good' is the touchstone, the criterion. The good, returning under a thousand names and forms, remained always the presupposition, remained the dogmatic fixed point for this criticism, remained – the fixed idea.
>
> (Stirner, 2006:309; emphasis in original)

It is clear from the quote above that for Stirner any disobedience, even if it is for the sake of reaching for a more equal polity, works against reaching self-ownership. Instead, it subjects the individual to the idea or structure that the commonwealth strives to achieve. Love does not have the self as an object but rather it has transformation as an objective, let's say a socialist society. In this scenario, according to Stirner, we get entrapped by the object we are following and thus never truly own ourselves. Nevertheless, Stirner differentiates between this type of criticism, which he considers to be servile and dogmatic (indeed he calls it *servile* criticism) and what he approves as criticism which he calls *own* criticism (309). So, not all criticism dispossesses us from ourselves, only criticism that is prompted by presuppositions that emanate from the commonwealth and not the individual. *Own* criticism emerges from thinking that has not been influenced by presuppositions and is able to emanate from itself (310). As Stirner writes, '[t]hinking and criticism could be active only starting from themselves, would have to be themselves the presupposition of their activity, as without being they could not be active' (310). He does not provide us with any example of criticism or thinking that may emanate from itself but invites us to think about it in antithesis to thinking and criticism that emanates from a presupposition, which as we have already noted he understands as not only not being able to provide us with ownership of ourselves and actions, but additionally being dogmatic and static. We can imagine then that own criticism could be the type of thinking that brackets out any ideology. Own criticism considers that we can be unique individuals only when we free ourselves from ideological positions. For example, as an anarchist if I am to be free I will need to rid myself from even the ideological positions of anarchism. I will return to

Stirner's critique of radical understandings of property and his own ideas about property, but I would first like to draw our attention to the ways in which he sees *own* criticism as being able to leave behind the entrapments of disobedient practices.

When it comes to own criticism, Stirner tells us that the measure of criticism is no longer man or the human but rather myself (311). '[W]hen I criticize,' he writes '[I] do not even have myself before my eyes, but am only doing myself a pleasure, amusing myself according to my taste; according to my several needs I chew the thing up or only inhale its odour' (311). We can try and imagine how this person, let's call them the *own* critique, is enjoying the activity of criticising or, as Newman suggests, creating for themselves 'new modes of subjectivity, new behaviours and ways of life which evade, undermine and destabilize the subjective positions established by power' (Newman, 2011b:201). But how would this self-creating individualistic subjectivity be able to bracket out what already exists, those 'subjective positions established by power' (201) and create for themselves a world that is bereft of power, privilege and all that enslaves us? I give Emma Goldman as an example of own criticism.

On 6 September 1901, US President McKinley was assassinated in Buffalo, New York by the anarchist Leon Czolgosz. When questioned by the police, Czolgosz said that Emma Goldman had put him up to assassinate the President (Goldman, 1970a:296). Goldman had not done such a thing but was nevertheless arrested and kept in jail until she cleared her name. During her stay in prison, she was interviewed by a number of papers about the assassination and her connection to Czolgosz. She repeatedly said she did not tell Czolgosz to assassinate President McKinley, but as Czolgosz was an anarchist she sympathised with him (306). However, she also told a reporter that she would also nurse President McKinley (306). It is important to note that Goldman was a nurse by training. Goldman as an anarchist and an advocate of the withering of the State was not expected to offer her assistance to the President, the figurehead of the State. However, for Goldman, what appears to be a paradox to most people has a reasonable explanation. As she stated to a reporter who asked her about this seeming contradiction:

> Now listen and see if you can get it. The boy in Buffalo is a creature at bay. Millions of people are ready to spring on him and tear him limb from limb. He committed the act for no personal reasons or gain. He did it for what is his ideal! On the other hand ... William McKinley, suffering and probably near death, is merely a human being to me now. That is why I would nurse him.
>
> (Goldman, 1970a:306)

We witness in Goldman's words a type of thinking that it is not bound to normative reasoning. Goldman was an avowed anarchist, as we know, and therefore was expected to act according to her ideals, which included anti-authoritarianism and, like Czolgosz, to be antagonistic towards the President of the US. In this case she defies this expectation. She puts aside the anarchist ideology and offers as a nurse to take care of President McKinley. On his sick bed the President takes up a different subjectivity, he is 'suffering ... merely a human being ... now' (306), and in Goldman's eyes is stripped of the decorum of presidency. If we wanted an example of own criticism, this is a good one, where Goldman demonstrates how we can show that a different world is possible, one that can be caring to human beings even if they are on a different ideological spectrum to us. She proves to herself that she is not a dogmatic anarchist and her reasoning shows us a different and new way of being with each other in the world. Stirner talks of own criticism, as we have seen, as thinking that is playful and non-dogmatic, thinking that springs from itself and not from some presupposition that we will need to follow unquestioningly as the truth. It is the truth or the idea of the truth that is based on presuppositions that appears to be problematic for Stirner. I will now turn to the problems that Stirner identifies regarding truth.

Disobedient subjects tend to pride themselves on talking truth to power. Recall the anti-World Trade Organisation (WTO) demonstrations in Seattle in 1999, where demonstrators displayed the slogan 'This is What Democracy Looks Like'. The slogan, which points to the people as being the essence of democracy, has become a common utterance in anti-globalisation and anti-G8 demonstrations since Seattle. The slogan and demonstrations, as I have argued elsewhere, speak truth to power (Loizidou, 2011:167–87). The slogan first alerts us to the fact that our polities are increasingly being managed by private organisations such as banks or the WTO and the backbone of democracy, the people, is being sidelined. The slogan and demonstrations were not, however, just making public the democratic deficit that we increasingly find ourselves in, but more actively telling the world that 'we the people refuse to be governed in this way'. This means that the people are no longer willing to be governed by private organisations, corporations, banks or parliaments and other public institutions such as courts that they see as servicing global finance capital and its accomplices. The slogan and demonstrations of this kind demonstrate that polities should and can be governed by the people themselves. The slogan is a performative speech act (Butler, 1993:2) that brings into being the true essence of democracy: 'the people'. But in Stirner's opinion, the truth – even talking truth to power – does not, as we often think and imagine, empower people. On the contrary, Stirner worries that the search for truth disempowers people (2006:311–13). Here is how he presents his argument against the valorisation of truth as the ultimate good:

> truth is only a – *thought*; but it is not merely 'a thought', but the thought that is above all thoughts, the irrefragable thought, it is *the* thought itself,

which gives the first hallowing to all others; it is the consecration of thoughts, the 'absolute', the 'sacred' thought …

I will answer Pilate's question: What is Truth? Truth is the free thought, the free idea, the free spirit; truth is what is free from you what is not your own, what is not in your power. But truth is also the completely unindependent, impersonal, unreal, and incorporeal; truth cannot step forward as you do, cannot move, change, develop; truth awaits and receives everything from you, and itself is only through you; for it exists only – in your head. You concede that the truth is a thought but say that not every thought is truly and really a thought. And by what do you measure and recognize the thought? By *your impotence*, namely, by you being no longer able to make any successful assault on it! When it overpowers you, inspires you, and carries you away, then you hold it to be the true one. Its domination over you certifies to you its truth; and when it possesses you, and you are possessed by it, then you feel well with it, for then you have found your – *lord and master*.

(Stirner, 2006:311–12; emphasis in original)

We noted earlier that for Stirner thinking, thinking that emerges out of *own* criticism, is something that demonstrates to us that the ego is free from all things (ideology, the State, religion, love, etc.) that enslave us. So for Stirner thought per se is a positive practice. However, when it comes to thinking that seeks the truth, when it comes to thinking that puts truth as its object, this type of truth is enslaving. It has the same effects as *servile* criticism. It is fairly obvious that in addressing his critique to Pilate (known for presiding over the trial of Jesus and allowing his crucifixion when the people decided to send Jesus to his death despite Pilate's reluctance to do so), Stirner thinks that truth-seeking is associated with religion. Indeed this becomes apparent when at one point in his address to Pilate he says:

The truth, my dear Pilate, is – the Lord, and all who see the truth are seeking and praising the Lord … As long as you believe in the truth, you do not believe in yourself, and you are a – servant, a religious man.

(2006:312)

As the Black studies and political theorist Cedric J. Roberts writes in *The Terms of Order* (2016), Stirner reaches this conclusion because he 'refus[es] to accept an identity or a proximate relationship between social freedom and individual freedom' (175). We may agree with Stirner that if we live in a Christian State and within legal frameworks, for example, or the general organisation of life is affected by Christianity, then it may have adverse effects on individuals who do not espouse this faith. For example, Christianity considers abortion murderous, and even now, despite the passing of legislation that allows for the termination of a pregnancy within the first 24 weeks of pregnancy and under certain circumstances,[4] some Christians are trying to revoke abortion laws or prevent the legalisation of abortion. In this case, what a religious Christian State would consider to be the truth regarding pregnancy and life would be against the individual interests of women who would like a termination of their pregnancies. So Stirner, if we take this as our example, may be right in saying that there is no correlation between individual freedom and social freedom. Why is the Christian truth more of the truth than a woman's desire to terminate her pregnancy? Even if we did not take the Christian State as our example, and instead took as our example the Western democratic and liberal State, we can see how Stirner's suggestion, namely that social freedom and individual freedom are not always compatible, holds some truth. Legislative and medical frameworks on abortion do not allow women to terminate a pregnancy merely because they want to do so and at any time. Nevertheless, what Stirner leaves unexplained is how one's ownership of oneself, and consequently one's ownership of one's thinking, is an ownership that does not take into account that the social may relate to other unique individuals. We have seen earlier that Stirner writes that he anticipates no problem arising in a world or polity that is made up of unique individuals, for they 'have nothing in common … and therefore nothing divisive or hostile either …' (186) and he imagines an exchange based on these very non-commonalities. However, he does not explain adequately, or convincingly for that matter, how two or three or an association of unique individuals will come to share the world and its resources. In other words, he does not address the ethical practices of living together without reducing everything to the commons. Whilst I am convinced by his suggestion that violence can only be reduced if we realise ourselves as unique individuals and live with other unique individuals precisely because of our lack of commonalities, I am not convinced that we can do so without developing some practices that somehow address the issue of sharing resources. Stirner's lack of clarity on this issue becomes apparent when he talks about property.

Stirner begins his reflections on property by offering us a critique of the conceptions of property held by liberals, communists, socialists and anarchists like Proudhon. I will return to his critiques of these ideologies below, but before doing so it is important to note that for Stirner there are two types of properties that we own. The first type of property is 'inward *possessions* …. spiritualities, thoughts, convictions, noble feelings' and the other is 'outward' ownership, which relates to things we possess (2006:218; emphasis in original). When it comes to inward possessions, Stirner argues that they are not our own

---

4   Abortions are legal in England, Wales and Scotland and are governed by s.1 (1) of The Abortion Act 1967. The act decriminalises women who seek abortion if the abortion is performed by two medical practitioners who determine that the pregnancy has not exceeded 24 weeks, that the pregnancy will put at risk the mental and physical health of the woman, that the termination will prevent serious mental and physical harm to the woman or that the pregnancy puts at risk the life of the woman and the child.

possessions but rather they belong to the spiritual realm such as that of religion or the State. We need to disown possessions such as honour, for example. We may believe that to be honourable is an attribute that we possess but in reality, Stirner suggests, it belongs to the religious sphere that through its sermons and pedagogy has made it its own (218–19). Whilst religion may be free, we become its servants. So, we are not in actuality possessors of honour; religion is. Similarly, the liberal State through rights that tend to protect our decency, for example, gives us the illusion that our decency belongs to ourselves, although it is the State that owns it at the end of the day (218). So, to become owners of ourselves, Stirner suggests we need to take ownership of our interiority. This thought is shared by Phillips, whom we encountered earlier – if we are to be a subject that is not subjugated to the realm of the forbidden we need to bracket out from our living those institutions that possess and enslave us. So, the process of self-creation that Stirner proposes requires us to pay attention to even the most taken-for-granted inward affinities, to critique them and thus discover what inward feelings, thoughts, etc. belong truly to us. As you may have noticed, Stirner has a two-pronged approach to discussing ideas, first he offers a critique and then he proceeds to state his own position. This is also how he writes in relation to outward property. He critiques the anarchist, communist, socialist as well as liberal positions on property and then offers us his own belief regarding property and our relationship to it. It is to his account of outward property that I turn now.

The liberal understanding of property, according to Stirner, would have everyone own their own property, and each one of us respect the property of others (2006:219–20). Stirner calls this reciprocal relationship between the ownership of property and respect for it the liberal civic concept of property. The State imposes a civic condition upon each one of us if we own property. If we disrespect our neighbour's property, by vandalising it or trespassing on it, we are to face criminal or civil sanctions. Stirner, who was in favour of the private ownership of property, is critical of the liberal concept of private property. Why? First, this concept of property does not allow the owner to enjoy their property freely – enjoyment of one's property has to fall within the liberal framework. This concept of private property additionally disguises a crude reality, namely the existence of inequality in private property ownership. Some people, big landowners for example, will always own more land than their tenants even if the tenants have been given the right to buy and own property. Moreover, the 'great proprietors' can buy out the 'small proprietors' at any time (220). The 'small proprietor', therefore, ends up being enslaved to a liberal ideology of property that in the end they do not have access to. We can still see this concept of property operating in our contemporary societies. We are all free to buy property, but given the rise in prices in the housing market, for example, only the privileged few are able own their own property, and simultaneously a great number of us are captured by the idea of owning our own property and working towards realising this goal. 'Property as the civic liberals understand it', Stirner writes, 'deserves the attacks of communists and Proudhon' (221). But, although it deserves the attacks of anarchists, socialists and communists, their critiques of liberal property did not gain Stirner's approval.

Proudhon is the first to face Stirner's sharp criticisms. Pierre Joseph Proudhon, one of the most prominent anarchist figures, proposes in his essay 'What is Property?' (2011b:87–138) that we should abolish the ownership of property. Instead, he proposes a new way in which to relate to property, one that is not based on ownership of property but instead on the benefit that we can gain from property. Property is not presented as a thing, with its value emanating from being either individually owned or possessed. On the contrary, its value emanates from the benefits it can provide for all. We can cultivate land as a society, for example, and benefit from its produce without owning it. He builds this argument around the presupposition that society itself, not individuals, is the owner of property. So, if we are to reverse the individual liberal conception of property, Proudhon suggests that we should form a union, form a society and take private property back and then benefit from it individually and as a social group without owning it. Property was stolen from society. Consequently, as property belonged to society originally any form of individual property is considered by Proudhon to be theft. Stirner is dissatisfied with Proudhon's critique of property on the grounds that the proposition that society is the owner of property is 'a spook' (Stirner, 2006: 222), an apparition. Proudhon, Stirner caustically remarks, would have been more accurate if he had argued as follows:

> 'There are some things that belong only to a few, and which we others will from now on lay claim or – siege. Let us take them, because one comes to property by taking, and the property of which for the present we are still deprived came to the proprietors likewise only by taking. It can be utilized better if it is in the hands of us all than if the few control it. Let us therefore associate ourselves for the purpose of this robbery (*vol*).' – Instead of this, he tries to get us to believe that society is the original possessor and the sole proprietor, of imprescriptible right; against it the so-called proprietors have become thieves (*La propriété c'est le vol*); if it now deprives of his property the present proprietor, it robs him of nothing, as it is only availing itself of its imprescriptible right.
>
> (Stirner, 2006:222)

It is the social aspect of property that Stirner finds problematic in Proudhon's proposition. He does not believe that property is social. He nevertheless recognises that there is an inequality in the ownership of property, and it is for this reason that he considers Proudhon's proposition to take back property as a fair solution. Nevertheless, he does not believe that property should become a social good. Recall that for Stirner the social, like the State or any ideology, jeopardises the autonomy of the auto-poetic ego. In other words, the idea of an ego being subordinated to society and not owning property but enjoying its goods is, for Stirner, another form of enslavement.

Moreover, Stirner also critiques Proudhon for his very understanding of what counts as property. If all property is theft, then, Stirner suggests, that means that somehow property must belong to somebody in order to be appropriated. If property belonged to everyone then it could not be appropriated. Even if the idea of property ownership is nothing but a legal fiction as '[p]rivate property lives by grace of the *law*. Only in the law has it its warrant – for possession is not yet property, it becomes "mine" only by assent of the law; it is not a fact, not *un fait* … but a fiction, a thought' (Stirner, 2006; 223; emphasis in original) then what Proudhon fails to consider is a particular aspect of this so-called legal fiction that stems from Roman law. In Roman law, 'property' is understood to be that which 'I can judge and dispose of as seems good to me' (223). Roman law thus has at its very basis property ownership that can be established by the usurpation of land (223). Stirner is correct; Roman law recognised the usurpation or colonisation of property (Bhandar, 2018) as ownership of property; however, this is not the full story regarding the concept of property within Roman law. In *The German Ideology* (1998) Marx and Engels critique Stirner for not paying proper attention to history and presenting opinions that have not been checked, and for *not* attending to material and relational issues regarding property (369–426). They sarcastically explain, for example, that Stirner fails to understand that property is *relational*: 'Saint Sancho only knows "things" and "egos", and as regards anything that does not come under these headings, as regards all relations, he knows only the abstract concepts of them, which for him, therefore, also become "spectres"' (384). Moreover, Marx and Engels critique Stirner for not knowing that private property was not the original form of property in Rome or other European communities: 'For recent investigations into the history of right have established that both in Rome and among the German, Celtic and Slav peoples the development of property had as its starting-point communal or tribal property …' (386). Agamben (2013) also informs us that in Roman law there were three types of property: property by occupation or usurpation, obligation and use, though the latter was not explicitly defined (123–43).

Stirner could of course be critiqued for his inattention to historical fact; Marx and Engels are right. However, even without taking account of this misdemeanour, we can critique him for his inability to provide us with a clear account of how the union of egoists, the individuals who would have shed religious, liberal, etc. incorporations of inward property, could share the world. Whilst Stirner's concept of disobedience and withdrawal from all ideologies is consistent with a lot of anarchist writings, Emma Goldman being a good example, the second part of purely following just one's own interests falls short even for the most individualist of anarchists, like Goldman, who always had the social at the foreground of their emancipatory practices (Hemmings, 2018).

Marx and Engels are correct in pointing out that Stirner is unable to see the relational aspect of property. Even if he does, or even if his union of egoists is, as Clark suggests, relational (1976:84), and, as we saw earlier (Stirner, 2006:186) Stirner anticipates them relating on various issues based on their non-commonality through a contract (Clark, 1976:84), I cannot personally see how a concept of outward property based on occupation cannot entertain the possibility of violence. Stirner, like Proudhon, considers that the liberal conception of property lies in the appropriation of property. Consequently, a social revolution that requires the re-appropriation of property is as important for Stirner as the theorists that he critiques. Nevertheless, even if they do so as unique individuals within a union of egoists and other unique individuals, this still does not explain how this occupation of property or understanding of our relation to property is any different from the ones that he critiques.

According to Stirner, the difference lies in the relationship between the individual and the union. He demonstrates this by contrasting the union of egoists to society, a liberal society, and so he writes:

> You bring into a union your whole power, your competence, and *make yourself count*; in a society you are employed, with your working power, in the former you live egoistically, in the latter humanly, that is, religiously, as a 'member in the body of this Lord'; to a society you owe what you have, and are in duty to it, are possessed by 'social duties'; a union you utilize, and give it up undutifully and unfaithfully when you see no way to use it further. If a society is more than you, then it is more to you than yourself; a union is only your natural force; the union exists for you and through you, the society conversely lays claims to you for itself and exists even without you; in short, the society is sacred, the union your own; the society consumes you, you consume the union.
>
> (Stirner, 2006:277; emphasis in original)

According to Stirner, the difference between the union and society lies in our very relationship to these webs of socialisation. The union is our object that we can utilise as we please while society subjectifies and objectifies us. Still, even if it is important to retain the concept of the unique individual, and even if '[o]nly in the union can [one] assert [themselves] as unique, because the union does possess you, but you possess it or make it of use to you' (276), Stirner leaves unexplained why a possessive union and not a union of individuals who share cannot sustain the unique individual. Is the reason we cannot be unique precisely that we have done away with the possessive individualism that is inherent to capitalism? Stirner's egoist insurrection is poignant in some respects. It alerts us to the psychic and material ways in which we become servile to ideas, like Phillips or the French political theorist Etienne De la Boétie, who demonstrate to us how quotidian concerns (regarding survival, for example) and norms (for example, how to be a good son or daughter) make us servile to a world that reduces us to being a cog in the machine. Nevertheless, a disobedience that produces a political system (union of egoists) that could give rise to the servitude of others, as I have shown through Stirner's understanding, critique and reconstruction of property, is myopic to the possibility of uniqueness existing in a polity whereby individuals relate to property through use rather than individual ownership of it. In other words, Stirner fails to grasp that the capitalist system that he very much criticises feeds on an idea of the individual, and perhaps if we are to undo the capitalist ideology, we need also to do away with the idea of the individual. We will need to hold onto the idea of uniqueness; Stirner is incisive in insisting that uniqueness should be very much part of a new polity that is free from the ideology of the liberal state or religion. Indeed, he is right to point out that we need to pay special attention to our lack of commonality (Stirner, 2006:186) and work to form a better world from the position of our disparities; but this unique self does not need to operate within an individualist self. Stirner himself somewhat *contradictorily* writes that only in the union of egoists can one assert oneself as being unique (276) or, put otherwise, uniqueness can make itself visible beyond an atomic political structure. Let's also not forget that one of the positive contributions of Stirner's unique self is his attempt to relate this concept to material life. Even if, as I suggested earlier, I disagree with his individualist notion of property ownership, one manifestation of this material life, his unique egoist is not just a psychic idea of self, despite Marx and Engel's (1998) criticisms (384).

Truth, or rather talking truth to power, what has come to be known as *parrhesia*, has been a common practice of disobedience amongst anarchists. Stirner, who has been claimed as an anarchist (Guérin, 1970:27–33; Clark, 1976; Woodcock, 1983:87–97; Ferguson, 2011b:167–88; Newman, 2011b), as we have already seen, was suspicious of the work of truth. *Parrhesia* however offers a different insight into truth, speaking and idealisation. *Parrhesia* was a way of speaking, practised in Ancient Greece and Rome which, as we will see in more detail below, challenged positions that were attached to idealism, misconceptions or unfairness. Foucault, who I will draw upon to show that *parrhesia* is a constitutive element of an anarchist art of living, notes that '[t]he word *parrhesia* [παρρησία] appears for the first time in Greek literature in Euripides [c.484–407 B.C.] and occurs throughout the ancient Greek world of letters from the end of the Fifth Century B.C.' (2001:11). With *parrhesia*, Foucault sets out to provide us with an access to the ethical and political questions that we face when we govern ourselves and others. Whilst Foucault is wise enough to be aware of the fact that the ancient concerns regarding government of self or others cannot be transposed to our times or modernity, he nevertheless did engage with Kant's 'What is Enlightenment?' in the 1982–3 Lectures at the Collège de France (Foucault, 2010:1–40). According to Frederic Gros, Foucault re-engaged with Kant in this essay to answer a slightly different question to Kant, namely, 'What government of self should be posited as both the foundation and limit of the government of others?' (Gros, 2010:379).

74 Disentangling the psyche

Foucault is interested in exploring *parrhesia* to figure out what are the limits of government (personal and public) in the hope that this will enable him to trace our relation to truth, how we refuse to be governed in ways that we consider corrupt and unacceptable, and when we place restrictions on government. Acts of disobedience, as we have already seen, are expressions of our intolerance of certain ways of government. *Parrhesia*, I argue, does more than just point to the limits of certain modes of government. The use of *parrhesia* by anarchists or anarchist-affiliated groups becomes exemplary of life lived parallel to the political regimes that it is contesting. If we observe anarchist parrhesiatic utterances, we will notice that they exhibit a different form of governing. We begin to observe a different ethical and political way of being in the world, an anarchist way of being in the world. In order to understand what anarchists and their use of *parrhesia* offer us, I will first look in some detail at Foucault's writings on *parrhesia*.

Parrhesia as a way of life

Foucault's 1982–3 and 1983–4 Lectures at the Collège de France focused on *parrhesia*. In the first set of lectures, which are entitled *The Government of Self and Others* (2010), Foucault moves from exploring *parrhesia*'s characteristics (e.g., frankness) to *parrhesia* as a political act or as a speech act that is addressed to the public. In *The Courage of Truth* the 1983–4 lectures (2011), Foucault looks closely at the differences between *parrhesia* and other truth-telling speeches such as teaching, to reveal the importance of *parrhesia* for democracy in its transformation from Ancient Greece to Christianity. Foucault explores *parrhesia* by looking into Euripides' *Ion*, Socrates, Alcibiades and the Cynics, amongst others. *Parrhesia* also plays a central role in the lectures that he gave in the autumn of 1983 in California. Some of the Berkeley lectures, entitled 'Discourse and Truth', were published in 2001 as *Fearless Speech* (Foucault, 2001). Here Foucault provides us with a handful of characteristics that we can use to differentiate between *parrhesia* and other forms of utterance that may lay claim to truth or be made publicly. It is important to note also that in *The Government of Self and Others* (2010) Foucault differentiates between performative speech acts and *parrhesia*. Performative speech acts, as Austin and Searle explain, are public utterances, unlike *parrhesia*, that do not lay any claim to truth; indeed, what performative speech acts do is contribute to our understanding that not all utterances are truthful but rather that some utterances are effective (61–74). *Parrhesia*, as Foucault tells us, 'is ordinarily translated into English as "free speech"' (2001:11). *Parrhesia* is also different from other forms of free speech, such as rhetoric, prophesy, wisdom and pedagogy. Let's see how Foucault differentiates between these different modes of public speaking.

'[R]hetoric', Foucault observes, 'is basically a technique concerning the way that things are said, but does not in any way determine the relations between the person who speaks and what he says' (Foucault, 2011:13). Moreover, and this is what fundamentally distinguishes *parrhesia* from rhetoric,

Rhetoric is an act, a technique, a set of processes which enables the person speaking to say something which may not be what he thinks at all, but whose effect will be to produce convictions, induce certain conducts, or instill certain beliefs in the person ...

(3)

Whilst *parrhesia* is a type of speech that bonds the speaker to the speech, 'rhetoric does not involve any bond of belief between the person speaking and what he [states]' (Foucault, 2011: 13). Foucault distinguishes between *parrhesia* and prophesy (15). We are all familiar with the truth that the genre of prophetic speaking is supposed to utter. We may say that precisely because of their claim to truth, prophesies are parrhesiatic speech acts. Nevertheless, as Foucault suggests, the difference between these two modes of speaking – the prophetic and the parrhesiatic – lies in the difference in their posture (15). As he explains, whilst parrhesiastes speak the truth for themselves, the prophet is a simple mediator of truth; '[t]he prophet, by definition, does not speak in his own name. He speaks for another voice; his mouth serves an intermediary for a voice which speaks from elsewhere' (15). Moreover, parrhesiastes, unlike prophets, are not known for foretelling the future, nor do they speak in riddles. So, there are substantial differences between *parrhesia* and prophesy. Similarly, Foucault insists that we can distinguish between *parrhesia* and wisdom. A wise person or a sage, like the parrhesiastes, speaks in their 'own name' (16) and is recognised as telling the truth. However, the main difference between the sage and the parrhesiastes lies in the fact that the sage

> keeps his wisdom in a state of essential withdrawal, or at least reserve. Basically, the sage is wise in and for himself, and does not need to speak. He is not forced to speak, nothing obliges him to share his wisdom, to teach it, or demonstrate it.
>
> (17)

And unlike the parrhesiastes, when the sage speaks they are not responding to anything or anybody. The teacher or the technician is the last figure that Foucault contrasts to the parrhesiastes. The teacher or technician – teachers, professors, doctors all fall into this category – are figures that the hold specialist knowledge in their hands (Foucault, 2011:24). Therefore, 'they possess this knowledge, they profess it, and they are capable of teaching it to others. The technician, who possesses a *techne*, has learned it and is capable of teaching it, [and] obliged to speak the truth ...' (24). But yet again, unlike the parrhesiastes, the 'teacher, this man of *tekhne*, of expertise and teaching, does not take any risk in the truth-telling he has received and must pass on ...' (24). So, a professor who is transmitting 'true knowledge' to their students is not risking anything in doing so, unless of course they are doing this under conditions of censorship. In these circumstances they will become a parrhesiastes. By directing us to the differences between it and other truth-telling speech acts Foucault is able to give us a clear picture of what *parrhesia* is. You may have guessed by now what the main attributes of *parrhesia* are. But let's turn to the list that Michel Foucault provides us with in *Fearless Speech* (2001).

In this text we find a useful summary of attributes of *parrhesia* collected by Foucault from Euripides, Plato, Aristotle and other Ancient Greek and Roman writers and philosophers. *Parrhesia* is free speech that is frank, truthful, critical, puts the speaker in danger and is duty bound. Let's take each one of these attributes in turn and see how Foucault relates them to *parrhesia*.

Parrhesia, he writes, means not only free speech but also to say everything. The speaker speaks his opinion about a subject matter. As they are doing so they show that their actual utterance is strictly linked to what they are saying. It is a direct way of showing what one believes. Of course, for *parrhesia* to be recognised as such we need the other attributes to be present (Foucault, 2001:12–13).

Parrhesiastes do not only have to be frank, they also have to be truthful. 'To my mind', Foucault writes,

> the parrhesiastes says what is true because it is really true. The parrhesiastes is not only sincere and says what is his opinion, but his opinion is also the truth ... there is [thus] always an exact coincidence between belief and truth.
>
> (14)

Parrhesiastes are courageous and their courage stands as evidence of the truth of their utterances.

Parrhesia is not just any type of true utterance. *Parrhesia* wants the speaker to be in danger, risking their life or putting a friendship at risk. In other words, in *parrhesia* by simply saying words the speaker is putting themselves at risk of losing something very valuable to them, including their life (15–17). A philosopher or any of us telling a tyrant or a dictator that they are perpetrating injustice are examples of parrhesiastes (16). As Foucault explains, 'the *parrhesiastes* primarily chooses a specific relationship to himself: he prefers himself as a truth-teller rather than as a living being who is false to himself' (15–17).

Parrhesia exposes a particular relationship between the speaker and their interlocutor. And, as Foucault explains, the danger in *parrhesia* 'always comes from the fact that the said truth is capable of hurting or angering the *interlocutor* (2001:17; emphasis in original). Moreover,

> [p]arrhesia ... may be the advice that the interlocutor should behave in a certain way, or that he is wrong in what he thinks, or in the way he acts, and so on ... So you see, the function of *parrhesia* is not to demonstrate the truth to someone else, but has the function of criticism ...
>
> (17)

Parrhesiastes are also in a less powerful position than their interlocutor. Nevertheless, none of the parrhesiastes in Ancient Greece were from a lower social status. Neither slaves nor women could be parrhesiastes, nor could they be citizens in Ancient Greece, so they did not have the status that allowed them to speak out formally.

And the last characteristic of *parrhesia* is that of duty. Parrhesiastes feel that it is their duty to speak the truth. They are compelled to say the truth (Foucault, 2001:19). So, as Foucault writes:

> *parrhesia* is a kind of verbal activity where the speaker has a specific relation to truth through frankness, a certain relationship to his own life through danger, a certain type of relation to himself or other people through criticism (self-criticism or criticism of other people), and a specific relation to moral law through freedom and duty. More precisely, *parrhesia* is a verbal activity in which a speaker expresses his personal relationship to truth, and risks his life because he recognizes truth-telling as a duty to improve or help other people (as well as himself). In *parrhesia*, the speaker uses his freedom and chooses frankness instead of persuasion, truth instead of falsehood or silence, the risk of death instead of life and security, criticism instead of flattery, and moral duty instead of self-interest and moral apathy.
>
> (Foucault, 2001:19–20)

Anarchists do not shy away from talking truth to power. Anarchist parrhesiatic utterances are not just occasional speeches but rather a way of life. Anarchists do not recognise authority, so when they speak to figures of authority, they do not try to convince them of their position, but rather they expose to them and consequently to us the limits of their authority, the lack of foundation for their authority and contradictions between their beliefs and what they do. In addition, *parrhesia*, like other *technes* that Ancient Greeks and Romans practised (as part of caring for oneself), was concerned with not subjugating oneself to the juridical order (Foucault, 1991:348). The parrhesiatic examples below demonstrate clearly how anarchists are free from the enslavement of the juridical order.

Parrhesia, an anarchist techne of living

My first examples of anarchist parrhesiatic speech are drawn from Emma Goldman, while my more contemporary example comes from the UK Uncut group and its sit-in at Fortnum and Mason on 26 March 2011. Goldman was an anarchist. UK Uncut, a UK-based group that was formed in 2010 to protest against tax evasion and austerity cuts, are not openly an anarchic group. I have argued earlier that unlike the postanarchist Newman, who would consider UK Uncut an anarchist formation, I do not, as there is nothing in their public statements that enables me to say that they want to see the withering of the

State, one of the major anarchist principles; nor do they publicly state that they want a life without law. Nevertheless, as their actions revealed inequality in tax paying, pointing to the deceptive ways in which corporations evade tax and exposing the way in which the State ignores such practices, without fear and with courage, we can also call them parrhesiastes. Their organisation (horizontal decision-making), ethos (speaking truth to power) and their detesting of the State enables us to see their affinity with anarchism without calling them anarchists. Their actions are exemplary of what Kinna (2019) calls the 'anarchization' of socio-political formations and groups, individuals giving up their time, risking themselves to form a collective, speaking truth to power and revealing the wider influence of anarchist ideas. It is for these reasons that I investigate their actions here, along with those Emma Goldman, to which I will turn now.

Let's begin with the background of one of many of Emma Goldman's parrhesiatic utterances. On 6 April 1908 Goldman was returning to the US from Canada after giving a series of lectures on anarchism 'including discussions encouraging street railway employees to strike for an eight-hour workday'.[5] She was held at the village of Noyes, in the State of Minnesota, where inspectors questioned her US citizenship. Goldman was a US citizen through her marriage to Jacob A. Kershner. She married him in 1887 and left him in 1888. They had never officially been divorced. In September 1908 the US government brought legal proceedings against Kershner challenging his citizenship. The inspectors' ultimate aim was to remove Emma Goldman's citizenship and deport her. They were of the opinion and had evidence to the effect that Kershner had gained his citizenship by fraud and perjury. When he applied for his citizenship, Kershner was not yet 18 years of age and had not lived in the US for five years, the required period for applying for citizenship. This evidence was enough to remove his citizenship. Kershner had disappeared. The Department of Justice did not notify Goldman of their case against Kershner in the hope that she would not find out that she had had her citizenship removed and so she could be arrested at the border and deported. Kershner was not denaturalised until 8 April 1909. Goldman's arrest in Noyes and her appearance before the Board of Special Inquiry (Bureau of Immigration) was to establish to what extent she was a US citizen and therefore had permission to enter into the US.[6] Goldman was examined by Walter E. Carr, chair of the

---

5   See Falk, *Emma Goldman: A Guide to Her Life and Documentary Sources: Chronology 1901–1919*, at www.lib.berkeley.edu/goldman/pdfs/EG-AGuideToHerLife_Chronology1901-1919.pdf p. 10. Accessed 16 December 2021.
6   This information is taken from the explanatory note: 'Denaturalization of Jacob Kersner September 24, 1908' (on file with me) and retrieved from the Emma Goldman Archive at the International Institute of Social History, Amsterdam. The transcript of the 'Examination of Emma Goldman before Board of Special Inquiry, 6 April 1908' has been retrieved from the Emma Goldman Archive at the International Institute of Social History, Amsterdam, document 830214126 (on file with me).

Board of Special Inquiry, Person A. Robbins and Shirley D. Smith. I am not interested in the legal ramifications of the investigation but in the way in which Goldman responded to the questions that were put to her. If we were to be stopped at the borders of our country of citizenship and threatened with removal from it, I think we may be afraid and not be in a position to give the response that Goldman gave in front of the Board of Special Inquiry. Goldman, as you will witness in the extensive quote recording the interrogation before the Board, makes a free, frank and courageous speech, which reveals that she was in a subordinate position to Walter E. Carr and the other two inquisitors, and that she was speaking out and responding in the way she did out of a sense of duty, a duty to tell the truth. Carr begins the inquiry with a series of banal but perfectly legitimate questions about her date and place of birth, her first entry to the US, her marriage to Kershner and her naturalisation. To all the questions she responds with frankness and sobriety, and without being afraid to explain that she does not remember certain details. Consider this interaction, for example, between herself and Carr, where Goldman provides him with true, frank and duty-bound answers, in line with what Foucault calls parrhesiatic speech, in response to questions about her acquisition of US citizenship:

Q: Are you a citizen of the United States?
A: Yes, sir, I am.
Q: In what manner did you acquire citizenship?
A: Well, through both my father and my husband.
Q: Has your citizenship ever been questioned?
A: It is being questioned now I suppose.
Q: How old were you when your father took out his papers?
A: I wasn't 18. I was less when he took out his first papers, but as to the second I can't remember exactly. I don't know.[7]

As you can see, Goldman answers frankly the questions that Carr puts to her regarding acquiring her citizenship via her father and husband. Goldman truthfully tells him that she cannot remember when her father took out his second citizenship papers. Carr then proceeds to ask her specific questions about her marriage to Kershner, which she answers again with frankness:

Q: How long after you landed at New York were you married?
A: Well I was married in February 1887. I was just past sixteen when I came to this country....
Q: In what church were you married?
A: I was not married in a church, I was married civilly.

7 See 'Emma Goldman before Board of Special Inquiry, 6 April 1908', which has been retrieved from the Emma Goldman Archive at the International Institute of Social History, Amsterdam, document 830214126 (on file with me), 250.

Q: What do you mean by "married civilly", by a Justice?
A: Yes, by the courts.
Q: How long did you live with your husband?
A: Two years.
Q: Did you ever source a divorce?
A: No.
Q: Well then, to all intents and purposes the marital relationship seemed to exist two years after the marriage ceremony. Is that a fact?
A: Not necessarily. I was not divorced, at least not legally so.
Q: Have you anything of a documentary nature to substantiate your claim as to marriage?
A: No.[8]

After the interrogation regarding her marriage and how she had acquired her citizenship, Carr turns to question Goldman's qualities as a citizen and her ideological positions. It is rather refreshing to read her answers. As you will see, the questions are once again answered with fearlessness:

Q: Did you ever take the oath of allegiance to the United States?
A: No, sir.
Q: Have you taken an oath of allegiance to any other country or government since the time of the naturalisation of your father and your marriage with your husband?
A: No, sir.
Q: Where you married before or after your father took out his second papers?
A: Before.
Q: Then you could hardly claim to partake of the naturalisation of your father, and therefore your claims to United States Citizenship must rest upon that of your husband absolutely. Is that not so?
A: I suppose so.
Q: Are you an anarchist?
A: I am.[9]

Similar answers in relation to her marriage to Kershner were pursued by Inspector Robbins. The replies given where again direct and parrhesiatic in manner. The most courageous answer to the questions of Inspector Robbins was the one given to him regarding her understanding of government and anarchism:

8   See 'Emma Goldman before Board of Special Inquiry, 6 April 1908', which has been retrieved from the Emma Goldman Archive at the International Institute of Social History, Amsterdam, document 830214126' (on file with me), 250 and 251.
9   See 'Emma Goldman before Board of Special Inquiry, 6 April 1908 has been retrieved from the Emma Goldman Archive at the International Institute of Social History, Amsterdam, document 830214126' (on file with me), 252.

Q: As an anarchist, I understand that you believe in no Government? Is that correct?
A: Exactly, I believe in man governing himself. Each man.
Q: Do you also believe in the overthrow of existing governments by force or violence or otherwise?
A: I believe in the method laid down by the Constitution of the United States, that when the Government becomes despotic and irksome the people have the right to overthrow it. You will have to hold the Government of the United States responsible for that. The Government of the United States was formed by the people uprising to crush a despotic power.
Q: You refer to the Declaration of Independence rather than to the Constitution do you not?
A: It is the Declaration of Independence instead of the Constitution but the Constitution provides for it too.
Q: Do you believe that the Government of the United States has reached such a stage as you describe now?
A: Well, the people haven't reached the stage of overthrowing it, and therefore I suppose they are satisfied.
Q: That hardly answers the question. You only evaded it. I asked you whether, in your opinion, or belief, the Government of the United States has reached that stage where it should be overthrown by force or otherwise?
A: I believe that if America goes on very much further it will reach that point. It is on the way.
Q: Now Miss Goldman, the question is, do you or do you not believe that the Government of the United States has reached such a stage that the present time as would warrant its overthrow by force or violence or otherwise. It is only delaying matters when you insist upon evasive answers.
A: I would much rather not express an opinion or a belief on that matter at all. It hasn't much farther to go. I think it is fast on the way, that is certain.[10]

All three inspectors agreed to allow Goldman to pass through into the US and they did not revoke her citizenship. Inspector Robbins' evaluation of Goldman is exemplary of how they received her words as truthful:

> From the general attitude of Miss Goldman before the Board, and her evident willingness to answer questions, and her manner of answering those questions, I am inclined to the belief that she is telling the truth. Her answers appear to me to have been straightforward and honest.
>
> (254)

---

10 See 'Emma Goldman before Board of Special Inquiry, 6 April 1908', which has been retrieved from the Emma Goldman Archive at the International Institute of Social History, Amsterdam, document 830214126 (on file with me), 253–4.

On 27 June 1917 Emma Goldman and Alexander Berkman stood trial in the District Court of the City of New York on charges of conspiracy relating to their anti-conscription activities prior to and after the signing of the Selective Service Act 1917 (hereafter Conscription Act) on 5 June by President Woodrow Wilson. Their arrests took place on 15 June, on the day that Wilson signed the new Espionage Act which rendered, amongst other things, any anti-draft activities illegal. Goldman and Berkman were arrested in the offices of their respective magazines, *Mother Earth* and *The Blast* at 20 E, 125 Street, New York. Their trial lasted from 27 June until 9 July 1917. I have explained elsewhere (Loizidou, 2011:167–87; 2020:181–93) and in Chapter 2 of this book how Goldman and her associates explained during the trial that law is not part of the arts that organise anarchist life, pointing to the limitations that law imposes on an anarchist life and life in general.

The incident that I am about to introduce takes place at the moment of Goldman's arrest. Again, Goldman addresses figures of authority with courage:

> The leader of the party excitedly cried: 'Emma Goldman, you're under arrest! And so is Berkman where is he?' It was the United States Marshal Thomas D. McCarthy. I knew him by sight; of late he had always stationed himself at our No-Conscription meetings, his whole attitude one of impatient readiness to spring upon the speakers. The newspapers had reported him as saying that he had repeatedly wired Washington for orders to arrest us.
>
> 'I hope you will get the medal you crave,' I said to him. 'Just the same, you might let me see your warrant …'
>
> McCarthy declared that no warrant was necessary for us; *Mother Earth* contained enough treasonable matter to land us in jail – for years. He had come to get us, and we had better hurry up.
>
> Leisurely I walked towards the stairs and called: 'Sasha, Fitzi – some visitors are here to arrest us.'
>
> …
>
> I started for my room to change my dress, aware that a night's free lodging was in store for me. One of the men rushed up to detain me, taking hold of my arm. I wrenched myself loose. 'If your chief didn't have the guts to come up here without a body-guard of thugs,' I said to him, 'he should at least have instructed you not to act like one. I'm not going to run away. I only want to dress for the reception awaiting us, and I don't propose to let you act as my maid'.
>
> (Goldman, 1970b:610–11)

Foucault explained that *parrhesia* can take any form as long as it conveys a truth frankly and courageously or, as he put it, 'in the form one thinks necessary to say it' (2005:372). In the quote above we witness Goldman speaking courageously; she was about to be arrested when she asked the police officer who tried to stop her from getting changed, to see his warrant, talking truth to power. Telling the instruments of law and order, the State apparatuses, that the way they operate is against the very oath they have taken – namely, to serve and protect the people – reveals the empty promises of law. It also reveals how anarchists like Goldman are not afraid of being arrested and put on trial for their truth – exposing the failures and limits of representative democracy and its institutions. We have seen in the previous example from Goldman how in the face of a possible deportation she not only gives truthful answers to her interrogators but makes no attempt to hide her anarchist beliefs, her belief in self-government. Foucault (2011:33–55) tells us that in democracy it is not possible to have *parrhesia* '[b]ecause one cannot distinguish between good and bad speakers, between discourse which speaks the truth and is useful to the city, and discourse which utters lies, flatters, and is harmful' (40). Democracy, as we know from Plato's Book 8 of *The Republic* (2006), is a form of polity where the people rule and are entitled to express their opinion, and

> *democracy* is not the place where *parrhesia* will be exercised as a privilege duty but the place where *parrhesia* will be exercised as the freedom for everybody and anybody to say anything, that is to say, to say whatever they like.
> (Foucault, 2011:36)

So, truth speaking is open to everybody and thus it makes it difficult to decipher who is telling the truth and who is not (36). As everybody has this right to tell the truth, orators with better rhetorical skills will seduce the people (37). Therefore, we can conclude that in a democracy the freedom to speak overrides the principle to speak the truth. We have seen more recently how the Breitbart News Network and Donald Trump have operated within this framework. What makes Goldman's speech parrhesiatic is the sheer fact that she criticises the very institutions – here the police, representative government in the earlier quote – that are the bastions of Western democracy. We witness anarchists like Goldman disentagling their psyche from normative structures, whilst they put their lives at risk. Parrhesiatic speech is one of the ways in which we see how this disentangling of the psyche takes place.

UK Uncut is not an anarchist group per se. Kinna, described groups like UK Uncut as exhibiting 'anarchist' qualities. A similar point was also made by the political theorist Saul Newman, who encourages us not to think of anarchism 'as a distinct project' (2016:13) but 'in terms of a certain mode of thought and action through which relations of domination, in their specificity, are interrogated, contested and, where possible overturned' (13), As I have already explained, I do not consider UK Uncut to an anarchist group, but their acts, organisation and parrhesiatic speech reveal anarchist influences and tendencies, and it is for this reason that I chose them as an example. They offer glimpses of a parallel anarchist life, the life that Goldman and other anarchists lived or live, that necessitates truth speaking and fearlessness.

So who are UK Uncut? As their website suggests the group 'is a grassroots movement taking action to highlight alternatives to austerity' which 'use[s] acts of creative civil disobedience to show [their] opposition to the Government's cuts to our public services'.[11] The group was formed on 27 October 2010 after the UK Conservative government introduced severe austerity measures that were harmful to the lower economic strata of UK society. Through various acts of civil disobedience UK Uncut took it upon itself to expose corporations and individuals that evade paying their taxes, such as the telecommunications company Vodaphone, Boots (the British beauty and health retailer and chain), Starbucks (the multinational coffee and roastery chain) and Top Shop (the British multinational fashion retailer). UK Uncut are horizontally organised; indeed they encourage individuals to form groups locally and expose the scandal of tax evasion and the power of the 1 per cent to impoverish the rest of the population.

One of their most exemplary actions was their occupation of the luxury food store Fortnum and Mason, which they took over during the anti-austerity march on 26 March 2011. They entered the store holding placards publicising that Fortnum and Mason where tax evaders and started playing with inflated volley balls as well as chanting 'If you don't pay your taxes, we'll shut you down', Whose shop? Our shop!', and 'Occupy, occupy, pay your taxes'.[12] This was a peaceful act of civil disobedience, talking truth to a tax evader and reminding the State of its duties to make sure that all taxes are collected despite the economic power of the taxed. Ten of the demonstrators were arrested and charged with 'aggravated trespass with intent to intimidate' (No Author, 2011).[13]

They were initially found guilty. As the *Telegraph* reported, the district judge who handed down their sixth-month conditional discharge and legal costs of £1,000 found their course honourable,

> [t]he District Judge Michael Snow, sitting at Westminster Magistrates Court, said the defendants were 'united by their common sense of decency'. 'Civil disobedience has a long and entirely peaceful history in this country,' he added. 'History often vindicates those involved in such acts. I have read a series of glowing references on behalf of every one of you.'
>
> (No Author, 2011)

---

11 'About UK UnCut', at https://www.ukuncut.org/about. Accessed 16 December 2021.
12 See 'Judge Praises Fortnum and Mason Protesters for "Common Sense of Decency"', *The Telegraph* (17 November 2011) at https://www.telegraph.co.uk/news/uknews/law-and-order/8896852/Judge-praises-Fortnum-and-Mason-protesters-for-common-sense-of-decency.html. Accessed 16 December 2021.
13 Ibid.

Moreover, Judge Snow told the activists: 'One often hears complaints of disengagement with the political process. That's clearly not an accusation that can be levelled at you' (No Author, 2011).

Protester Oliver Pope, 20, read a statement outside the court on behalf of the group:

> We were standing up, or more accurately sitting down, against our government making harsh cuts to public services, whilst letting big companies get away with dodging a total of tens of billions of pounds of tax every year.
>
> We are supposed to have a democratic right to protest yet people like us, exercising that right and expressing our discontent feel the force of the law and receive harsh and disproportionate sentences.
>
> We will, of course, continue to fight this and will be appealing the judgement.
>
> (No Author, 2011)

The activists had their convictions quashed a year later. What interests me here is not why this happened but rather the courage that the protesters exhibited in talking truth to power, in being parrhesiastes and exposing the hypocrisy of the UK State when it comes to taxation, namely allowing all those corporations to get away with paying little or no tax while introducing cuts under the guise of a financial crisis. I do not think I need to say much more regarding their parrhesiatic stand, a stand that they have sustained in various ways, even taking Her Majesty's Revenues and Customs Office (HMRC) to court over letting Goldman and Sachs, the US multinational investment bank, not pay £20 million interest in tax. Though they lost the case they succeeded in having the HRMC chief sacked and the HMRC receiving a reprimand from the courts. If the heart of the State is the financial world and economy then the parrhesiatic actions of UK Uncut enable us to see how, whilst they may not embrace the whole of the anarchist project, they certainly defend the idea of social and economic inequality. If they were to take it a step further and begin imagining a world without centralised government, they would be part of the more expansive and integrated anarchist project.

Disobedience, as we have learned from Etienne De la Boétie and Adam Phillips, is necessary for our social and psychic or individual growth. We have been warned by Max Stirner that disobedience, or disobedient acts, risk making us subordinate to the cause, idea or political system that we are contesting. However, *parrhesia* and those who practise it show us the way to something different. Parrhesiastes, in our examples of Emma Goldman and UK Uncut, put themselves at risk (in the case of Goldman, losing her citizenship and being deported from the US; in the case of UK Uncut, incarceration) to speak truth to power and simultaneously reveal the corruption and hypocrisy of the authorities that they addressed (border control, minister of justice, HMRC and the corporations). In doing so, they did not simply disobey authority, they also revealed a life that can be lived with honesty (Goldman) and decency (UK Uncut), qualities that impressed both the US Board of Special Inquiry and the UK courts respectively. With their speech they did not just challenge the normative ways of doing things, through obedience and even deception, but showed us that some are able to live lives parallel to these norms. For this to happen, though, we need to disenentangle ourselves from those habits and fears that keep up us attached to obedience. For that, as we have seen, we need to train our body, our speech, our psyches to be courageous. Some, like Emma Goldman, use their faith in the idea of anarchism to fortify themselves with courage, and others, like UK Uncut, rely on collective solidarity. It may not be easy to disentangle ourselves from known paths, habits and patterns of thinking, but I hope I have somehow convinced you that it is possible to do so, that it is possible to have different lives from the ones we have.

Chapter 4

Anarchism and love

When we ask someone to describe love we tend to receive a variety of answers: love is 'surprising', 'unpredictable', 'sensational', 'hmm…a feeling', 'damaging', 'devastating', 'delicious', 'exhausting', 'consuming', 'calming', 'stormy', 'fuzzy', 'the meeting of two fantasies', and this can continue as long as we keep falling in love or remain curious about it. Indeed this is what Socrates discovered when he asked the guests at Agathon's gathering to praise love. The outcome is 223 paragraphs of praise and discussion about love, which came to be known as the *Symposium* (Plato, 1925:III,172–223). Furthermore, love has not just preoccupied philosophers, it has been the theme of an endless list of literary works, poetry, art, cinema, psychoanalysis, science and commerce.[1] Nevertheless, when we are asked to describe love, or account for the feeling of love, we seem to be unable to settle with *a single* definition or description of love.[2] In his *A Lover's Discourse: Fragments* (2002) the late cultural theorist Ronald Barthes insists that this is because love is a unique and singular experience for each one of us (2). He invites us to read the fragments on love in his book *as* animated figures, movements, where the lover grapples with the difficulties, ambivalences and energy that love induces in them. Thus, whilst we may not be able to articulate a single description of love, we may be able to account for the variety of experiences, effects, sensations that we recognise as 'love'. In saying this I am not only stating that there is a relationship between love, law and anarchism but furthermore I am articulating how an individual and unique experience of erotic love can act as a critical tool, revising ideological positions such as that of anarchism. Moreover, when interrogating the relationship between anarchism and love we witness a permeable anarchist subject able to absorb the criticisms that love levies upon anarchism and use them to reconstruct anarchism. As we see, this is less possible in the case of law and other radical political ideologies such as Marxism.

1 I am specifically referring to the commercialisation of love through various objects such as cards and gifts that we particularly witness on Valentine's Day (a day dedicated to the celebration of love). For more on this, see Hochschild (2003).
2 Despite the fact that love may be something that we may all experience, and in this sense it is a universal phenomenon, the experience of love is unique for each one of us and it cannot be reduced to one all-encompassing description.

DOI: 10.4324/9780429952692-4

In the last few years there have been two significant books that draw on the similarities and relationship between love and radical politics. The first is Srećko Horvat's *The Radicality of Love* (2016), which proposes that revolutionary politics need to embrace radical love – a universal type of love that constantly reinvents itself, freeing us from habitual ways of relating to each other – if we are to ensure that politics remain radical. As you may have guessed, the book contours a symbiotic relationship between radical love and radical politics. *The Radicality of Love* does not spell out the characteristics adorning radical love, but Horvat provides us with some clues; radical love, he writes, does not share the characteristics of commercialised love, nor those of 'free love', that is, love that is freed from the shackles of possessive relations, an idea present in anarchism and practised by hippy communities in the 1960s and queers (2). To be clear, Horvat does not identify radicality in such expressions of love which, as we realise as we work our way through the book, he finds fickle and distant from the spirit of radical politics.[3] We get a glimpse of how he imagines radical love to be when he introduces us to Che Guevara's attitude towards revolutionary politics and love, and particularly his love for Aleida March. For Guevara the love for revolution and erotic love were inseparable, and their presence was necessary for a radical transformation of society. The same fidelity and passion required in one's love life needed to be present in the revolutionary cause and the people behind it, as Guevara writes: 'At the risk of seeming ridiculous', Guevara writes, 'the true revolutionary is guided by great feelings of love. It is impossible to think of a genuine revolutionary lacking this quality' (quoted in Horvat, 2016:109). For Horvat, therefore, love and passion are necessary ingredients for the revolutionary cause. This of course, as Horvat finds out from Guevara, is not quite so straightforward; it requires a constant negotiation between desire and obedience to the cause, as well as self-sacrifice and conflict with others. Nevertheless, as the book points out, not every revolutionary project shared Guevara's view about the interconnection between radical love and radical politics. The book identifies moments when love was prohibited, and individuals engaging in extra-marital sexual activities were put on trial as love was seen as diverting radicals away from revolutionary projects (Horvat, 2016: 80–8). Communist USSR exhibited such a tendency. Whilst at the start of the Russian Revolution, bourgeois values associated with love and sex (e.g., abortion) were decriminalised and sexual permissiveness was encouraged, not

---

3   It is important to note that the idea of 'free love' as non-possessive love, love that does not reduce any of the beloved to the property of the other, decouples love from the idea of marriage, which is identified as being one of the principles that reproduces capitalism. The idea of 'free love' was offered as a critique of capitalism. For more see Emma Goldman's essay 'Marriage and Love' (1969d: 227–40). Horvat's understanding of love is also heteronormative. In the interview he gave to the magazine *Gai Pied* in April 1981, Michel Foucault, points out that fleeting homosexual relations register a different way of life, one that confronts convention and opens up friendship as a way of life (Foucault, 1997:135–40).

Anarchism and love 89

long into the revolution the situation changed and the revolution reverted to the very bourgeois values that it opposed (80). Individual sexual freedom was seen as an obstacle to the communistic politics that the revolution aspired to build. Therefore, sex acts (e.g., masturbation, sex before marriage) and objects associated with sex (e.g., erotic literature and images) were prohibited or discouraged and sexual abstinence championed. The banning of love from radical politics, Horvat concludes, made both love and politics dogmatic and stale. For radicality to flourish, sustain and reinvent itself, he suggests, we need radical love and revolutionary politics to realign with each other or, as he puts it, 'To be devoted to the Beloved one and the Revolution at the same time is the true Radicality of Love' (162).

Richard Gilman-Opalsky's *The Communism of Love* (2020), the second of the recently published books that tackle the relationship between love and radical politics, revisits the idea of love in philosophy (e.g., Plato, Merleau-Ponty, Blanchot, Levinas, Nussbaum, Badiou), political theory (e.g., Arendt, Kolantai, Jenny Marx), and sociology (e.g., Bauman), cultural studies and psychology (e.g., Bauman, Barthes, Fromm) to identify commonalities in their understanding of the relationship between love and politics. Gilman-Opalsky observes that despite the theoretical differences that are present in the writings of the theorists he engages with, all note that love and capitalism do not share the same values (2020:5) 'Capitalism', he writes, 'as both an ideological position and as an actual power that organizes life, cannot satisfactorily encompass the psychosocial and emotional needs of everyday people' (5). This allows Gilman-Opalsky to conclude that the essence of love is the opposite of capitalism. The essence of love is communistic, and radical events (uprisings, riots, rebellions, insurrections) are read as attempts to restore love as an organising principle of life whilst simultaneously protecting us from the grasp of capitalism (5).

My focus is slightly different from those offered in these two important books. I am not suggesting in any way that love cannot be realigned to radical politics, nor am I suggesting that love's essence is not communistic. Both propositions, made by Horvat and Gilman-Opalsky respectively, are certainly appealing and worthy, and preoccupied theorists (such as, for example, Alain Badiou and Truong (2012)) prior to these two recent books. My intention is much more modest. I am interested in tracing how erotic love challenges radical subjects and, more specifically, how love challenged the anarchist Emma Goldman.[4] Goldman did not only published an essay about love and anarchism (1969d:227–39), an essay where she explains anarchism's ideological objection to marriage and its critique of any form of possessive love; she also left a record of her own erotic escapades and views on love and anarchism in her two-volume

---

4 Neither Horvat nor Guilman-Opalsky engage with anarchism and love. Guilman-Opalksy refers to anarchism in passing, stating the reasons for not doing so – communism having a more systematic critique of capitalism and a refined concept of community – and his affinity to anarchism (2020:11).

autobiography *Living My Life* (1970a and1970b). Although erotic love may be moving, in the same way that radical politics move us to action, it is not akin to, nor can its movement be compared to, that of radical politics. The reducibility of love to politics or vice versa – a reducibility that can easily be made when we misidentify the *euphoric* feeling of a radical event such as love – increases, I suggest, the possibility of radical politics absorbing love, and as a result becoming totalising or closed. If Horvat and Gilman-Opalksy had turned their attention to anarchism – as an ideology that calls for non-possessive love – and to the lives of anarchist subjects, as I do here by drawing on the amorous relations of Goldman, they would have noticed that love cannot be reduced to politics, duty or command. Other disciplines, Critical Legal Studies, for example, have attempted to develop a discourse on law and love with the objective of freeing legal scholarship from its positivist genealogy. In doing so they have expanded our understanding of legal discourse and enriched the theoretical framework of law but simultaneously, as I explain later, have subjugated love to law. My aim here is to show that by not subjugating their erotic lives to the ideology of anarchism, anarchist subjects are able to constantly *question* their actions and their beliefs. Horvat suggests that radical love can have this pedagogic role for radical politics, but he has also argued that love has to be dutiful to change in order to achieve this. This chapter differentiates itself from this position; it does not imprison love to duty of any variety, but rather follows the movement of love and its effects to get a different and more lived-based understanding of anarchism and its relationship to norms and ideology.

This chapter is organised around three figures.[5] Figure One presents love through the work of the poet, essayist and Professor of Classics Anne Carson. Carson does not describe love, but instead provides us with an account of effects that are associated with love. In doing so she tracks various shifts in the journey to falling in and out of love, and I suggest that she presents love as *movement* (i.e., not static) in terms of sensations, experiences and effects, as well as being *ambivalent* (i.e., not certain), as not something that once you have 'tasted' it you can possess forever. Figure Two provides an account of the engagement of Critical Legal scholarship with the matter of love. Love is once more presented *as* a movement, but it is arrested within the fishnet of legality or law. The work of Peter Goodrich is exemplary in its attempt to bring the *question* of love into conversation with law. Whilst his endeavour is undoubtedly honourable, exposing law's universalising claims, he simultaneously provides us with an account of love *as* law, a provision that, as I will argue, somewhat obstructs love from its movement. Even when Critical Legal scholars such as Maria Aristodemou (2014) set out to discern the belief that law can deliver equality and justice if it adopts a model of relationality akin to the one

5 Barthes suggests, and I am following his suggestion here, that we should understand the figure not 'in its rhetorical sense, but rather in its gymnastic or choreographic acceptation; ... the body's gesture caught in action and not contemplated in repose' (2002:3–4).

when we are in love, she traps love – and law for that matter – in the psychoanalytic understanding that presents it as being unchanging and structured by lack. But love, as we shall see in the following section, is both movement and ambivalence. Finally, in Figure Three, I revisit the movement of love through the biography of the anarchist Emma Goldman. On this occasion love retains its movement. It is not reduced to Goldman's ideological beliefs – that is, anarchism – but instead it challenges the fundamental beliefs within anarchism, such as the belief in 'free love'.

One of the focal aims of this chapter is to alert the reader to the possible pitfalls of the ways in which legal scholarship brings together the themes of law and love. There is a tendency to introduce the theme of love in legal scholarship as a way of pointing out the 'limits' of law, or the injustices that are inherent in legal codes. I would like to suggest that legal scholarship must, *not* arrest love within legal principles and practices such as contractual principles or the practice of judgment. For, as Critchley puts it, 'love [cannot be] reduced to coercive control, to contractual obligation and command' (2015:31).

As Alain Badiou points out, Plato tells us that 'Anyone who doesn't take love as a starting point will never understand the nature of philosophy' (Badiou and Truong, 2012:3). This chapter draws on figures of love in order not to just present how such themes are taken up in literature, law and anarchism, but also to offer a critique of the Platonic ideal of love. For Plato love 'is not love of an individual person, but either (ideally) love of beauty itself ... or at best love of the cluster of beautiful and desirable qualities instantiated in the individual' (Soble, 1989:151). Whilst the proposition that love can provide us with a better understanding of philosophy may stand, the idea that love is or should be about the love of beauty, or the love of an ideal, is more questionable, if love is to be viewed as just an idea and not as a movement, embodied and ambivalent. Instead, through the discussion below on anarchism and love,[6] it will be suggested that an embodied account of love acts as a critique of ideality and simultaneously opens us to the possibility of relating to the world without the burden of wanting to rid it of any ambivalence and contradiction. It is by critiquing ideality and, in this instance, the Platonic idea of love, with reference to three figures of love that are conceived as very much embodied and in movement, that I want to show how love contributes to the refinement and transformation of ideality and ideology, in our case anarchist ideology. As you will see in the next section, in following Carson's interpretation of love as both ambivalent and everchanging we gain a more embodied understanding of love,

---

6 Anarchism, in general, offered a critique of institutional love (marriage) and promoted the idea of 'free love'; see for example Goldman's 'Marriage and Love' (1969d), 227. Here I am focusing on Goldman's lived experience of love and how she used her experience as a means to critique anarchism. For more on Goldman's philosophy emerging from a synthesis of embodied lived experience and Nietzschean philosophy, see Rossdale (2014:116–33).

one that enables us to evade the possibility of idealising love but also one that does not have love being absorbed by an ideology.

Figure One: love in a fragment

Although there are multiple reflections/writings on love that I could have chosen to engage with in drawing an account of love, I have chosen to focus this initial engagement on Carson's particular account of love in *Eros the Bittersweet* (1998). Like Barthes (2002:3–9), Carson does not set out to describe love but rather to alert us to the sensations, movements and intensities that love produces. In *Eros the Bittersweet* Carson offers an account of erotic love drawing on classical philosophy and literature. She begins her account by introducing a fragment by the archaic Greek poet Sappho. In this fragment, Sappho writes: 'Eros once again limb-loosener whirls me | sweetbitter [*glykinpikron*], impossible to fight off, creature stealing up' (Carson, 1998: 3). Carson begins with this fragment and although she translates the meaning of *glykinpikron* (γλυκύπικρον) as 'sweetbitter', she does not do so with the intention of defining love, but rather with the intention of drawing the reader's attention to the taste of love, a taste that we should never assume, as the word designates, to have a stable consistency. Both Sappho and Carson, want us to remember that falling in love may begin as a sweet delight, but bitterness may slip in as time goes by. By choosing to begin her account of love with this fragment from Sappho's poem, Carson skilfully avoids providing a definition of love. Instead, she leaves us with an account of love that tracks the movement of love, or what love *does*. And whilst there is no evidence in the book that Carson chose the poem deliberately, since poems are demonstrative of words in movement, I suggest that by choosing to organise the whole book around this fragment she consciously draws our attention to the word 'poem', which in Greek is *poiema* (from Agamben, 1999:68). This drawing is indicative of the movement in the noun *poiesis*.

So once Carson has alerted us to the movement (that forces our limbs to loosen), the sensational and paradoxical figurations (the word sweetbitter captures two incongruent tastes in one) of love, she invites us to follow her account of what Eros stands for, as a series of unfoldings whereby we evidence, amongst other things, the lovers' undoing. How does this unfolding play out? Let's hear Carson.

First, she writes, 'Eros moves or creeps upon its victim from somewhere outside her: *orpeton*. No battle avails to fight off that advance: *amachanon*' (Carson, 1998:4). Eros is an external energy, or even a force that ambushes the lover, allowing no space for resistance. It is a movement that renders the will of the lover null and void, or as Carson puts it, '[f]oreign to her will', and consequently 'forces itself irresistibly upon her without' (4). The externality of eros figures '[e]ros [as] an enemy' (4) allows Carson to conclude that we can understand Sappho's reference to love as being bitter as 'the taste of enmity. That would be hate' (4). In the first instance, lovers experience eros unexpectedly and the feeling or sensation that overwhelms their bodies and soul is that of unfamiliarity or enmity. One no longer recognise one's self when in love. And as this surprising, ambushing experience of eros is experienced as an invasion of one's body and soul, it leaves a taste of bitterness in the lover's mouth, akin to the unexpected taste of a bitter almond from a mixed packet of otherwise delicious nuts. Carson insists that Sappho, and many other writers in the archaic period after her, never provide us with a concept of love, but rather with its *physis*: 'The moment when the soul parts on itself in desire is conceived as a dilemma of body and senses. On Sappho's tongue, ... it is a moment bitter and sweet' (7).

But the particularity of eros does not stop with its bittersweet taste, nor with the surprising movement that takes over its subjects' souls and bodies. Carson explains that the scene of love witnesses an array of emotions and the total undoing of the subject. In Gilles Deleuze's terms this is a 'becoming imperceptible:[7]

> In Greek the act of love is a mingling (*mignumi*) and desire melts the limbs (Lusimeles, cf. Sappho fr. 130 ...). Boundaries of body, categories of thought, are confounded. The god who melts limbs proceeds to break the lover (*damnatai*) as would a foe on the epic battlefield.
>
> (Carson, 1998:8)

Moreover, Sappho – Carson writes – introduces us to the *ambivalence* of emotions. It is eros that introduces ambivalence. 'Love-hate', 'bitter-sweet' are some examples of the ambivalent, yet all too familiar, emotions that we experience when in love. We love and want someone, we desire them, we pursue them, but once we 'get' them we may stop wanting them. This ambivalent movement towards the one we love, our love-hate relationship with them, demonstrates that our affection fills a hole in us for, as Carson puts it: 'erotic desire can only be for what is lacking' (1998:9). When one is in love, one does not desire the other because of who they are, but rather because a hole in one's own self is filled. There is, we may say, a hole in me that the lover will fill. Carson explains that this bittersweet movement of love, a love that takes us by surprise, fulfils a lack in us, eros as lack, that mingles or brings bodies together, that ambivalence plays a role in how we relate to the world, and simultaneously defaces the fiction most commonly depicted in popular culture that depicts the two people being in love as being one. In contrast, Carson suggests that Sappho's fragment shows that we are two in love, or in the pursuit of love (16–17).

---

7   Deleuze and Guattari, (1999:232–309). The term 'becoming imperceptible' refers to the dismantling of the subject, the dismantling of agency, intentionality and the individual ego. As we have seen in Sappho's reference to love as melting one's limbs, we experience the melting of the subject. For more on this, see Braidotti (2006:133–59).

The most important move that is revealed in Carson's *Eros the Bittersweet* is that of the indication of the ambivalence of love. Furthermore, this ambivalence is presented almost as a law, but as we shall see this is not in the manner of a juridical law. It is more in the sense of a way of doing things, an ethic, as Carson calls it. In making this point, Carson draws upon classical Greece's mores around same sex love. She writes:

> Upper-class mores encouraged men to fall in love with and lay suit to beautiful boys while at the same time commending boys who spurned such attentions. 'It is no simple thing' to understand or to practice such an ethic, says Pausanias (183d) and he attaches to it the interesting label *poikilos nomos*.
>
> (Carson, 1998:24)

In Classical Greece it was common practice for older men to pursue younger men amorously, but it was equally common for the young and beautiful men to reject their advances and consequently their love. This practice is described by Pausanias as *poikilos nomos*. According to Carson, '[t]he phrase *poikilos nomos* sums up the problem of erotic ambivalence' (1998:24) And as she correctly explains, '[n]omos means "law", "custom", or "convention"' whilst '[p]oikilos is an adjective applicable to anything variegated, complex or shifting' (24). So, as she writes, '[n]omos implies something fixed firm in conventional sentiment and behavior' and '*poikilos* refers to what scintillates with change and ambiguity. The phrase verges on an oxymoron; or at least the relation between noun and adjective is a richly devious one' (24). This paradoxical or oxymoronic practice of love in Ancient Athens has another purpose. It symbolises or implies that eros's 'essence and loveliness is in its ambivalence. The erotic code is a social expression of the division within a lover's heart. Double standards of behaviour reflect double or contradictory pressures within erotic emotion itself' (24).

Carson has introduced us to love as movement here. To love which in its movement takes one by surprise, melts one, but simultaneously fills a lack. in other words, when one is in love, one is never in love with another, but rather with oneself. The taste of love produces ambivalence; love *is* ambivalent and for this reason it cannot ever become a law. Law has been presented in positivist jurisprudence as producing certainty and consistency. When writing about postcolonial law and drawing upon the work of Boire, the Critical Legal theorist Peter Fitzpatrick argued that law's failure to live up to its universalising image results in an ambivalence in law (2004:215–29). However, there are two significant differences between Fitzpatrick's understanding of law's ambivalence and love's ambivalence. Ambivalence is not the foremost constitutive element of law but rather a quality that makes itself manifest in law when law fails to deliver what it claims it does ideally: universality, fairness, etc. This ambivalence reveals that law can be repressive, arbitrary and enslaving. Love's ambivalence towards the other is a constitutive element of love that does not fix the subjects and thus enables them to be free and not fixed. In Carson's account eros is inconsistent, uncertain and varied. Eros is *poikilos*, differing, and whilst there may be codes of practice between the pursuer and the pursued, as was the case of love between men in Classical Greece, we cannot expect this to ever be a law, i.e., a fixed law. In order for love to keep moving, to retain its force, it needs to remain open; at least, this is what Carson's figure of love tells us. To what extent do Critical Legal discourses on love offer us an ambivalent, varied and uncertain concept of love? Or to what extent do they reduce love to a command, a contract and thus a law? To what extent, in other words, does Critical Legal discourse not reduce love *to* law? I turn to these questions in the next section.

Figure Two: law and love

The Critical Legal Studies movement in the UK includes multiple facets and directions.[8] Nevertheless, despite its multifaceted history and constant metamorphoses it has always remained committed to exposing the limits of the law and moreover the limits of legal justice; and it has simultaneously sustained an opening of legal study to other fields, such as literature, politics, philosophy, ethics, feminism, queer theory, critical race theory, postcolonial theory, psychoanalysis, science and history. This opening of law to other fields was done with objective of, as Goodrich indicates, challenging 'the narrowness of the substantive dogmatics of the doctrinal tradition of scholarship as well as the "inadequacy" of juridical elaborations' (1992:196). Indeed, it was hoped the impact of Critical Legal Studies, 'whether theoretical or substantive' (197), would be noticed by 'educational and scholarly moments or institutions of the legal profession' (197). It is within this vein of thinking that Critical Legal scholarship[9] introduced the concept of love into its discussion of law. Including love as an object of study within law was meant to shed light on the limits of institutional law and doctrine, revealing the injustices that come about when law ignores the domain of love in its judgments. More generally, at the intention was to take the intimate sphere into consideration within legal scholarship. Goodrich sums up this project aptly when he writes that the taking on board of love within Critical Legal Studies 'aspires to reopen questions of jurisdiction and of the plurality of laws, interior and exterior, past and future, imagined and real' (4).

At this point I engage with one of the most radical troubadours of love in Critical Legal Studies, Goodrich. Subsequently, I turn to the Critical Legal scholarship of Aristodemou and her critique of law and love. Goodrich has

---

8   For a useful trajectory of the movement, see Murphy (1999:237–78); Goodrich (1992:195–236); and, generally, Stone, Wall and Douzinas (2012).
9   See Meyer, (2006:431–47); Khan, (2000); Gearey, (2004:3–23); Goodrich, (1996); and Aristodemou, (2014).

provided us with a sustained account of the relationship between law and love. However, I argue that his engagement with love ends up capitulating *love* to *nomos*, to law, and loses the ambivalence which is essential both to keep love unfixed and in unveiling law's limitations. Let's see how the figure of love is portrayed in Goodrich's writings. In *Law in the Courts of Love* (1996) Goodrich tells the story of the jurisprudence (decisions) of the High Court of Love in Paris (established on Valentine's Day 1400) (1). This court was made up of women judges:

> The High Court of Love was to have jurisdiction to determine the rules of love and to hear disputes between lovers. It was also, as a court of last instance, to adjudicate appeals from decision in first instance courts of love.
> (1)

The High Court of Love was organised in a non-hierarchical way and '[t]he justice of love was an art of singular and heterogeneous decisions on disputes ranging from violence between lovers to amorous defamation, from breach of erotic confidences to release from unfair contracts of love' (1). It is important to note that Goodrich presents us with this study as a 'minor jurisprudence … or [a] form of legal knowledge that escape[s] the phantom of a sovereign and unitary law' (2). As Goodrich insists, a minor legal literature does not deface the claim that there is only one law or a 'universal jurisprudence' (2). While this may indeed be a 'minor jurisprudence' wherein the decisions of the Court were singular, responding to the particular situation that they were addressing; and while the Court was unusually constituted by women who were selected on the basis of the poems they read out (1), the logic of the decisions was steeped in the laws of contract and not necessarily an ethics of, for example, sexual difference.[10] While the content of adjudication may be different from decision to decision what we witness in these decisions are not figurations of love, but a love subjugated to law.

How is this played out in Judgment xvii of the Court of the Countess of Champagne? In this case a man was pursuing a woman who already had a lover. The woman did not completely fend off the advances of the man but instead told him that '[i]f she were ever to be deprived of, or more literally disappointed or frustrated by her present love … then she promises that she would undoubtedly take the suitor as her lover' (29). Shortly after she made her promise to the suitor, the woman marries her lover 'and the suitor demands that she keep her word' (29). As Goodrich informs us, perhaps not surprisingly:

---

10 Here I am referring to Irigaray's influential book *An Ethics of Sexual Difference* (1993), and the idea that Western culture (which includes legal culture) has not addressed women's sexual difference and continues to treat women unjustly. We could only redress this if we take into account that women are sexually different from men.

[t]he woman denies this claim on the ground that she has not lost her lover. The dispute is presented to the Court of Queen Eleanor of France where it is decided in favour of the suitor. The ostensible ground of the decision is a precedent judgment delivered by the Court of the Countess of Champagne, a court composed of some thirty women who collectively debated the distinct principles of love and marriage. In the precedent decision, handed down on the 1 May 1174, the Court of the Countess of Champagne had stated that love and marriage were mutually exclusive: 'Lovers give all they have to each other freely, and without any consideration of necessity, whereas married partners are forced to comply with each other's desires as an obligation, and under no circumstances can they refuse each other.' Principally on that ground, the Court found that the promise of love should be kept for the simple reason that when her lover became her husband, the woman lost her lover, and thus fulfilled the condition of her promise.

(Goodrich 1996:29)

At first glance, it may appear that this decision pays homage to eros; it recognises after all that lovers give all to each other. But upon reflection we can see that what this decision does is precisely the opposite. Instead of celebrating the ambivalence of eros – recall Carson's account of love, i.e., love as the movement that takes us by surprise and which is ambivalent, or 'sweetbitter' – we observe the movement of love (the woman in question marrying her lover) being subjugated to the logic of law. Consider the decision then once more: at no point in the decision do we have an account of the woman's desire. We just have a judgment that reinforces what the law does, making decisions based on the application of certain categories: 'lover becomes husband therefore no longer lover'. Here, the woman is forced to take the suitor as her lover *despite* her desire. The courts could equally well have decided that given the fact that love is ambivalent, or given the fact that love is always in movement, the new position as a wife/lover (a position that it seems the woman presented) frees the woman from her promise; after all, as Critchley reminds us, love is neither a 'contractual obligation' nor 'a command' (31). What we observe in this minor jurisprudence is law's persistent and universal desire to adjudicate over every part of life, to reinforce its sovereignty as an arbitrator of grievances and, in doing so, to remain oblivious to its inability to relate to the parties in dispute or in court. Furthermore, the case of a minor jurisprudence law is only concerned with the survival of the form of law, in this instance that of contract.

Love is also considered by Maria Aristodemou in *Law, Psychoanalysis, Society* (2014). I will come to how the book discusses subjectivity and love in relation to law and society, but let's first delve into the core argument and intention of the book. Aristodemou sets out to offer a critique of law, or more precisely of our relationship to law. We expect law to provide us with justice, reveal the truth, be sovereign and protect our human and other rights. This expectation, present in any subject, comes from our need to fill what we are missing, a lack or a loss that we all experience the moment we acquire or enter into language. Culture, society, politics and love are what we turn to in order to fill this lack or loss (7–16). Only by understanding how we relate to the social, where law is located (an understanding that can be facilitated by psychoanalysis), can we begin to unravel and wither our attachment to law and its promises (3), and perhaps a radical transformation may be achieved. Once we recognise the role that the lack plays in creating attachments that could fill what we are missing, the role our lack plays in creating our fantasises, we will stop seeing things through rose-tinted glasses and cease hoping that we will ever manage to fill the lack that is present in our psyches. Love, politics and friendship, Aristodemou argues, cannot fill our lack, nor can these discourses ever correct the failures and limits of law. Why? Because culture, society, love, politics and friendship, like human subjects, are also lacking. We might have expected, perhaps naively, that when it came to love we would not find the same lack as in politics. Romantic comedies, such as *Love Actually* (2003), have accustomed us to thinking that love is possible and real, despite the tribulations that we may go through in our attempt to find it. However, Aristodemou's psychoanalytic account of love digs deeper into love, revealing that our falling in love is somewhat selfish, we never fall in love with another, in the best case we fall in love with ourselves. Consequently, she writes:

> love is an illusion, or miracle, that makes up for the lack of the sexual relationship. We love, first and only ourselves and to make those selves loveable and remedy our lack, we claim or delude ourselves into thinking that we love the other. So the three words 'I love you', are a shorthand for 'please love me'. That is, we deceive ourselves into thinking we love someone so as to reflexively convince ourselves that we must, in fact be loveable. So love, like law, serves as a defence against the threatening lack that beseeches both us and the other. In effect, or in the end, all love is a form of self-love: we fall in love because we think we are worthy of being loved, and being worthy of being loved means that we are loveable.
> (Aristodemou, 2014:100)

So ultimately when we fall for another, when we move towards the other, we demonstrate not love for another, but rather love for ourselves. At least this is what Aristodemou via Lacanian psychoanalysis concludes. Aristodemou does not of course set out to provide us with a definition of love, nor to tell us that the limits of law can be supplemented by love in the same way that some Critical Legal scholars suggested that it can be supplemented by ethics (Douzinas and Warrington, 1996). On the contrary, she sets up to disprove such fantasies. What interests me in Aristodemou's thought and sharp observations is the link that she makes between law and love. So far we have seen how Goodrich, in analysing the relation between law and love, unintentionally subjugates love to law. In Aristodemou's case law and love, the movement of law and the movement of love – a movement that is prompted by lack, a lack that is present in all subjects when they enter language – is identical. Both law and love 'relate' to the outside, to justice or an object of desire, in order to fill their own lack. This simply means in the case of love, for example, that we never love another, our love for the other is prompted by the desire to satisfy our selves. In this way Aristodemou articulates a movement in love that is self-referential, closed, even fatalistic, shutting out any ambivalence, even the possibility of questioning the links that she traces between the subject, society, law and love. The Lacanian formula that she utilises not only fails to articulate the variations in love, types of love (friendship, parental, lover, stranger) and cultural differences, but moreover also to consider the possibility that the subject may not be lacking or to entertain a different image of what happens when one enters language. For example, she never considers the possibility that the acquisition of language does not cause a loss to oneself but instead offers a gain and augments oneself. She and, more specifically, Lacan fail to see that within this schema of theorising the lack can be the very fantasy that stops us seeing that no matter what love is or how it relates to us, to law, to culture and society, it can be movement – a movement that introduces ambivalence and prompts us to question who we are and what we believe and how these things relate to others and society. It fails in other words to entertain the possibility that love is neither self-referential nor narcissistic. Even if we stick to the belief that love could be these things, Aristodemou ignores the fact that erotic love is not static, and consequently ignores the way love's movement may affect her analysis of the relationship between law and society.

Aristodemou and Goodrich are two of the most insightful and critical scholars of law. Their legal theories are useful and important. But whilst Goodrich's account of love ultimately arrests love's movement to law and Aristodemou, in equating the movements of love and law, provides us with a rather universal and static (bereft of history) understanding of love, as we will see in the next section, love is much more versatile than Critical Legal scholars have suggested. Critical Legal scholars' reflections on love have either to subjugated love to law (even if the aim was the opposite) or rendered it static (by attaching it to the concept of lack). In turning to the biography and writings of Emma Goldman and her experience of love we will gain a glimpse of love confronting and questioning the 'ego' or the 'I'. In doing so I am not aiming to fetishise love, or to suggest that is an antidote to law, but rather to trace its movements and attend to the instabilities that are introduced when something that we call love enters our lives. This is not an attempt to rehabilitate law, to repeat myself once more, but rather to register a different relationship to our social and political lives, once law, law as command, is put to one side.

Moreover this non-possessive, critical and ambiguous movement (as we have seen in Carson's analysis of love but that is not present in the analysis of the Critical Legal scholars that I examined above or in the new political theory of Horvat and Gilman-Opalsky) does not just alert us to the idea that love is not static. Additionally, it makes us aware that if we are to have societies that are not trapped in competition, possessive individualism and overall inequality (material and social) we need to desire ideas of love that are arrested in commands or, as Horvat proposed, in fidelity. It is this very arrest of love, as we shall see in the next section through Emma Goldman, that sustains ideologies such as anarchism in ways that do not correspond to the flow of life, or are simply sclerotic. Love's movement reveals that if we are to address the deficiency of any ideology, we need to stay with the ambivalences that love and life throw at us, reflect upon them and revise what stops us from living a better and freer life. Of course, it goes without saying that, as Gilman-Opalsky suggests, this is only possible if we depose capitalism as the organiser of our lives. Capitalism is an ideology that thrives on the claim that it is flexible and agile, but it simultaneously wants to arrest and expel any ambiguity or ambivalence that may not espouse its belief system of competition, privatisation and profit. To put it simply: capitalism's embrace of ambivalence or ambiguity is one that arrests the critique of ideology, the movement of love and life, squeezing out of them every passion for profit, for a buck.

Figure Three: love and anarchism

In 1907 and 1908 the USA was going through a recession (Goldman, 1970a:413). A large part of the population was unemployed, living in terrible conditions and starving. Attempts made by individual people or groups to hold public gatherings to discuss the conditions that they were living in, and consider ways to support each other, encountered interruptions and interference by the police (413) or were simply banned (414). Nevertheless, gatherings did take place. For example, Voltairine de Cleyre (an American anarchist) and Harry Weinberg (a civil liberties attorney) addressed these issues at a gathering in Philadelphia where, at the end, the crowd called for an immediate demonstration although the organisers of the public gathering suggested otherwise. The demonstration went ahead and the police dealt with the demonstrators heavy-handedly; Voltairine de Cleyre and Harry Weinberg were arrested, charged with inciting a riot and given $1,500 bail each (413). Goldman was also invited to speak in Chicago about the recession and anarchism on 6 March 1908 (Falk, 2004:280). The authorities banned her from public speaking anywhere in the city because on 2 March 1908 a young Russian Jewish immigrant, Lazarus Averbuch, had knifed Chicago's chief of police (who answered to the name of Shippy) and shot Shippy's son and bodyguard.[11] However, Goldman insisted on going ahead with her talk. As venues were banned from hosting Goldman,

---

11 The reason for Lazarus Averbuch's visit to Shippy's house and the sequence of events is contested to date. There was no evidence that Averbuch was an anarchist though he was beaten at demonstrations. Some suggest that his killing was a racially motivated crime. See 'The Strange Death of Lazarus Averbuch', *Mysterious Chicago Tours*, 8 December 2014. Accessed 16 April 2021. https://mysteriouschicago.com/the-strange-death-of-lazarus-averbuch.

her anarchist friends in collaboration with Ben Reitman – a charismatic doctor who was at the forefront of taking care of the homeless itinerant workers and prostitutes in Chicago, as well as leading the recession demonstrations – took it upon himself to find a place for Goldman to speak. Reitman arranged for Goldman to give a public lecture at the Workingmen's Hall on 17 March 1908, without publicising her as the speaker.

The event was extremely well attended and the press and the police were in the audience, which came as a surprise to Goldman and her comrades, since nobody had notified either party. As soon as Goldman went on stage, the police dragged her off. They also got hold of and removed Reitman, who for some reason did not make any eye contact or exchange any words with Goldman. This distance that Goldman sensed in Reitman's posturing unnerved her. They had become amorously involved and, as she says, this incident '[…] affected [her] disagreeably' (Goldman, 1970a:418). When Reitman failed to turn up at the office where anarchists gathered to discuss how the press found out about the event, suspicion fell on him. Goldman, however, suggested that 'He must have been detained by the police' (418). Reitman returned the next day to explain that he could not come to the meeting for his own reasons, that he had not been arrested by the police and that he had not informed the press of the public lecture (418–19). Initially Goldman was reassured by Reitman's response, but later on during her stay in Chicago, while they were out drinking at a restaurant, she noticed that Reitman was being friendly with the police and this prompted her, as I analyse later, to question herself (421).

Right from the start, her ten-year love affair with Reitman challenged Goldman. Reitman's coming into her life, becoming her lover, challenged her senses, fulfilled her fantasies and needs and made her *question* the soundness of her judgement. Perhaps more importantly though, her encounter with Reitman made her question to what extent she could sustain an anarchist life as such, since his existence, the way that he related to the world and to her, brought emotions such as jealousy or possessiveness to the surface, which led her to *question* whether she could continue pursuing the anarchist cause with integrity.

Before I consider how love challenged and called into question Goldman's political beliefs, it is important to point out that anarchist political thought and practice are often guided by questions. Sometimes the *question* adorns titles of books and essays. Think, for example, of Pierre Joseph Proudhon's 'What is Property?' (2011b:87–138), Goldman's essay 'Was My Life Worth Living?' (1934), or Alexander Berkman's *What is Communist Anarchism?* (1989). They are using the *question* to criticise mainstream ideas and the status quo, understandings of property, punitive policies, political formations (democracy) as well as to propagate anarchist ideas. The *question* in most of these titles is used as a prop, to challenge the political status quo, as well as encouraging us to imagine that a different world is possible.

The *question* can reveal the limits of the political system. If we take, for example, Proudhon's 'What is Property?', by asking this question he is able both to show how private property sustains inequalities and is an infringement to justice (2011:87–8) and to call for the abolition of private property. His use of the question enables him to set up a test or a trial, where property and its effects are questioned and judged, a trial in which he is acting as the prosecutor: 'In writing this memoir against property, I bring against universal society an action pétitoire ...' which he anticipates will prove that 'those who do not possess today are proprietors by the same title as those who do possess ...' (91). The function of the *question* in this instance is to demonstrate the limits of social and economic government under capitalism and critique 'universal society' – or at least the society that has vested its energies, resources and intellect into both desiring and sustaining an unjust system where private property plays a pivotal role, producing inequities as well as propagating anarchism. More precisely, the *question* acts as a weapon against a system of thought, a politics, a social realm and an economy that lies *outside* anarchist ideas. Put another way, the *question* opens the door exposing the way a dominant system of thought that understands and presents itself is shambolic and unjust. Equally, this outside is not presented as a screen on which anarchist thought will be projected – and thus by mere force of its projection will destroy the outside. On the contrary, the *question* puts the anarchist, Proudhon in this instance, in relation to the outside, exhaling his ideas in the hope that the exhalation will reach out and convince the outside (universal society) of the abolition of property. It is not coincidental, I suggest, that his writing is directed towards an addressee that he hopes to convince:

> If I fail to win my case, there is nothing left for us (the proletarian class and myself) but to cut our throats: we can ask nothing more from the justice of nations; for, as the code of procedure (art.26) tells us in its energetic style, *the plaintiff who has been non-suited in an action pétitoire, is debarred thereby from bringing an action possessoire*. If, on the contrary, I gain the case, we must then commence an action possessoire, that we may be reinstated in the enjoyment of the wealth of which we are deprived by property.
> (Proudhon, 2011b:91; emphasis in original)

We are equally able to observe that for Proudhon the *question*, or rather posing the *question*, does not guarantee an outcome – convincing the outside (universal society) of the importance of the abolition of property in this case – but rather throws him towards that possibility.

It could be said that the question in anarchist political thought, as we have seen, points to the limits of the outside, opens up the possibility of a different thinking, demonstrates that such thinking is relational – it relates rather than imposes itself on the outside. The *question* never guarantees a resolution or a solution in advance, but rather depends on the very thing that it criticises, the outside, shifting.

Emma Goldman never ceased to *question* the outside. Both in court and outside court, she posed a challenge and constantly exposed the outside to its limits. Her whole life was punctuated with posing uncomfortable questions to the outside. Here is one example from her speech in the trial against conscription, where she is pointing out to the jury how the trial that she and Alexander Berkman found themselves in did not follow a legal logic but rather followed political expediency, which was mainly aimed at stopping any form of action that would jeopardise the US from entering into World War I, and at taking any opportunity to clamp down on anarchism:

> The meeting of May 18th was held before the Draft Bill had actually gone into effect. The President signed it late in the evening of the 18th. Whatever was said at that meeting, even if I had counselled young men not to register, that meeting cannot serve as proof of an overt act. Why, then, has the Prosecuting Attorney dwelt so much, at such length, and with such pains on that meeting, and so little on the other meetings held on the eve of registration and after? Is it not because the District Attorney knew that we had no stenographic notes on that meeting? He knew it because he was approached by Mr. Weinberger and other friends for a copy of the transcript, which request he refused.
>
> (Berkman and Goldman, 2005:60)

In exposing the ways in which the criminal justice system, the police and the Prosecuting Attorney and its administrative office selected evidence that brought her and Alexander Berkman to trial, Goldman uncovers the limits of the administration of justice or more precisely she indicates that what passes as 'legal truth' is not changed within the parameters of legal knowledge (doctrine application, evidence selected on the basis of evidential rules) or due process, but rather is corrupted by an outside – in this case by politics (the politics of the persecution of anarchism, as well as the politics of war). In this case, as the quote above indicates, Goldman points out to the jury that even if in her speech she encouraged men of conscription age not to register, she would not have been breaching the law because the Selective Act of 1917 had not passed through Congress. On the afternoon when the 'No Conscription' lecture was to be held, 18 May 1917, the No Conscription League – a group set up by Goldman and Berkman, to enable, through written material and lecturing, those who were to be drafted to make an educated decision as to whether they would object to the conscription or not – had secured no stenographer, so there is no transcript of the lectures and discussions that took place. The Prosecuting Attorney and his office therefore were accusing Goldman and Berkman of conspiring against the draft on the basis of oral statements made by witnesses that could not be cross-checked with a written document.

The question does not merely appear in anarchist political thinking as a challenge and an exposition to the limits to what that stands outside anarchist thinking and ideality. Anarchist political thinkers and activists question their own beliefs, their own idealism, when the outside challenges the limits of how they understand and experience themselves in relation to the world and life. Their overall positions may be solid – the anarchist quest for the amelioration of suffering, the abolition of the State, the creation of non-hierarchical political and inter-personal relations, social and economic equality – but this solidity is not left unmoved, nor is it left stagnant. For, as Goldman repeatedly articulates, life (outside) moves at a different pace from whatever thought has managed to capture in words or has solidified. When a question comes up and challenges anarchists' beliefs, as we will see, such a question is not discarded, but rather is allowed to disturb (as if access to the disturbance that a cutting question could be denied), to send a body into turmoil, to change its pace of breathing, to reassess the ideal from the vantage point of what disturbs. Goldman's life and writings are exemplary of noticing the *questions* posed by the outside on anarchism. These questions are most vividly demonstrated through Goldman's intimate life. Love and desire, as we will see, shake her body and make her question the extent to which she can call herself an anarchist.

When Emma Goldman met Ben Reitman, she was consumed by his personality, his being, as she writes: 'I was enthralled by this living embodiment of the types I had only known through books, the types portrayed by Dostoyevsky and Gorki' (Goldman, 1970a:420). Reitman turned Goldman's world upside down and made her 'crave [for] love and life' (420). She was aware from the start that their worlds were very different, but she 'yearned to be in the arms of the man who came from a world so unlike …' hers (420). Reitman became her lover and her only love for a period of ten years, as well as her manager. Reitman was very competent at organising and securing spaces for Goldman's political campaigns as well as manage the distribution of *Mother Earth*, Goldman's very successful magazine. *Mother Earth* had over 10,000 subscribers. Ben Reitman was nevertheless not an anarchist; his world was very different from Goldman's.

Reitman was a doctor and became so in the most unusual of circumstances. Candase Falk informs us that while Reitman was working as a cleaner at Chicago's Polyclinic Laboratory, he often listened to the lectures given in the hospital by doctors, especially those given by a Viennese visiting doctor (Falk, 1999:47). One day when the Viennese doctor was late for his class, Reitman took it upon himself to dress like the doctor, by wearing a white coat, impersonate him and deliver a lecture based on what he had already memorised from the doctor's past lectures. As expected, the officials at the hospital were outraged; but at the same time, they were struck by his ability to absorb technical medical terms. As Falk tells us, 'Professor Leo Loeb, a pathologist at the College of Physicians and Surgeons, was impressed by Ben's zeal and ability despite his lack of education, and urged him to become a medical student, even paid his tuition' (47). After graduation Reitman opened a private practice, which he often closed and went off travelling (47). He was cosmopolitan, he cared and supported the 'Hobo' community; but although he was a socialist in practice he never had any political affiliations until he met Goldman.[12] It could be said that Reitman was a man who was an anarchist in spirit, but who nevertheless cared more about himself and how to sustain his independence than succumbing to any ideological position. Goldman found the way he approached the world refreshing, despite their differences.[13] He offered what her political activities could not: intimacy, companionship and his managerial skills (Goldman,1970a:425). Moreover, by her own admission, with his own primitive sexual vitality, Ben Reitman had aroused in her an 'elemental passion' (420) that she 'had never dreamed any man could rouse in' (420) her. She knew when she accepted his offer to become her manager, to be her companion, that Reitman and what she felt around him 'was a new and great force, which ... had come to stay' (420).

While Goldman had experienced disappointments throughout her political activist career, they never diverted her from her political activities; nor did they make her question anarchism as a political ideology that could bring about personal, social, spiritual and economic emancipation. The only encounter that constantly made her question both herself and anarchism was her personal amorous relationship with Ben Reitman. In her exquisite *Emma Goldman: Revolution as a Way of Life* (2011), Vivian Gornick suggests that despite her passionate attachment to Reitman's erotic love and the challenges that love and anarchism brought to each other, Goldman was never ready to abandon the ideal for the reality (90) but instead she allowed 'sexual passion ... to be in touch with the primeval at the heart of politics' (90). Gornick's interpretation of Goldman's relationship to love and politics is not inaccurate. Nevertheless, I would like to suggest that Gornick significantly plays down the fact that throughout the ten years of her turbulent relationship with Ben Reitman, Goldman constantly questioned both anarchism and herself because of the challenges that this relationship threw upon her anarchist beliefs. I will come to the way in which this is shown in Goldman's writings, demonstrating her questioning of her relationship to anarchism later in this section, but it is worth noting that Gornick's assessment is not absolutely correct. In 1909 Goldman

---

12 As Falk tells us, Reitman described himself in an unpublished essay in the following way: 'an American by birth, a Jew by parentage, a Baptist by adoption, single by good fortune, a physician and teacher by profession, cosmopolitan by choice, a Socialist by inclination, a rascal by nature, a celebrity by accident, a tramp by 20 years of experience, and a Tramp reformer by inspiration' (Falk, 1999:46).

13 Throughout her biography *Living my Life* (1970a and 1970b) Goldman tells us that she was very conscious of their differences. For example, when she first met Reitman and became enamoured of him, she describes her longing to be with him but she also writes 'I yearned to be in the arms of the man who came from a world so unlike mine' (Goldman, 1970a: 420). Later on in the biography, she accepts Reitman's offer to become her manager, although she initially hesitated, *not* because she would *not* like his love, companionship and management (425) but rather because his beliefs were contrary at times to those of her comrades who had worked with her for years propagating anarchism; because, as she puts it, 'He was from another world; moreover, he was impetuous and not always tactful (425).

was planning to go on a tour of Australia with Reitman. Goldman says as much in her biography when she writes:

> I ... wanted to get away from the disharmony and the censure of the people nearest to me.
>
> The previous year I had received an invitation from Australia. J.W. Fleming, our most active comrade there, had even raised enough money for the fare. At that time I could not decide to go away so far and make the long journey alone. With Ben at my side the voyage would be turned into a joy and give me a much needed rest, *free* from *strife*.
>
> (Goldman, 1970a:436; my emphasis)

Drawing upon Goldman's and Reitman's private letter correspondence, Falk enforces Gornick's observations. This correspondence suggests that by 1909 Goldman was exhausted by her political activities as well as her turbulent relationship with Reitman (she was aware of his promiscuity) and was willing to abandon activism in an attempt to give their love a chance, for as she wrote in a letter to him, 'I shall probably never again know such a love, or feel anything for any other man' (Falk, 1999:78).

Gornick may be right, if we observe the whole trajectory of Goldman's love life, we will be probably able to concur that she has never abandoned her political ideals for her intimate or erotic life. Indeed, in *Living my Life* (1970a) Goldman expresses her disappointment at not finding a long-lasting love,

> The stars could not be climbed by one rooted in a clod of earth. If one soared high, could he hope to dwell for long in the absorbing paths of passion and love? Like all who had paid for their faith, I too would have to face the inevitable. Occasional snatches of love; nothing permanent in my life except my ideal.
>
> (Goldman, 1970a:343)[14]

Goldman may have abandoned her hope for a permanent love, or a long-lasting love, in exchange for flashes of intimacy and erotic entanglements and anarchism, but she never allowed herself to stop allowing love, the force of love, to question the flow of anarchism. Love for her was this force, this vital element that gave food to her politics and kept her going, not despite but perhaps because of the turbulences that it created. Not despite the torments that it caused her, especially when love came in the figure of the 'primitive'

---

14 Gornick, (2011) uses this quote from *Living my Life* (Goldman, 1970a) to suggest that Goldman would not abandon her ideal for love. It is important though to note that the quote comes quite early in the biography and before Goldman meets Ben Reitman. As I indicate, in the text, when she met Reitman and accepted his offer to be her companion, manager and lover, Goldman thought that her life was changing, this man was here to stay (Goldman, 1970a:425).

vitality of Ben Reitman, but because of them. Goldman was well aware that life was constantly in flux, forces upon forces working with or against each other, possessing and dispossessing bodies and individuals. She thought of anarchism as an ideology that was moving with the flow of life, ever changing, unlike any other political ideal, unlike law for example (Berkman and Goldman, 2005:63). She thought of love in a similar way; when she accepted Reitman to be her companion and lover she wrote: 'This was a new and great force, which I knew had come to stay' (Goldman, 1970a:425). In her private correspondence to Ben Reitman, we find her describing him as a force, an irresistible force:

> What a terrible force love is and how it does make one a mere tool, absolutely dependent. Or, is it only because I am so insatiable? ... So here we are, the beginning of the road, each pulling in a different direction yet unable to go quite apart. Our only hold must be the few rare moments, rare but sublime ...
>
> (Quoted in Falk, 1999:98)

A force then, an outside force, love and desire, prompt a question, a series of questions that render Goldman breathless, sleepless, questioning her commitment to anarchism, her ability to live her life as an anarchist, her ability to have at least two 'forces' working together – bringing about the changes in the world and in her life.

Ben Reitman, the force (the *outside*) made Goldman question her judgement as a political activist from the very beginning. Not because he was different – that she was aware of and found attractive, and moreover his socialist practices (establishing the Hobo Centre) convinced her of his care for the world and his sensitivities – but rather because she could not believe that *her* body could deceive her. Just days after she met Reitman, Goldman was in Minneapolis at a social gathering with fellow anarchists where they reminisced about the hardship that they had faced in Chicago. Goldman noticed that Reitman, who was also part of their gathering, was friendly with the police officers, the same police officers who had crashed the event at the Workingmen's Hall on 17 March 1908 where he and Emma Goldman were stopped from talking. Here is how she accounts for this incident:

> Ben Reitman, whose embrace has filled me with mad delight, chumming with detectives! The hands that had burned my flesh were now close to the brute who had almost strangled Louis Lingg, near the man who had threatened and bullied me in 1901. Ben Reitman, the champion of freedom, hob-nobbing with the very sort of people who had suppressed free speech, who had clubbed the unemployed, who had killed poor Averbuch. How could he have anything to do with them? ... Was it Reitman who informed them? Was it possible? And I had given myself to that man!

I, who had been fighting the enemies of freedom and justice for nineteen years, had exulted in the arms of a man who was one of them.
(Goldman, 1970a:421)

Ben Reitman's friendliness with the police put doubt in Goldman's mind, made her question herself. And indeed it is she herself who puts into question, her body, her sensuous world. His hands electrified her body. She was engulfed by delightful sensations in his arms. She was 'exulted' (Goldman, 1970a:421) by his embraces. The erotic encounter with Reitman made her 'ecstatic' (420), noticing his friendliness with the police 'dazed' her (421). Both encounters with Reitman, who came to epitomise erotic love for her, drive Goldman outside the comfort of what her body, with its years of activist experience, had come to know and understand as comradely ways of relating with the social world. Comrades, anarchists and socialists whom she had known and known erotically would never have encountered police officers with friendliness, most of them had suffered at the hands of police authorities, herself and others had been persecuted by them; rather they would either have ignored the police or treated them with disdain. Her senses had never before been tested by somebody with whom she had been in proximity, in close association and moreover in an amorous relationship. What it is quite important to note here is that the questioning of herself of her bodily knowledge is inextricably linked with her politics; we may say that her body and politics were one and the same thing. So when Goldman questions Ben Reitman's friendliness with the police she is not merely questioning him; as we can see from the quote she questions herself, she is asking herself how she could have had a sexual encounter with somebody who is friends with the enemy. Goldman's evaluation of Reitman's act, that questioning of herself, enables us to see also that Goldman that when she assesses an external situation, she does not do so through reason (inside). For Goldman, the inside that names or relates to the outside appears to be inextricably linked to the sensual, to the sensations that move her body – ecstasy, exultation, bewilderment, enthusiasm, depression, to name but a few. The *question*, then, in the case of anarchist political theory, seems to make apparent to us, to Goldman, the limits not only of knowledge but of reasoning – the limits of reasoning prompted, propped up by the sensual. The 'question' questions reason.

It is true that early anarchist political thinking aimed to counter the prejudices that the pre-Enlightenment period had force upon the world through the force of reason. But in Goldman we observe a subtle but vibrant reliance on the sensory world, and a critique of reason – a critique of the enslavement that reason *can* bring. Goldman left Minneapolis 'with a storm in [her] heart' (1970a:421). In this storm she was left to consider, to think to what extent she wanted Ben Reitman in her life, to what extent he was an enemy, a police informer, to assess the telegram that she received from him in Milwaukee where she was engaged in her political activities, telling her 'I love you, I want you. Please let me come' (421–2). She struggled to make a decision, to believe in him – to believe that he was not a friend of the police officers but rather somebody who came into contact with the police because of the nature of the work he did, helping the homeless, vagrants and sex workers, tramps and prostitutes. At the end she tells us that her struggle – her questioning, the limits of reason – provided her with an opening, an opening that came in a form of a dream, and an opening that resolved her struggle, resolved the questioning about Ben Reitman and herself:

> Ben was bending over me, his face close to mine, his hands on my chest. Flames were shooting from his finger-tips and slowly enveloping my body. I made no attempt to escape them. I strained towards them, craving to be consumed by their fire. When I awoke, my heart kept whispering to my rebellious brain that a great passion often inspired high thoughts and fine deeds. Why should I not be able to inspire Ben, to carry him with me to the world of my social ideals?
> (Goldman, 1970a:422)

Goldman pursued the call of the dream with a telegraph asking Reitman to 'Come' (Goldman, 1970a:422). The *question* for the anarchist political activist and thinker, who here is epitomised by Goldman, does not merely interrogate the *outside* (social, economic, legal), though it does that also (how could the socialist Ben Reitman be associated with the police?). It puts into question political convictions; it tests, turns their world upside down[15] (Goldman could not sleep or find rest until she found an opening, an aperture) and reveals to us how at the limits of knowledge – knowledge of oneself, of the world, of oneself passing through the world – the opening appears precisely when one allows the fire, the elemental, to guide us. The fire here is the one that Ben Reitman's hands roused in her body, the dream repeating the passion that becomes the passage to a different way of being in the world. This different way also opens up the possibility of hope, but it is one where hope can only be guaranteed through another question: 'Why should I not be able to inspire Ben to carry him with me to the world of my social ideals?'

Reitman had left her 'with a storm in [her] heart' (Goldman, 1970a:421) that enabled her to put aside her concerns about Reitman (that had arisen from the very start of their affair), take into account that they were different and allow him to remain in her life for ten years. This question enables Goldman to allow Ben into her life despite their differences, alas hoping that they will become more politically aligned over time. The question becomes the prop that keeps the movement of love going.

A couple of years into their relationship, and at a time when Goldman was aware of Reitman's promiscuity, she was forced to ask yet another question in relation to Reitman. Upon reading *The Power of a Lie* by the Norwegian writer and dramatist Johan Boyer (published in 1903 and in English, in 1909),

---

15 As we will see throughout the book, for Goldman the world is an embodied world, where her political and intimate life coincide.

Reitman was so affected by the book that he decided to confess all the lies he had told Goldman. So he admitted to her that although he had not leaked the meeting to the police back in Chicago, he had leaked it 'confidentially' to a reporter who must have in turn leaked it to the police. Reitman never returned to meet her and the other activists after the disruption of the Chicago event because he was with another woman he had arranged to meet; he was borrowing money from *Mother Earth* to pay for his mother's 'bills' and at every lecture Goldman had given and he had attended, he had managed to seduce a woman (Goldman, 1970a:439). When she read his confessional letter, Goldman's whole being was placed in turbulence. Reitman, of course, was asking for forgiveness, confessing his love and expressing his wish to be with her (439), but his repentance and the reassurance of his love and devotion to her did not stop her from feeling as if she had been thrown into the gutter:

> I had the feeling of sinking into a swamp. In desperation I clutched the table in front of me and tried to cry out, but no sound came from my throat. I sat numb, the terrible letter seeming to creep over me, word by word, and drawing into its slime.
>
> (440)

Goldman was unable to orient herself, or to scream – experiencing not just a challenge from the *outside* but its repressive force manifesting itself as an inability to express the very primal sound, the echo of natality (Heidegger, 2004:58–60), of creativity. Unable to scream, her voice was disabled from orienting herself to an opening, so to find a way to herself; numb-stripped from the power to feel any sensation – Reitman's letter shut her down, dragging her into an elemental quality, that of 'slime', something slippery and elusive. And then she was interrupted: 'I was brought back to myself by Sasha's arrival ... I broke out in uncontrollable laughter' (Goldman, 1970a:440). The appearance of a familiar face – that of her good friend and erstwhile lover, Alexander Berkman – returned Goldman to herself, to a way out: 'I must get out on the street or I shall choke' (440). So she went out, and walked and walked for hours in search of some air, to 'breathe', to find a pathway to her heart. Days passed by and she was still preoccupied with the letter. Trying to find a way out. She repeated to herself over and over again that Reitman is from a different world, with different ideals, turning the repetition into a question, a question that put on trial the very core of anarchism, the creation of new values: 'What right have I to condemn, I who claim to teach new values of life?' (420) In answering the question about her own sexual encounters and looking for answers there she observes her own promiscuity and notices a difference between her own promiscuity and that of Reitman. Her sexual encounters are accompanied by love, whilst his are accompanied his inability to control himself, by his 'nature' (420). She remained indecisive until another question made its appearance, a question which would not, however, provide her with a guarantee but would enable her to make a decision, or at least to find herself, to find a pathway to her heart, and back to Reitman: "'Is my love for Ben so weak that I shall not be able to pay the price his freedom of action demands?' 'There was no answer'" (421). There was no answer *but* there was an answer: she had to trust herself in the very way she embodied anarchism – to find a way that would enable her to love and not enslave Reitman's 'nature'. Indeed, we then find out that she asked Berkman to take her to Reitman. She forgives him.

The question reveals to her and to us that anarchism as a way of life is not free from turbulence; that anarchism as a way of life requires, for its revival, questioning that in turn triggers a series of affective sensual disturbances, disturbances that challenge the ideal, a sensational movement that constantly renews the ideal.

By allowing the ambivalence of love to disturb her and her ideals more generally, by allowing constant questioning to remain present throughout her relationship with Reitman, Goldman can question not only Reitman but anarchism itself, and see its limits. Anarchism may suggest that a fairer world may be achieved through the abolition of marriage and the practice of 'free love', but she learns that possessiveness and jealousy are not so easily disparaged. She learns from this encounter with love that the ideal of love that anarchism promotes is not so ideal after all; yet that is precisely what breathes new life into anarchism as such.

Conclusion

I have indicated that it is possible to talk about love by focusing on its movement, rather than attempting to define it statically. Such a reading of love can enable one to see not only that love resides in ambivalence – as Carson suggests – but that it can in fact enable us to love and be in multiple ways in the world. For Carson, love moves one away from law. I would add that love's movement reveals to us the never-ending enigma of who we are and are constantly becoming.

For Critical Legal scholars, as I have noted, the reference to love confines love in the framework of law. The ambivalence of love that Carson writes about gets confined to a court where the ambivalence that love creates recalls, in turn, the case of the woman with the two lovers, a case that is decided or framed in a decision. Law's role is to stop the ambivalent movement of love. As I have suggested Goodrich frames love, or even frames law, in such a way that the movement and unpredictability, or ambivalence that Carson introduced, vanish. Aristodemou's critique of law's faith in love may disparage the myth of love leading law to deliver justice, but it suffers from producing a static representation of love.

When it comes to anarchism and love I hope to have shown, through Goldman's experience of love, how her falling in love with Reitman moved her personally; the experience was recorded on her body, but also moved her to question her political beliefs, and anarchism in particular (a movement that aims at the social, political, economic and spiritual emancipation of the human race, without a ruler or master), a life lived without 'oughts' (Goldman, 1969a:227). In doing so, I hope I have indicated that Goldman shows both the limits and the possibilities that love can foster. She shows the ambivalence of love, but at the same time she exposes the startling difference between the subject in love, the anarchist subject and the subject of law. The anarchist subject uses the turbulence of love to question itself. Love becomes a residence in this turbulence – an ethos of living well with ambivalence.

Chapter 5

Humour and the uncommon of laughter

In 1981 Steven Fischler and Joel Sucher released the documentary *Anarchism in America* (1981). The documentary provides a well-rounded history of the US anarchist tradition since the nineteenth century. *Anarchism in America* attempts to dispel a couple of myths about anarchism: (a) anarchism promotes disorder and violence by introducing the ethical beliefs and ideas of anarchism to a wider audience, and (b) anarchism is alien to the American way of doing things, or more precisely to the US ideology. One of the ways of going about disproving the second myth is to point out that the American idea of doing things for yourself is akin to anarchism's autonomous impulse. The documentary acts as an introduction to American anarchists, their ideas and struggles. For example, *Anarchism in America* is 'illustrated' with rare footage of anarchist struggles, such as the eight-hour working day struggles, anti-World War I and anti-fascism/imperialism demonstrations as well as interviews with well-known US anarchists such as Emma Goldman, Mollie Steimer[1] and Murray Bookchin.[2] We learn about Bookchin's ideas on social ecology, the journey that led him to the realisation that the working class was not a revolutionary class, his critique of Marx and his embrace of anarchism as the true

---

1 Molie Steimer (21 November 1897–23 July 1980) was of Russian origin and emigrated to the US at the age of 15. She became an anarchist and a friend of Emma Goldman, and was part of the anarchist collective Frahayt (Freedom) and worked on the magazine of the collective, which was published under the same name. She was a strong critic of the US entering World War I as she, like her fellow anarchists, considered the war to be an imperialist war. She was arrested, tried and eventually deported to Russia in 1921 for her anti-World War I activities.
2 Murray Bookchin (14 January 1921–30 July 2006) was a US anarchist of Russian Jewish origins. He was both an activist (working in the 1940s as a shop organiser at the United Electrical Workers) and a political theorist/writer. Bookchin proclaimed himself an anarchist in 1958, as he found anarchist ideology to be close to the environmental concerns that he prophetically could see threatening the world. His most notable books are *Toward an Ecological Society* (1980), *The Ecology of Freedom: The Emergence and Dissolution of Hierarchy* (2005), *Post-Scarcity Anarchism* (2004) and *Social Anarchism or Lifestyle Anarchism: An Unbridgeable Chasm* (1996).

DOI: 10.4324/9780429952692-5

revolutionary ideology to address the problem of hierarchy in society – what he considered to be the heart of the problem in capitalist societies.

In *Film and the Anarchist Imagination* (1999), Richard Porton critiques Fischler and Joel. He argues that in their eagerness 'to convince the audience that anarchism is as American as apple pie' (36) the documentary makers focus primarily on the history of individualist anarchism (33–41) and consequently fail to represent the more collective anarchist groups in the US. Although Porton's observation holds true (the film does lean towards depicting the more individualist strand of anarchism), the documentary does not shy away from showing collective anarchist struggles, such as the anarchist anti-fascist efforts. Despite Porton's valid criticisms I am drawn to *Anarchism in America* because of its archival material relating to the American anarchist movement, the variety of anarchist manifestations being depicted – from the early anarchists associated with Emma Goldman to Karl Hess, a broadcaster, tax resister and free-market anarchist – and above all because it includes the only image of Emma Goldman on film.

This image of Goldman not only provides us with access to the relationship between anarchism and comic/humour/wit[3] – to this effect, as we shall see, Simon Critchley (1999; 2007) writes incisively – it also, most significantly, enables us to review critically the philosophical claim that comedy is the most Universal of arts. The theme of this chapter is humour/wit/comedy, laughter and anarchism. The chapter sets out to undo the claim that the comic (and its variations, humour and witticism) has a Universal reach (Kierkergaard, 2013; Kant, 1987; Bataille, 2000:59–63; Aristotle, 2005; Zupančič, 2008). In making this point I focus particularly upon two scenes: Emma Goldman's humorous responses to the journalists interviewing her upon her arrival in the US in 1934 in *Anarchism in America*; and the clown actions of the Clandestine Insurgent Rebel Clown Army (CIRCA)[4] in Scotland during the anti-G8 demonstrations in July 2008. Despite Goldman's witty remarks to the press and CIRCA's humorous actions, it is noticeable that neither provoked laughter from State functionaries (the press, the police). The absence of laughter, as I explain in this chapter, enables us to understand the failure of the Universal claim relating to humour. This observation may not be of great importance for those who are interested in the literary study of humour, comedy and laughter; but if one is interested in the political significance of the absence of laughter from the State holders that surround my two examples, as I am, this absence enables us to see how a world that does not operate through mastery, control, surveillance, authority and profit (certainly the police and the press are heavily invested in

3 As I explain later on in the text, I am using these three terms interchangeably despite their technical differences.
4 CIRCA is a formation of clowns that was formed in the UK in 2003 that intervenes at protests and has an anti-authoritarian and anti-capitalist stance. There are global 'factions' of CIRCA. The artist and activist John Jordan was involved in them. See Jordan (2005) and CIRCA, 'About the Army' (No Date).

these) is possible. Such a world is an anarchist world. Such a world, as we will see, is not utopian in the sense that it is in the future but instead it exists in parallel to the world of authority, hierarchy and capitalism.[5]

Let's return to the first scene that prompted this observation. What is it about Goldman's moving image that will enable me to point to the collapse of Universal claims? If we take a preliminary look at the actual image, what do we observe? Around 18.11 seconds into *Anarchism in America* we are presented with footage of the anarchist Emma Goldman. This footage was filmed on 2 February 1934 when Goldman returned to New York.[6] In the footage we see her being interviewed by three newspapermen. Goldman is seated. The newspapermen are also seated. Goldman has a glass of water on her left. The newspapermen proceed to ask her questions about the countries she has travelled in and her convictions. Goldman directs her look to the camera and consequently away from the newspapermen, betraying her unease with the camera, and replies sternly to their questions one by one.[7] Her answers, which I will turn to later in the chapter, were humorous. However, to my surprise, we witness no burst of laughter from the immediate circle of newspapermen that surrounded her. How can we interpret the failure of Goldman's humorous replies to provoke laughter? What does this lack of laughter tell us about the philosophical claim that comedy (and its variations witticisms and humour) is of Universal reach? And, more importantly, what does anarchism's use of the comic tell us about its view of life and its organisation?

---

5 As I have argued elsewhere (Loizidou, 2021), the idea of the norm is a myth. If, as Foucault proposes, the norm operates 'as the Universal prescription for all' (2008: 55), the existence of concrete lives that are different from the norm challenges its Universality or at least the operation of the norm.

6 Emma Goldman was exiled from the US to Russia in 1919 with Alexander Berkaman and another 249 anarchists. She and Berkman had been found guilty by a New York court on the count of conspiracy against the draft. She was allowed to return to the US for just 90 days to give lectures promoting her biography *Living my Life* (1970b), visit family and friends and lecture on literature and drama. The group of civil liberties attorneys and literary figures that invited Emma Goldman to the US, including Harry Weinberger, Roger Baldwin and Arthur Leonard Ross, had to negotiate with the Immigration and Naturalisation Service on the conditions of the visit. Despite the negotiations, the Service granted her a visitor's visa for 90 days. There was a certain amount of hysteria about her visit. Even Eleanor Roosevelt received a letter from a group of women protesting against Goldman's visit to the US and expressing their fears: she might orchestrate the assassination of the president. Mrs Roosevelt replied, 'He is very carefully protected and, in any case, Emma Goldman is now a very old woman. I really think that this country can stand the shock of her presence for ninety days' (31 January 1934) (in Falk, 1999:252).

7 In her excellent book about Emma Goldman, *Emma Goldman: Political Thinking in the Streets* (2011a) Kathy E. Ferguson also writes that Goldman appears stiff and uncomfortable in this footage (185). Goldman, she explains, had a general dislike of the moving image and was suspicious of the role of machines in political communication.

You may be thinking that I am making too much of this one moving image of Emma Goldman, her humorous replies and their failure to produce any laughter from people who are part of the State apparatus, the newspapermen.[8] You may be mumbling under your breath that we cannot make generalisations and say that anarchists use humour to disarm or neutralise the State, or exhibit the State's social and political values. You may also be wondering whether humour is an exclusive characteristic of anarchism. Isn't humour, you ask, part of our everyday life? It is, and nobody can deny this. Indeed, in their introduction to the ground-breaking special edition of *Critical Inquiry*, 'Comedy an Issue' (Berlant and Ngai, 2017:233–49) Lauren Berlant and Sianne Ngai note that in our times 'the presence of comedy as weapon and shield, pedagogy and performance *saturates* the most *ordinary spaces* (236; my emphasis). This is uncontestably true. Moreover, comedy, jokes, witty comments and statements have the propensity to trouble and test boundaries. Political cartoons like those produced by the French satirical magazine *Charlie Hebdo* caricaturing the Prophet Muhammed – depicting the prophet as either gay or naked kneeling on all fours – raised dismay and anger amongst the Muslim population in France and globally, and gave rise to demonstrations and an armed attack at the Charlie Hebdo headquarters that resulted in the death of 12 people, including five of the magazine's staff cartoonists. It goes without saying, therefore, that comedy, jokes and witty comments do not produce the same reaction in all; they can be either insulting or funny. What is funny or comic, Berlant and Ngai emphasise, 'is sensitive to changing contexts' (234). Humour, comedy and wit 'remind us', according to them, 'of forms of intersubjectivity we usually don't think about, but we discover as presupposed by our very compulsion to make jokes and judgments in the first place' (235). They remind us, in other words, that in making, for example, humorous remarks we imagine that the recipient will find them funny, and they will either provoke laughter or some reaction that shows our connection to the recipient or a challenge from them. Such remarks unveil our own presuppositions about our audiences, which we imagine hold the same cultural sensitivities as ourselves. There is, in other words, an expectation of a reaction at the hearing of a joke. I will return to this shortly. But if you are wondering whether I am about to grossly exaggerate Goldman's, and by extension anarchism's, attachment to humour, it is important to note that the footage archiving Goldman's witty remarks is not the only record of her propensity for humour.

This is not the first time that I have noticed Emma Goldman using humour to answer questions or diffuse a tense situation. But this is indeed the first time

---

8 The press is the fourth estate of government. In *Reviving the Fourth Estate* (1998), Juliana Schultz informs us that during a parliamentary debate in the House of Commons in 1787 Thomas Carlyle referred to the press as the fourth estate. We are informed that Carlyle attributed this observation to the political theorist and philosopher Edmund Burke (Schultz 1998:49).

that we have a moving image of her using humour to address questions, or somewhat tricky questions, as you will witness later. There are numerous instances in her biography, *Living My Life* (Goldman, 1970a and 1970b), where Goldman uses humour to relate to organs of the State, such as inspectors or police offices. If you were also wondering whether this could be a particular characteristic of the charismatic anarchist Goldman, I can assure you that this is not the case. The use of humour to relate to organs of the State apparatus is a general anarchist trait. Anarchists do not just *critique* the State and its apparatus, or those who present themselves as having some form of authority more generally (political, cultural, economic, etc.), they also exhibit humorous *disregard* for the State, its institutions and anybody who assumes a position of authority. CIRCA , Ya Basta[9] (Critchley, 2007:123–4), UK–Uncut[10] and the Precarious Workers Brigade[11] are examples of contemporary anarchist formations that have used humour in their political actions in such ways. In *Infinitely Demanding: Ethics of Commitment, Politics of Resistance* (2007) Simon Critchley sets out to demonstrate not only that anarchist activists embrace humour as a political technique but also that humour, and specifically the way in which anarchists deploy humour as a political form, can enable us to decelerate the politics of destruction and death that we have been witnessing globally since 11 September 2001. As he writes, the uses of humour by anarchist groups or associations 'hide a serious political intent: they exemplify [the] forging of horizontal chains of equivalence or collective will formation across diverse and otherwise conflicting protest groups' (124). Moreover, as he identifies, through the '[d]eploy[ment] of a politics of subversion, contemporary anarchist practice exercises a satirical pressure on the state in order to show that other forms of life are possible' (124).

As we will see in the last section of this chapter, when we will be looking more closely at the use of humour by Goldman and CIRCA, such use displays a disregard for the status quo, authority, sovereignty and normative propositions of life. Critchley is correct to write that the use of humour by anarchist groups and individuals makes it possible for us to see that 'other forms of life are possible' (124). Nevertheless, Critchley, like many philosophers, political theorists and theorists of humour, builds his arguments around an almost unquestionable belief that every humorous and witty comment will produce laughter in those to whom they are immediately addressed. There is not a single instance, for

9 Ya Basta Association is an anti-globalisation group that engages in direct action. It was very visible in the 2001 Anti-G8 demonstrations in Genoa, Italy. It was formed in 1994. See Associazione Ya Basta (No Date).
10 This is a left-wing activist group formed in 2010 to protest against various public cuts.
11 Precarious Workers Brigade is a UK-based activist group that works in the arts and cultural industries and runs campaigns primarily to transform working and payment conditions within these industries. For more, see Precarious Workers Brigade (No Date).

example, where Critchley is concerned with the possibility of a humorous remark failing to provoke laughter, with what such a failure may teach us about these 'other forms of life …' (124) or what the characteristics of such alternative forms of life might be.

Henri Bergson suggested in his philosophical essay on laughter, published in 1900, that the role of laughter and comedy in society and life (the latter understood by him as a constant movement or flow) is to reveal the mechanical aspect in our lives or, more precisely, that we are like machines (2008:18–34). Comedy, and consequently the laughter that ensues, emanates from gestures, movements, words that tend to be repetitive, mimicking our slips, base characteristics or imperfections (amongst other things); but it doesn't generate growth, change or originality. For Bergson comedy stifles life, 'for to cease to change would be to cease' (19). So whilst philosophers like Critchley do not refer to this aspect of comedy, or as I have already suggested do not address the failure of a comic act, statement or gesture to produce laughter (here prompted by the footage of Emma Goldman and my observations of CIRCA), I would like to point out that the lack of reaction from the audience – there is no laughter, disdain or opposition – is an attempt to allow life to grow, to free it from repetition, convention or, as Bergson would say, the mechanistic aspect of life. Emma Goldman was clear about the need to grow as a human being bereft of restrictive conventions or normative values, and it was this aspect that she focused on in a speech that she gave in London at Foyle's Twenty-Ninth Literary Luncheon on 1 March 1933 at Grosvenor House:

> Most people who look at life never live it. What they see is not life but a mere shadow of it. Have they not been taught that life is a curse visited upon them by a bungling God who has made man in his own image? Therefore most people look at life and upon life as a sort of stepping-stone to a heaven in the hereafter. They dare not live life, or get the living spirit out of life as it presents itself to them. It means a risk; it means the giving up their little material achievements. It means going against 'public opinion' and the laws and rules of one's country. There are few people who have the daring and the courage to give up what they hug at their hearts. They fear that their possible gain will not be the equivalent for what they give up. As for myself, I can say that I was like Topsy. I was not born and raised—I "grewed." *I grew with life, life in all its aspects, in its heights and in its depths.* The price to pay was high, of course, but if I had to pay it all over again, I should gladly do it, for unless you are willing to pay the price, unless you are willing to plunge into the very depths, you will never be able to remount to the heights of life.
>
> (Goldman, 1933; my emphasis)

Boris Johnson assumed his position as prime minister of the UK on 24 July 2019. His supporters (which extended beyond the Conservative Party [Gimson,

2016] that he represents) voted for him because he was humorous and witty, and as such someone to whom they could relate. He was trusted not only to complete Brexit but also to restore the island to is former glory – the result of forceful colonial endeavours as we know – to improve the economy, increase the level of employment. Johnson's humour produced laughter amongst his supporters and disdain from the opposition. In all cases it produced a reaction. As Bergson tells us, laughter connects us to this mechanistic aspect of ourselves; it is a reaction to repetitions and the familial and not the source of life. In 2018 when he was foreign secretary, Johnson compared Muslim women to letter boxes and bank robbers, a 'joke' that anti-Islamic citizens enjoyed and the Tory Party did not consider to be in breach of the party's code of conduct (Hughes, 2018). However, if we detach it from the bodily pleasures it may have brought to those who enjoyed such a joke, and reflect upon the socio-political values that the so-called joke carries, it is clear that it is not life affirming. On the contrary: its aim was to denigrate Muslim women who wear the burqa. The laughter or pleasure provoked brought to the surface the rigid norms that re based on anti-minoritarian beliefs, the same beliefs that impede Muslims, women, LGBTQ citizens and any other minoritarian groups from having liveable lives (Butler, 2004). Indeed, the prime minister may score high on cracking jokes but his score as regards protecting lives is pretty dismal. The tardiness of both his reactions and those of his ministers to Covid-19 – delayed lockdowns, lack of personal protective equipment (PPE) and denial of the seriousness of the disease – have to date cost the lives of over 170,000 people in the UK.[12] So, humour, jokes, witticism and laughter need to be placed in a political and social context in order for us to assess whether they are life affirming or deadening in the sense of conserving the status quo, as Bergson suggested. What interests me here is the significance of the lack of laughter in Goldman's witty remarks in the film footage, and the lack of reaction to anarchists' humorous provocations generally from State holders, such as the police, media, etc. I argue, as you will see in the third section of this chapter, that this unresponsiveness directs us to a different socio-political framework, one that has life and growth as its guiding principles as the quote from Goldman shows.

The idea that anarchists' use of humour can be life affirming has been explored by Critchley in *Infinitely Demanding* (2007). The book focuses on the significance of anarchism and humour in our contemporary political lives, as well as humour's life-affirming potential. The book's emphasis is slightly different to mine. It does not concern itself with the significance of the lack of uproarious laughter in response to a joke. Instead, it explains how humour, and specifically anarchist humour, can curtail catastrophe and wars, events that are dominant in our times. In addressing this topic Critchley turns to philosophy. Critchley argues that subjects feel a loss of meaning during periods of war and catastrophic times, when the meaning of our lives or life per se it is at stake.

12 See Gov UK (2021).

Consequently, as he explains, we witness two types of philosophical response. The first is that of 'passive nihilism' (4). When subjects find themselves in this state, they tend to focus on achieving maximum pleasure and improvement of themselves through self-help classes and physical exercises (e.g., yoga) and disengage from politics. The second response he identifies as being that of 'active nihilism' (5). 'Active nihilists' believe that it is possible to bring meaning back into their lives by destroying the existing world and replacing it with a new one. Al-Qaeda, the Italian Red Brigades (5) and militant groups are more exemplary, according to Critchley, of 'active nihilism'. Even if these responses are diametrically opposed to each other – one being a private response ('passive nihilism') and the other public ('active nihilism') – they both share one attribute, namely that they both acknowledge that the world is meaningless. *Infinitely Demanding* discerns that these two philosophical responses do not contribute to the dissolution of warring times. It is obvious why. For purposes of clarity, though, let us see how these two approaches may sustain or exasperate the warring impetus that surrounds us. If for example subjects focus on improving themselves and disengage from politics, as happens when they embrace 'passive nihilism', they then allow the existing status quo to sustain if not proliferate bellicose politics. Doing nothing, in situations where some intervention may be required – for example, when we know that our male neighbour is hurting his female partner – whilst we are focusing on getting our bodies to be more flexible through yoga, will neither stop the female partner from being injured nor contribute to transforming our patriarchal societies. If, on the other hand, we engage in 'active nihilism' through militant activities that aim at destroying the existing status quo, such actions also proliferate destruction. If we are to pause these catastrophic times, Critchley suggest, we need to 'create' an *ethical* subject that can disrupt the politics of warring.

What would such an ethical subject look like? Would it resemble widely recognised ethical figures such as that of Antigone? The *ethical* subject in philosophy, as Critchley correctly observes, has always been recognised in the figure of the *tragic* hero/ine. Whilst we may admire ethical heroes and heroines, whilst we may find moral satisfaction in the actions of Antigone, for example, Critchley argues that tragic figures are unable to stop warring politics. We may ask why is this the case What is the problem with the tragic figure/subject of ethics? Drawing upon Levinas, Critchley argues that the philosophical ethical subject is understood to be the subject that responds to the call of the other, that is infinitely responsible for the other. Once again we may ask ourselves why it is a problem that ethical subjects respond, for example, to a cry for help. Shouldn't such responses be admired and emulated? We may at first glance look upon Antigone with admiration. The problem with tragic heroines like Antigone, as Critchley argues, is that although they may invoke an admirable ethical stance, such a stance does not guarantee the heroine's survival. As we know, Antigone takes her own life in defiance of Creon's edict against the burying of her brother Polynices.

Let's explicate this more carefully through Sophocles' *Antigone* (1984). Recall that in the play Antigone refuses to obey her uncles and the king of Thebes, Creon's edict not to bury Polynices. Polynices was an enemy of Creon as he led an army against him. Antigone defied Creon's edict. Her punishment for defying this edict was to be buried alive in Polynices' tomb. Instead of waiting for Creon's army to carry out the punishment, Antigone hangs herself in the tomb. Lacan, as Critchley reminds us, sees the 'the tragic hero [as being] possessed by até, the free and violent drive for truth that leads them to "ruin and disaster"' (76). I don't think any further explanation is necessary why tragic heroes and heroines (like Antigone) and their ethical stance lead to their destruction. It is self-evident from the play. The tragic subject in philosophy is additionally presented as an authentic subject. For Critchley however the authentic subject of tragedy is *not* the only ethical subject. For him 'original inauthenticity' (2007: 73) also opens the subject to ethical demand (73). Humour is a type of ethical demand that travels under the banner of 'original inauthenticity'.[13] 'Humour', he proposes, 'is a more minimal, less heroic form of sublimation that allows the subject to bear the excessive, indeed hyperbolic, burden of the ethical demand without that demand turning into obsessive self-hatred and cruelty' (73). The 'main task' of Critchley's book is ' [to] offer ... a theory of ethical experience and subjectivity that will lead to an infinitely demanding ethics of commitment and politics of resistance' (3). Thus we may conclude that, for him, proposing an ethic of inauthenticity is exemplified by humour that will create a politics of resistance that is not premised upon death politics and will show us the way to alternative ways of living.

Critchley presents us with anarchist humour as an alternative ethic, an ethic of inauthenticity. However, although humour, and specifically anarchist humour, may be life affirming, Critchley, like so many other theorists of humour, considers it to be of Universal reach. As I have already indicated, theories of comedy, laughter, humour and wit (most of the time these terms are discussed interchangeably) have been part of philosophical discussions since Aristotle's *Poetics* (2005). Irrespective of what philosophical trajectory we pick and follow – (a) superiority (Aristotle, Hobbes), (b) relief (Spencer, Freud), (c) incongruity (Kant, Schopenhauer and Kierkegaard) – we will notice that these philosophies of humour, comedy and witticism present the production of laughter as the commons of values, beliefs and comradeship.

If laughter, as some philosophies suggest, rejoices in the drawing together of the commons of life, coalitions of relief, can the absence of laughter merely suggest a failed joke, an unfunny joke, a lack of common values or goals, a strained coalition of relief or just an existence that performs (in the utterance of

---

13 Critchley is implicitly suggesting that our current world is being governed by the ethics of tragedy rather than those of comedy. A law is one of those institutions that identifies itself with tragedy and its ethics. For more on law and repressed humour, see Goodrich (2016)

a joke that provokes no laughter) a parallel life with values, ideas, aesthetics and imagination? While all these suggestions may be plausible, it is with the latter that I will grapple in this chapter, proposing that this absence of laughter points to a parallel life trajectory. Bergson, as we have already seen, made similar remarks regarding the meaning of laughter, without invoking anarchism as part of his philosophical analysis.

I turn my focus next to some theories and theorists of laughter, witticism, humour and jokes. In doing so I hope I will be able to show how Universal claims are made through these theories. I also aim to demonstrate how the claim that humour has a Universal reach is a myth that sustains the political status quo and, following Critchley's observations, contributes to proliferating war and destruction.

Humour, wit, comedy, laughter

A failure to laugh at an anarchist joke or witty comment (the focus of our investigation) provides us with a way of seeing *how* our attachment to the status quo or a particular way of life is built. As we shall see, sovereignty and Universality are two terms associated with comedy, wit and humour that also conserve and retain the status quo and a way of life. A failure to laugh at an anarchist joke or witty comment provides a vision of what a parallel way of life could look like. Whilst I will be using the terms wit, humour and comedy interchangeably, it is important to see how a distinction is made between them in Freud's theoretical oeuvre. It is to this topic that I turn now.

In his essay 'Humour' (1928) Sigmund Freud focuses primarily on the topic of humour. In his earlier work, *Jokes and Their Relation to the Unconscious* (Freud, 1905 [2001]) Freud attempted to approach humour 'from an economic point of view alone … to discover the source of the pleasure derived from humour … and … was able to show that pleasure proceeds from a saving in expenditure of affect' (1928:1). In his 1928 essay Freud focuses on exposing the differences between humour and wit. As he explains, both wit and humour provide us with a sense of freedom or, as he puts it, give us a 'liberating effect' (2). He says humour both liberates and uplifts the subject uttering such a comment. If, for example, the humorous comment is uttered as a response to a difficult situation that the subject is facing in real life, then the humorous utterance can be seen as evidence of overcoming any difficulties that external reality may have imposed upon the humorous subject (2). Putting it more precisely, Freud explains that the subject that is humorous 'insists that it is impervious to wounds dealt by the outside world, in fact, that these are merely occasions for affording it pleasure' (2). The subject that makes such a humorous comment draws some form of satisfaction from the joke. Freud identifies satisfaction as being narcissistic (2). But this is not the main difference between the witty and the humorous comment. We are informed also that humorous comments, unlike witty ones, do not channel 'aggressive tendencies' (3) and exhibit 'dignity' (3) instead. We can interpret this to mean that instead of attacking somebody the humorous subject that finds itself in unfortunate situations uses humour to overcome the feeling of desperation that such circumstances may give rise to. Those that use witty comments, on the other hand, exhibit a feeling of antipathy 'either to afford gratification, or, in so doing, to provide an outlet for aggressive tendencies' (3). We will elaborate on Freud's understanding of humour and laughter later in the chapter. I have introduced his distinction between humour and wit not because I will be focusing or engaging with these differences in the chapter, *nor* because I want to argue that anarchists are humorous and not witty, but because I want to draw your attention to the way I am engaging with wit, humour and comedy, and how I differ from Freud in this respect. First, I will be using these terms interchangeably and not drawing on their categorical differences. Second, as we have seen, Freud draws our attention to the difference between humour and wit because he is ascertaining how they function in our psychic world, whereas I am more intrigued in finding out how we can interpret their failure to produce laughter, and what social and political conclusions we can draw from this. Moreover, I am curious to know, as I already indicated, what the failure to laugh at a joke tells us about the claim that humour, jokes and wit are Universal.

Before we turn to the theories, philosophical or otherwise, about the comic variety let us briefly remind ourselves of the philosophical idea of the Universal. The Universal in metaphysics, 'the philosophical investigation of the nature, constitution and structure of reality' (Audi, 2001:563), is engaged in considering the qualities and characteristics that things, entities or relations have, and looks at their commonalities or alikeness (565). If we take the example of a book as the object of our investigation, we may conclude that what constitutes a book is that it is made of white pages with printed ink letters, and these characteristics are shared by all books. This description of a book is Universal as it captures the qualities of a book. The philosopher Judith Butler has explained how such claims to Universality cannot hold in 'Restaging the Universal: Hegemony and the Limits of Formalism' (2000:11–43). Kant's principle of Universality – '[a]ct only on that maxim that you can at the same time will to be Universal law' (1993:30) – sees our moral actions being directed by *reason*. Kant *also* distinguishes between moral actions that are particular to the reasoning subject – e.g., I want to pass my exams with an A, I need to study – and those that are more general – e.g., when we don't have money and we are hungry we don't steal to satisfy our hunger, as stealing is not Universalisable. By the use of reason, Butler suggests that Kant builds a justification for moral action that it is based on already prejudged principles and values (15). It goes without saying that if it is reason that directs us to act then undoubtedly such a process blocks out particular or concrete considerations. Kant's Universality is abstract and formal. Hegel, Butler writes, observes that Kant's Universalised action is mobilised by the pronoun 'I'; the 'I' is the vehicle of the volitional subject (2000:16). This 'I' for Kant is pure reason, cut off from sensations, feelings and any other attributes or qualities that a subject has. For Hegel this is paradoxical. If Kant's Universality is mobilised as we have already noted through a formal Universal 'I', then there must also be a concrete 'I', a concrete Universality that draws upon those attributes that Kant excludes. And although a concrete Universality may not be able to exist on its own it is nevertheless constitutive of the abstract formal Universality:

> not only is the thinking self fundamentally related to what it seeks to know, but the formal self loses its formalism once it is understood that the production and exclusion of the 'concrete' is a necessary precondition for the fabrication of the form. Conversely, the concrete cannot be 'had' on its own …
>
> (Butler, 2000:18)

The use that Butler's makes of Hegel's critique of Kant's concept of the Universal enables us to see that there are two types of Universality, an abstract and a concrete Universality. These two types of Universality are both constitutive of each other and in antagonism to each other. For example, abstract human rights have been exposed as inadequate by concrete entities pointing to their limits. Whilst rights like, for example. the right to marry (article 12 of the Human Rights Act 1998) is a formal right, it has not always been available to people of the same sex, indeed it was not until 2013 that same-sex marriage was recognised in the UK, through the Marriage (Same Sex Couples) Act 2013. And there are many countries in the world that still do not recognise same-sex marriage. I am using the example of marriage here to demonstrate the relationship between the Universal and the concrete that Butler alludes to, not because I endorse the institution of marriage in general per se, but rather because it is an example that readers will be familiar with. The right to marry is an abstract and formal right that was revised precisely because of the challenge of the concrete. Article 12 of the Human Rights Act 1998 could not have been constituted without the concrete (same-sex couples, in this case, who wanted to get married) showing us its limits. Simultaneously, as there were limits, the concrete challenged the abstract Universality and brought about the inclusion of same-sex marriage within the ambit of article 12 in the UK. This process of mutual constitution and competition between the two Universalities will obviously continue over time. Undoubtedly what we observe here is a very poignant understanding of the Universal, one that makes the concrete an important collaborator in the constitution of Universality. This type of Universal is also constituted by what it does not include or what is absent. Butler does not tell us anything about the commonalities of lack or commonalities between these two Universalities. We can assume that there are no formal commonalities between the two types of Universalities, but we can also assume that there is a common goal here, the goal to make sure, if we stick to the example of rights, that human rights continue to be sustained in the form that they are. In her impressive book *The Odd One In* (2008), Zupančič follows a Hegelian analysis of comedy and reaches the conclusion that 'comedy is', as she writes, 'the Universal at work' (27). Unlike Butler though, as you can see from the quote below, Zupančič does not suggest that the concrete is competing with the abstract Universal. Consider her words:

> When comedy exposes to laughter, one after another, all the figures of the Universal essence and its powers (gods, morals, state institutions, Universal ideas, and so on) it does so, of course, from the standpoint of the concrete and the subjective, and, on the face of it, we can indeed get the impression that in comedy, the individual, the concrete, the contingent, and the subjective are opposing and undermining the Universal, the necessary the substantial (as their other). ... Hegel's point, however, is that in this very 'work of the negative' (through which comic subjectivity appears) comedy produces its own necessity, Universality, and substantiality ... it does so by revealing the figures of the 'Universal in itself' as something that is, in the end, utterly empty and contingent.
>
> (Zupančič, 2008:27)

Zupančič explains how Hegel prompts us to think of comedy as producing its own Universality, one where abstract Universality and the concrete coincide, or merge into one another, by drawing our attention to the difference between Ancient Greek tragedies and comedies. When it comes to tragedy, Zupančič explains, Hegel suggests that the duality of abstract Universalism and the concrete do not coincide (25). This becomes apparent when we observe the relationship between the actor and the character that they represent in tragedy. When it comes to tragedies the mask that the actor puts on may enable them to be other than themselves, e.g., Oedipus, and in doing so they represent abstract Universality; but simultaneously the actor ceases to be themself, the concrete (25). When it comes to comedy, however, as the quote above suggests, once the comic moment produces laughter, the actor/performer does not represent another character, but instead the subject becomes the Universal. The laughter that is produced because of a comic statement – not always guaranteed (contingent) – binds the subject to itself and reveals the Universality of comedy. Zupančič does not explain what happens in the absence of laughter, but she does say that there is a false comedy (30–1). False comedy happens when the abstract concrete and the Universal do not swap positions and the concrete remains outside the Universal (30). Zupančič describes these types of comedies as conservative comedies, comedies that enable the audience to identify with the Sovereign that flatulates and to see them as human-like (30–1). Such comedies conserve existing values and impede us from challenging the political status quo. Let's take, for example Boris Johnson, the joker. It could be said that Johnson's jokes are false jokes. They portray Johnson as an ordinary man whom we can all identify with (at least his supporters) and hence leave untouched his political and social programme that caters for the few. A true comedy, in contrast, will present the Sovereign believing that he is a Sovereign bestowed with superior powers, whereas the audience will laugh at this situation because we are able to see that the Sovereign is like anyone else, a human with human qualities (Zupančič, 2008:31). Such comedies are subversive, as the concreteness (the humanness of the Sovereign) contains within it the Universal. While this proposition, the proposition that the concrete holds the Universal, and that comedy is Universal, does not have the production of laughter as the epitome of what is true or false comedy, as both types can produce laughter; it does nevertheless show that a true or subversive comedy is one that reveals the failure of power to recognise its weakness, that it is the concrete (weakness, humanness) that is Universal and not some abstract faith in superior power. But we can see that Zupančič's analysis of true and false comedy, eloquent and sharp as it may be, has one objective: to reveal to us that every concrete comic event carries the Universal. It seems that in either scenario we can observe an investment in producing the Universal. To be precise, there is no question or ambivalence about the *existence* of the *Universal*. This is true in both Zupančič's account of the relationship between the Universal and the concrete in comedy (one that sees the concrete becoming the Universal) and Butler's account of Universality (as competing Universalities). Here I am arguing that the absence of laughter in cases where a joke is being made does not necessarily put the joke into the category of a false joke, but rather helps us to see that there is no abstract or concrete Universality, but rather a *parallel* understanding of how the world both organises and makes itself manifest, and at no point can it be generalisable or static.

What follows is a critique of an eclectic array of writings about Universality. I focus on the limits of these accounts and the potentialities for a parallel account, one that emerges at the moment when comedy and its various manifestations fail to procure laughter.

Within the Western philosophical tradition Aristotle was one of the first philosophers to reflect on comedy. We find only fragmentary references to comedy in the *Poetics* (2005) despite Aristotle's declaration at the start of the book that he will discuss this genre of drama extensively (29).[14] The reason for not having an extensive discussion of comedy in the *Poetics* is because the book that was to be dedicated to comedy got burnt in the library in Alexandria

---

14 Aristotle also refers to comedy in *Nicomachean Ethics* (1934), *Art of Rhetoric* (2000) and *Parts of Animals* (1961). Despite the fact that we have lost the second book of *Poetics*, where Aristotle explicitly talks about comedy, we can still get a sense of his comedy based on these fragmentary extracts. First, Aristotle presents comedy in the same vain as in his analysis of tragedy that we have in full. As in the case of tragedy (which imitates superior action), comedy is an imitation of action, base action or base qualities. Second, comedy speaks to the Universal. Third, Aristotle distances himself from Plato, who wanted poetry to be banned (see Book X of *The Republic: Books VI–X* [2006]).

around 390 A.D. Despite this, Aristotle's fragmentary reflections on comedy have been very influential in our understanding of the genre. Commentators build a picture of Aristotle's views on comedy by comparing them with his overall philosophical thinking, especially his thoughts on tragedy (Watson, 2015). By using this comparative method, Watson goes as far as providing us with a made-up definition of comedy:

> Comedy is an imitation of action laughable and with no share in magnitude, complete, in speech made pleasing by accessories whose forms are different in different parts, by acting and not a narration, through pleasure and laughter achieving catharsis of such emotion.
> (Watson, 2015:179)

Watson's definition is close to what we get from the surviving book of *Poetics* commonly referred to as Book I, but it still remains a speculative definition. Below I engage with what has survived from Aristotle's writing on comedy. My aim here is primarily to show that he concludes that comedy is Universal and how such claims to Universality obscure the possibility of seeing that there are other *parallel* organisations of life to the one that is presented as Universal. So, let's turn to Aristotle's *Poetics* and see how he crafts his argument about Universality.

Poetry, Aristotle explains, is divided into two types, serious poetry and vulgar poetry. What these two types of poetry have in common is that they *mimic* life or people. As he explains:

> Poetry branched into two, according to its creator's characters: the more serious produced mimesis of the noble people, while the vulgar depicted the actions of the base, in the first place by composing invectives [satirical lampoons of individuals] (just as others produced hymns and encomia).
> (Aristotle, 2005:4.1448b, 23–9)

The first type of poetry, the one that mimics the noble characteristics of man, belongs to the genre of either epic poetry or tragedy. Comedy mimics what is 'the laughable' (3.1149a, 34). The dramatisation of the laughable, like any other poetic creation, mimics human action (2.1448a, 1–5) and does not rely on plot to deliver laughter (Watson, 2015:183). The production of the laughable mimics 'people in action' who are considered to be 'base' (2.1148a, 1–2). Both the depiction of base characteristics and the generation of laughter are produced in a variety of ways, for example using phallic songs (early comedy) (4.1449a, 10–12) or objects such as phallic icons (42fn.a).

As Watson reminds us, Aristotle is clear that 'the mother of comedy' *is* laughter (Watson, 2015:183). Aristotle is additionally very specific about the qualities of what is laughable; what is laughable are base characteristics – the joke that will aim to produce the laughter using base characteristics as its theme ought not to produce pain but shame in the one that has become the subject of such a comic utterance:

> Comedy ... is mimesis of baser but not wholly vicious characters: rather, the laughable is one category of the shameful. For the laughable comprises any fault or mark of shame which involves no pain or destruction: most obviously, the laughable mask is something ugly and twisted, but not painfully.
> (Aristotle, 2005:5.1149a31–6)

We are given no explanation as to why a shameful characteristic that is the theme of a comedy could not destroy the laughed-at subject, just an assurance by Aristotle that such mimetic action will not be painful.

However, whilst Aristotle can assure us that the depiction of base or inferior characteristics in comedy will not cause any emotional distress to the laughed-at subjects, he cannot confirm comedy's origins. As he writes, there are counter claims over the origins of comedy made by the citizens of Megara, the Dorian Greek ethnic group and the Athenians. The Megarians specifically argue that comedy was invented during their democracy. Aristotle comments that:

> they cite the names as evidence. They say they call villages komai, while the Athenians demoi; their contention is that comic performers [komodoi] got their name not from revelling [komazein] but from wandering through villages when banned from the city.
> (Aristotle, 2005: 3.1148a, 35–40)

It may be of no importance to us whether it was the Megarians or the Athenians (Ionians) who initiated comedy[15] or whether originally comedy was comprised of improvised phallic songs (4.1449a, 10–12), but I would like to suggest that these paremboles enable us to see how Aristotle slowly builds his understanding of the relationship between comedy and the Universal and comedy and the particular.

I argue here that Aristotle has provided us with not only an understanding of comedy as *contempt* for the base characteristics of the social, which forges a relationship between the producer of humour and the recipient of humour, but also an understanding of comedy as the terrain of the *commons* (bound or related by laughter). We see this effect of humour haunting philosophy. Contemporary philosophers, not just psychoanalytically informed philosophers such as Zupančič but also more radical post-Autonomist philosophers like Virno whom I engage with later in the chapter, are influenced by Aristotle's construction of comedy as Universal.

---

15 See Lever (1956, 15–18). Lever informs us that indeed Corinthian vases from the early sixth century depict comical scenes, phallic icons and other satirical gestures. In her opinion, this is evidence of the existence of the comic in Doric culture.

Let's see then how Aristotle introduces us to the idea that comedy is Universal. He builds his argument by first introducing us to poetry (*poesies*), a category of writing of which comedy is a part. Aristotle then argues that *poesies* is more philosophical than history (the recording of events we experience). Indeed, he insists that *poesies* lays claim to Universality while history claims the particular. For Aristotle, though, the Universal (*katholou* in Greek) takes a particular shape. Universality relates to sayings, sayings of a particular person that are *handy* to a particular person in making probable or necessary claims. Universality we may say 'captures' what is probable, expedient or necessary in its portrayal of the 'whole'. If we follow Aristotle's understanding of Universality, we observe that what is Universal does not refer to what has taken place (history), but rather to what 'could' take place, a fiction. Read his exact words:

> The difference between the historian and the poet is not that between using verse or prose; Herodotus's work could be versified and would be just as much a kind of history in verse as in prose. *No, the difference is this: that the one relates actual events, the other the kinds of this that might occur.* Consequently, poetry is more philosophical and more elevated than history, since poetry relates more of the Universal, while history relates particulars. *'Universals' means the kinds of things which it suits a certain kind of person to say or do, in terms of probability or necessity: poetry aims for this, even though attaching names to the agents. A 'particular' means, say what Alcibiades did or experienced. In comedy, this point has by now become obvious: the poets construct the plot on the basis of probability, and only then supply arbitrary names; they do not, like iambic poets, write about a particular person.* But in tragedy they adhere to the actual names. The reason is that the possible seems plausible: about the possibility of things which have not occurred we are not yet sure; but it is evident that actual events are possible – they could not otherwise have occurred.
>
> (Aristotle 2005:8.1451a39–9.1451b1–18; my emphasis)

We can see clearly from the above quote that for Aristotle comedy paints the possibility of the probable or the necessary, and it is *this* that he calls Universal. To repeat myself, comedy is a fiction. The Universal seems also to be enveloped in this attribute. While for Aristotle this demonstrates the expedience of words to the benefit of the speaker, later, as we shall see in the various theories of humour, this gets translated as the demonstration of *commonality*. What seems to be lost in translation is the non-common or non-probable. You may wonder why it is important to consider the non-probable or non-common. If for Aristotle the Universal captures what is *probable* and *expedient (handy)* to the comedian, there must also be a possibility of something that is *improbable not* being captured by the Universal. We find that the failure to laugh at anarchist witty comments or comic acts carries with it this *improbable* or *uncommon* which suggests that their sense of humour carries with it a set of values that are *parallel* to Universal claims about life and society. This in turn reveals how fictional is the belief that the Universal represents the whole. And if the Universal is a fiction, we might ask what other constellations and variations of life and values we can have. We have seen that Zupančič suggests that what the comic reveals to us is that the concrete holds within it the Universal. Butler critiques claims to Universality – *there are no such things as Universal values* – and proposes a different schema of understanding the organisation of life and society, one based on *competing* Universals. Both thinkers, Zupančič and Butler, hold onto the Universals in some way. What my examples – Goldman's witty comment that fails to produce laughter and CIRCA (as we shall see later) – reveal is that values are not common to all (Universal). Instead these examples reveal that they are societies or groups that live parallel lives to the hegemonic one, without the need to antagonise hegemonic life.

Before explaining how concrete examples of anarchist humour enable us to see both the fictionality of the Universal and the existence of parallel lives, let's look at how humour is categorised. In his edited collection *The Philosophy of Laughter and Humor* (1987), John Morreall provides us with three theories: (a) superiority, (b) relief and (c) f incongruity. Aristotle, Plato and Hobbes' theories of humour fall within the theoretical category of superiority. I have noted earlier how comedy in Aristotle demonstrates contempt for the ridiculous or base human characteristics. But as Aristotle did not provide any guidelines regarding the characteristics of what can be ridiculed, Renaissance humanists had the opportunity to elaborate upon what human characteristics are the subject matter of comedy. For example, Skinner (2009) informs us that Castiglione, in *The Book of the Courtier*, explained that it is not base human characteristics that are the subject matter of ridicule in comedy but rather 'affectation' (157). Other attributes that have become the subject of ridicule include avarice, portrayed in Molière's *L'Avare*, hypocrisy and vain gloriousness (158). Hobbes' additional insights into comedy can be found in paragraph 13 of the chapter on 'The Passions of the Mind' in *Human Nature and De Corpore Politico* (1999), where he suggests that the laughter that ensues as a result of a comical comment/gesture relates to an insistence on our own superiority (Skinner 2009:172). Hobbes comments:

> Men laugh often (such as are greedy of applause from everything they do well) at their own actions performed so little beyond their own expectation; as also at their own jests and in any case it is manifest, that the passion proceedeth from a sudden conception of some ability in himself that laugheth. Also men laugh at the infirmities of others, by comparison of which their own abilities are set off and illustrated. Also men laugh at jests, the wit thereof always consisteth in the elegant discovering and conveying to our mind some absurdity or another.
>
> (Hobbes, 1999:54)

In his excellent *Visions of Politics: Hobbes and Civil Science,* Vol. II (2009), Quentin Skinner points out that Hobbes, unlike Aristotle, sees laughter bursting out when one experiences a feeling of superiority. As the quotation above clearly indicates, laughter emerges on two occasions: (a) when we discover that we can perform less than our expectations and (b) when we laugh at others' physical weaknesses. *Human Nature* is not the only book where Hobbes discusses laughter. Skinner reminds us that laughter forms part of Hobbes' considerations in the *Leviathan* (1985); however, in this instance Hobbes is not in favour of any jests that provoke laughter at the expense of others. Jests that provoke laughter and gesture towards the superiority of the jester are described as being aggressive, a threat to peace and consequently a hubris towards the laws of nature (Skinner, 2009:172). You may ask why. As Skinner explains, laughing at somebody because we consider ourselves superior to them demonstrates inequality, the very opposite of the 'equality' that the *Leviathan* aspires to instigate (172). Moreover, the production of laughter on such occasions is seen as a revelation of a weakness of character (175). However, Hobbes' critique of laughter did not prevent him from using humour in the *Leviathan* to criticise clergymen and schoolmen (170 and 171).

While philosophies of superiority see humour and its effect, laughter, as a stain on character, a danger to peace or an immorality, the theories of relief offer almost the diametrically opposite explanation. It was not until the nineteenth century that philosopher and scientist Herbert Spencer initiated a scientific understanding of humour, later to be developed by Freud, based on relief. Such theories point to the limits of the superiority theory. For example, in his essay 'The Psychology of Laughter' (Spencer, cited in Morreall, 1987:99–110) Spencer refutes the superiority theory on two grounds: (a) there are various occasions that we *do not* laugh because of somebody's infirmities and (b) we may just laugh for *no* reason, just because somebody produced a 'pun' (Spencer, cited in Morreall, 1987:99). Instead, Spencer proceeds to explain that laughter is the result of the expenditure of tension that has become saturated in our nervous system. Spenser's theory stems from the scientific theory which explained the operation of the body based on hydraulic mechanics. In Freud's *On Jokes and Their Relation to the Unconscious* (1905) we find an elaboration of Spencer's relief theory. For Freud, there are three instances whereby laughter can be provoked: jokes or wit, comedy and humour. In each of these instances, when laughter is produced some psychic energy is saved that would have been used otherwise. As Morreall aptly summarises:

> In joking ... the energy saved is that which would ordinarily be used to repress hostile or sexual feelings and thoughts, and when we express what is usually inhibited, the energy of repression is released in laughter. In the comic, the energy saved is energy of thought: we are spared some cognitive processing that we have summoned the energy to perform, and we discharge this surplus energy in laughter. In humor, the energy saved is energy of

emotion. We prepare ourselves for feeling fear, pity, or some other negative emotion; but then we realize that we need not be concerned, so that the energy summoned for the emotion is suddenly superfluous and available for discharge in laughter.

(Morreall, 1987:111)

Freud teaches that jokes or witticisms release energy that would otherwise express itself in hostilities, of a sexual or other nature, in the form of laughter. Comedy saves us from thinking and the laughter that ensues from the comic spares us from energy that would have been used for thinking, whilst humour prevents us from processing negative emotions. On any occasion when laughter breaks out, nervous, thinking or emotional energy is being saved.

The incongruity theory suggests that laughter breaks out when we find something amusing. More specifically it contends that what provokes laughter is something that goes against our expectations in a particular situation. Kant, Schopenhauer and Kierkegaard were prominent advocates of this theory. They don't all consider comedy and laughter in a positive light. Let's take Kant, for example. Kant engages with jokes in the *Critique of Judgment* (cited in Morreall, 1987:45–50). According to him, jokes provoke laughter which in turn represents a physical manifestation of pleasure. However, Kant considers physical or embodied pleasure to be of the base variety in contrast to the pleasure that we receive from appreciating a beautiful object, which is associated with the faculty of the mind. Having construed laughter as a type of embodied pleasure that is inferior to any pleasure that we may have from thinking or of the mind, Kant nevertheless concedes that laughter does return subjects to a state of equilibrium. But Kant's denigration of laughter does not only stem from providing an embodied type of laughter. The pleasure gained from jokes or witticism, he suggests, is temporal and therefore a 'nothing' or inconsequential, as such pleasure does not emanate from reason (Kant, cited in Morreall, 1987:45). He writes:

> In everything that is to excite a lively convulsive laugh there must be something absurd (in which understanding, therefore, can find no satisfaction). Laughter is an affection arising from the sudden transformation of a strained expectation into nothing. This transformation, which is certainly not enjoyable to the understanding, yet indirectly gives it very active enjoyment for a moment. Therefore its cause must consist in the influence of the representation upon the body, and the reflex effect of this upon the mind; not, indeed, through the representation being objectively an object of gratification (for how could a delusive expectation gratify?), but simply through it as a mere play of representations bring about an equilibrium of the vital powers in the body.
>
> (Kant, cited in Morreall, 1987:45)

I drew attention to Kant's understanding of the role of comedy in the production of laughter and his assessment of it as an aesthetic reflex not because I was intending to offer an extensive analysis of comedy and laughter in Kant, but rather because I wanted to point out that he is of the belief that laughter can be produced as a result of incongruous events and that his appreciation of this has a Universal reach.

Kierkegaard also follows the incongruity theory of comedy (Morreall, 1987: 83–9). As he writes in *Concluding Unscientific Postscript*:

> The comical is present in every stage of life … for wherever there is life there is contradiction, and wherever there is contradiction, the comical is present. The tragic and the comic are the same, in so far as both are based on contradiction; but the tragic is the suffering contradiction, the comical, the painless contradiction.
>
> (Kierkegaard, cited in Morreall, 1987: 83)

In contrast to Kant, where humour is not an elevated pleasure but rather a 'nothing', something that emanates from an erroneous logic, for Kierkegaard the comic has an important role to play. For Kierkegaard, the comic and irony are close to the three spheres of life: the aesthetic, ethical and religious. Humour, as Morreall explains, 'marks the boundary between the ethical and religious spheres' and, as Kierkegaard concurs, 'Humor is the last stage of existential awareness before faith' (Kierkegaard, cited in Morreall, 1987:83).

With the sole exception of Kant (who more than any of the commentators on theories of humour holds no significant appreciation of comedy or laughter) we observe that despite their differences in their understandings of the operation, effects or meaning of humour, jokes, wit and comedy in our lives, all the other philosophies of the humorous share some similarities. They present comedy as *relational*, relating to the receiver of the joke but also relating to characteristics, occasions or instances that are appreciated because of some *common* reference they cognise. The production of laughter seals the relationality of a comical, humorous or witty utterance or gesture and reminds us of that we have a common evaluation of life. The superiority theory advocates that humour or comedy conveys the characteristics that humanity Universally considers to be debased, avaricious, super glorious. Laughing *at* these characteristics demonstrates that we commonly hold these characteristics to be debased. The relief theorists similarly talk of how the joker relates not only to the object of the joke, but also to the one who receives the joke. Consider Freud for a second: 'The process in the joke's first person produces pleasure by lifting inhibition and dismissing local expenditure; but it seems not to come to rest until, through the intermediary of the interpolated third person, it achieves general relief through discharge' (1905 [2001]:157–8). The evocation of a joke, Freud writes in 'Humour' (1928), may produce laughter from the one that hears the joke, even if they had not taken part in producing the joke (1). The recipient of the joke who laughs with pleasure demonstrates a commonality (at least temporarily) with the jester. The incongruity theory, as we have just noted, sees this relationship enveloping the spheres of ethics and religion and, again, the commonality of laughter bringing the jester and the spheres of religion and ethics nearer to each other. For Kierkegaard, laughter and the comic have a direct relationship to life in that they can demonstrate the common leap to faith.

Despite the differences in these theories of humour, there is no doubt that for all of them 'commonality' is a constitutive ingredient of their understanding of the operation of humour. The assumption that there is a 'commonality' is used to produce a Universalising narrative around the operation and effects of humour. Humour conveys what is common in humanity. We can even read this performatively, the effect of humour – laughter – brings into being what is common in humanity.

We talked earlier about what Aristotle had to say about Universality. Let's remind ourselves: '"Universals" means the kinds of things which it suits a certain kind of person to say or do, in terms of probability or necessity' (Aristotle, 2005: 8.1451a 39–9.1451b1–18). Universals are fictions of the general. Aristotle's elaboration on the Universal and the Particular in the *Poetics* comes after the paragraph where he discusses the unnecessary use of the particular in the mimetic arts:

> A plot is not unified, as some may think, if built round an individual ... But Homer, in keeping with his general superiority, evidently grasped well, whether by art or nature, this point too: for though composing an Odyssey, he did not include every feature of the hero's life (e.g. his wounding on Parnassus, or his feigned madness in the call to arms), where events lacked necessary or probable connections; but he structured the Odyssey round a unitary action of the kind I mean, and likewise with the Iliad. Just as, therefore, in the other mimetic arts a unitary mimesis has a unitary object, so the plot, since it is mimesis of an action, should be of unitary and indeed whole action.
> (Aristotle, 2005: 8.145a 16–17 and 8.1451a 21–30)

Aristotle is telling us that the experience of the name, Parnassus' injury, is not important for the unity of the plot. It is not important or necessary because what mimetic arts do is to represent actions, as in the case of comedy, and not all actions are necessary for the unity of the plot. Aristotle's understanding of the Universal survives to some extent in the writings on humour, comedy and wit of Hobbes, Kant, Kierkegaard and Freud. Let's see how.

Although Aristotle was interested in the way in which the mimetic arts represent human action, the aforementioned theorists of humour appear to have focused their attention less on the representation of action and more on the *effects* of humour, its moral lessons, and the common attributes of humanity that we can derive from a burst of laughter; laughter becomes either evidence of this commonality or it writes into humour commonality (if we read it performatively). The representation of *action* in the plot gets displaced onto the *effects*. Hobbes, Kant, Kierkegaard and Freud are more interested in what the effects of a joke can tell us about life and human subjects. *Action* is *not* something that is represented in the plot but rather an *effect* of the plot. The plot's unifying and Universal qualities are present not in the action but in the effect which in turn is used by these philosophers as a means to Universalise about individuals and society; jokes can be dangerous for society if they are excessive (Hobbes), beneficial to society as they relieve us from hostile feelings (Freud) or revealing of the borders between religion and ethics (Kierkergaard). And as for laughter, it is the *action* or *effect* that humour usually seeks. Laughter is the *effect* that cements the idea that jokes are both relational and convey the commonality of humanity.

Exodus and jokes

Given that laughter has consistently been interpreted as harvesting commonalities and Universalising properties between those who make jokes or produce a comical effect and those who receive them, it prompts us to ask how we should understand the absence of laughter when a comic act, a joke or a witty comment is made? How are we to understand, in our case, that no newspaperman laughed at Emma Goldman's witty response to the question: 'How do you find Italy?'

Let's return to Freud once more to see what he writes about the failure of laughter:

> there may be two people concerned, one of whom does not himself take any active share in producing the humorous effect, but is regarded by the other in a humorous light: To take a very crude example: when a criminal who is being led to the gallows on a Monday observes, 'Well this is a good beginning of the week,' he himself is creating humor; the process works itself out in relation to himself and evidently it affords him a certain satisfaction. I am merely a listener who has not assisted in this functioning of his sense of humor, but I feel its effect, as it were, from a distance.
> (Freud, 1928: 1)

Freud's example appears at first glance to address this issue. At second glance we observe that he is not actually responding to my query. The humorous utterance may not require a second person, as the utterer of the joke absorbs the pleasure of the utterance and somehow assumes the position of the second person. His example, at least at first glance, tells us more about the joker and less about the failure to laugh. And even when Freud places a second person at the scene, somebody who did not invest in producing the joke, we can see that they are still entertaining a joke at a distance. They still *relate* to the joke at a distance. A commonality emerges even at a distance.

As I have explained earlier this attachment to commonality has been recognised as a Universal attribute of jokes, comedy and witty comments. You may ask why this is a problem. Haven't we pursued theories of the commons for years to try and create an alternative political terrain, something that neo-liberalism has denied us? The problem with Universalist theories that present themselves as holding commonalities amongst us is that they are telling partial stories (see Aristotle's definition of the Universal), and in doing so they fail to notice what is non-common in our human existence, or in life more generally, a failure that, I argue, is not just textual but also material, as it harbours important insights regarding the organisation of our everyday lives. In other words, they project the idea that our lives are organised and built on common grounds, values and ideas. Despite our investment in the idea of commonality and the commons it is worth noting that we move along in life, we get by, because of our *lack* of commonalities. To want or desire to reduce everything to commonality and relationality impoverishes our understanding of who we are and how the world operates. Some may even argue that it endangers life, as Butler did in *Precarious Life* (2004: xi–xxi). The failure to laugh at Goldman's witticism conveys, I argue, that *irrelations* are a constitutive part of our lives.

T the Italian political philosopher Paulo Virno identified that jokes express this *irrelation* or, as he put it, a 'non dialectical relation with the negative' (2008:22). In *Multitude: Between Innovation and Negation* (2008), Virno set out to critique one of the most dominant ideas in political theory, that of Sovereignty, through his analysis of jokes. Virno offers a sustained critique of two groups of theorists who engage with the concept of Sovereignty: those who are advocates of Sovereignty, such as Hobbes and Carl Schmitt, and those who hold some optimism in a post-Sovereign constellation – such as the anarchist linguist and philosopher Noam Chomsky (21). Virno's critical analysis reveals that one of the major errors in the thought of post-Sovereign theorists is that their failure to notice the 'nature' of human subjectivity, which Hobbes suggests is enveloped in hostile and destructive drives. Therefore, Virno concludes that an Exodus from the State can only be achieved if we embrace the fact that life is ambivalent, oscillating and perturbing, and human subjectivity is equally complicated and ambivalent. If we are to exit the State formation, we need, according to Virno, to be more mindful of the playfulness of language and its rituals, a playfulness that allows ambivalence and complication to be part of it. Virno turns to Wittgenstein for assistance on this. He discovers that Wittgenstein's distinction between rules and regularities in language enables us to see and understand how we can exit from the State and Sovereign political formations, as both these concepts/structures offer us a limited way of organising and living our lives.

We have become accustomed to thinking, following Hobbes' *Leviathan* (1985), people or citizens give up their freedom to make decisions about their own lives to the Sovereign, who, in turn, is supposed to take care of their well-being and provide overall security. The Sovereign is thought to be the one that makes all the decisions about our lives. The exchange – of freedom for security – between the people and the Sovereign – explains to a large extent how modern States function. Carl Schmitt further developed the Hobbesian theory of Sovereignty. Whilst developing his theory of Sovereignty, Schmitt was concerned with the effects on the force of law and democracy in times of turmoil – i.e., exceptional times where different groups contest the Sovereign organisation of life. He questioned and investigated to what extent the law and the Sovereign lose their legitimacy during, for example, rebellions or civil wars. Schmitt thought that if both the rule of law and democracy were to lose their efficacy during exceptional times, then they would have detrimental effects for society. So, he went on to develop a theory of Sovereignty that turned Sovereign exceptional decision-making during times of turmoil into something with legal efficacy. We find his theory of Sovereignty in two books, *Constitutional Theory* (Schmitt, 2008) and *Political Theology* (Schmitt, 2005). In these he explains how, in a situation of a state of exception whilst the Sovereign suspends the law the Sovereign still retains, as Agamben wrote, its juridical essence (Agamben, 2005:25). In other words, when the Sovereign declares a state exception and suspends the law, this turns the unexceptional times into normal ones and by magic makes the declaration a legal one. For Schmitt, therefore, the Sovereign is no longer the one that just protects us during unexceptional times, but is also, as Agamben puts it, the one 'who decides the state of exception' (1998:12). We have witnessed how decisions to suspend the law after the terrorist attacks of 9 September 2001 generated widespread Islamophobia, accelerated the surveillance and policing of young Muslim men around the world and instituted new levels of control, fortification and surveillance of national borders. It could be said that the state of exception 'has now become the rule' (Agamben, 1998:12), and it could be argued that it haunts our democracies.

Virno turns to language, in an attempt to think of ways organising our lives without the figure of the Sovereign haunting them. Virno follows Wittgenstein's *Philosophical Investigations* into language games, in which Wittgenstein points out that the application of words does not have to follow rules doggedly (Virno, 2008:102), that linguistic games are not totally regulated and that 'a single movement of the game is not deducible from the move from which the movement is also the application' (102). This allows Virno to conclude that there is a gap between the application of rules and the rules themselves, a fact that in turn enables him to argue that despite our beliefs that it is impossible to change rules, or to escape from them, there is hope for those who are fighting against Sovereignty and for social and political justice. As Bratich explains, once Virno identifies that the possibility for an exodus resides in us understanding 'the distinction between rules (forms and codifications) and regularities (usage and customs)', a distinction that Wittgenstein made possible, we are also able to see that 'the state of exception is [not] an expansion of dominion' (Bratich, 2009:72). For Virno, the decision to declare a state of exception, which is understood to be a rule, is believed to be rooted in regularities. Regularities (usage, custom) are not static, they can be changed and are ambivalent, which for Virno signifies, as Bratich aptly explains, 'an openness to the world, fraught with uncertainty and danger, as well as being the source of innovation. These regularities ensure uncertainty, oscillation, and perturbance, thus providing the conditions not just for enhanced sovereignty but for exodus as well' (Bratich, 2009:71–2). For Virno, as Bratich writes, the 'constitution' of lifeworlds that are democratic and non-statist can be made by the 'human capacities to ward off, linguistically protect from, and ritualistically enact the worst of human traits' (72).

Jokes fall into the category of linguistic 'forms of verbal thought' (72) that are innovative and can ward off the routine of rules and open us in multiple directions. The very structure of jokes (or witticisms) for Virno, as Bratich explains, metamorphosise the direction of a rule:

> jokes take us from rules to regularity (custom, openness). A joke is an abrupt divergence from the expected application of rule, akin to 'changing topics'. This swerve, a surprising reaction to the norm, is the sources for exodus as well. The crisis that spawns innovation in political terms is a crisis of a form of life, one whose indeterminacy and precariousness can plunge into the worst totalitarianism while holding the promise of an abrupt way out. Jokes have a political function, as they make rules open to change, creating the conditions of new ways of thinking, specifically as public action.
>
> (Bratich, 2009:73)

Virno hopes that the structure of the joke can provide us with the ammunition for and lessons in how to exit the State and its apparatuses. Indeed, his position – like that of Critchley – is that the structure or the concept of the joke can enable us to escape the State formation. What distinguishes Virno's thoughts about jokes and comedy from other thinkers is his understanding that jokes can reveal non-commonalities or *irrelationship*, an irrelationship between the rule and its application. This irrelationship between the rule and its application is what opens up new directions and an exodus from the State. What is the significance of Virno's argument? By demonstrating that there is a non-relationship between the rule and its application through the structure of the joke, Virno alerts us to the fact that we cannot build a polity outside the State formation through the usual frameworks, e.g., elections, legal reforms; instead we need a quick move that takes the norm by surprise and enables the emergence of a political formation that is unlike that of the State. What this move will be and what it will look like is left unspecified by Virno. However, regardless of the powerful critique of the State and its operations, Virno holds on to the Universal (of the Aristotelian type) despite his attempts throughout the book to demonstrate that Aristotle's claim that jokes are not logical utterances is erroneous. We observe that on this occasion common effects and commonalities are still present in his philosophical conclusions. Ambiguity, oscillation, perturbance, innovation and the common desire for exodus become Universalised and common to all. Moreover, Virno's understanding of jokes, laughter and the potential they have to bend and change the direction of the rules may demonstrate the *irrelation* between the rule and regularities, but it leaves unexplained failed jokes and their political significance.

In the next section of this chapter, I focus upon Emma Goldman's and CIRCA's use of humour and the failure of laughter in their audience. As we shall see, such lack enables us to understand that an anarchist life exists parallel to the one promoted by the State formation. Unlike Virno, who wants to see in the structure of the joke the possibility of exiting from the State, I suggest that the lack of laughter in the two scenes that I will analyse demonstrates how an anarchic and a Statist life exist contemporaneously. They co-exist whilst having different living coordinates. Seeing the situation from this perspective enables us to recognise that the State may not necessarily be the only organiser of life. It is well known that critics of neoliberalism have, for example, suggested that capital or the finance world has replaced the State as the organiser and regulator of life (Brown, 2015; Harvey, 2007). The point that I am making here is somewhat different. I am not arguing that the State has been replaced by an anarchist polity. Nor am I arguing that capitalism has replaced the State. I am simply arguing that through the 'structure' of the failed joke or comic comment we can witness the existence of parallel and different living coordinates. It is true that when the humorous jest is addressed at the arm of the State machinery, such as the police as in the examples from CIRCA below, it may appear that the absence of laughter by the police demonstrates a competing way of life, and it is undoubtedly possible to see it that way. Indeed, how else could we see it we may ask? Doesn't the police's reluctance to engage with the jests of CIRCA suggest a denunciation of the way of life that they are promoting? Of course it does. But the persistent comical acts from CIRCA simultaneously articulate that a different parallel life exists from the Statist offering. In other words, despite the lack of laughter from the police, CIRCA's sheer existence and the projection of their life coordinates reveal an anarchist parallel life. The next section focuses on demonstrating the features of this parallel life. It begins with an exploration into the philosophical tradition of Cynical philosophy, a tradition which provides us with insights that are akin to the values and lives of anarchists, and then turns to Emma Goldman's failed joke and CIRCA's clownism.

The wit *not* to will

It is surprising that despite the witty remarks of Diogenes the Cynic none of the theorists of humour that I have discussed in this chapter looks at his witty comments and attempts to offer us a commentary on comedy, humour, wit or jokes as a philosophical trope emanating from Diogenes' way of living. This could of course be because he does not provide us with a theory of wittiness, humour, jokes or laughter. Nevertheless, his life is a testimony to wittiness. His wittiness or humour is a way of life that sets out to debunk philosophy's claim to Universalism, and simultaneously shows that word and deed can coincide.

Ancient philosophy was interested in bringing or showing a harmony between life and its doctrine. It proposes is that if one is truthful to one's philosophical ideas, one should also embody them. However, this not an easy task. The challenge, as Sloterdijk correctly points out in *Critique of Cynical Reason* (1987) is not only for an individual 'to live what they say' (101), but moreover to 'say what they live' (102). Consequently, failing to have our words and actions coincide exposes us to the corruption of the truth or a truthful life. Sloterdijk convincingly argues that the philosophical line that takes us from Plato to contemporary dominant philosophy – with the exception, I would argue, of feminist, queer, Black and decolonial philosophy – has produced disembodied high theory. The tradition of low theory (embodied) went in exactly the opposite direction and produced embodied philosophy.[16] The ancient roots of these types of philosophy lie in the Cynical tradition, the best-known activist of which is Diogenes the Cynic. It is an anti-dialogic tradition that, through embodied practices (masturbating in public, urinating in public and speech acts, wit and humour), exposes the hypocrisy of the dialogic discourse, which only lives what it says or preaches in hypocrisy. We can see this in the humorous exchange that Diogenes the Cynic has with Platonic-trained philosophers. In this exchange, we find Diogenes challenging the definition of human offered by Plato. Here is how Diogenes Laertius, the biographer of philosophers, tells the story: 'Plato had defined Man as an animal, biped and featherless, and was applauded. Diogenes plucked a fowl and brought it into the lecture-room with the words "Here is Plato's man". In consequence of which there was added to the definition, "having broad nails"' (Diogenes Laertius, 2005:6.2.40). Diogenes humorously exposes how Plato's description of man (the word 'man') fails once it is exposed by deed (presentation) of what a Man would look like if we followed Plato's description literally. If Plato's definition was to correspond to the thing Plato was describing, then the biped and featherless man would need to have bird-like nails. Diogenes the Cynic, and the Cynics more generally as Sloterdijk points out, expose us to what is lived (Sloterdijk, 1987:102) and simultaneously to the false ideality that Western metaphysics has been produced since Plato. The cynical tradition is an embodied philosophy. Recall earlier I pointed out that cynical philosophers tend to practise what they talk about; the example above of Diogenes both

---

16 For the embodied philosophy of feminist and queer theory see, amongst others, Butler (1990), and for the embodied philosophy of critical race theory, see Williams (1991).

challenging and reinventing the category of Man through the presentation of a fowl at the academy epitomises this embodied philosophy. This embodied philosophy then carries with it certain characteristics; it is shameless (in exposing the limits of other philosophers or speech acts), it is cheeky and satirical, uninhibited and above all resistant to the idealisation of life and idealism in general (Sloterdijk, 1987:101–3). This tradition is a tradition of anti-mastery, more precisely it exposes the powerlessness of mastery.

Emma Goldman belongs to the cynical philosophical tradition of defacing the posturing of totalising political regimes and their effects, as well as presenting us with an alternative political society. How does a cynical philosophy explain the absence of laughter in response to a joke or a witty comment? How are we to understand the fact that none of the newspapermen laughed at Emma Goldman's witty response to the question, 'How do you find Italy? – 'Beautiful country minus Mussolini'? Are we to understand this response as a failed joke, a failed comical act that conveys nothing about the world in which we live (or in the case of Goldman the world in which she was living)? We could, but I think that would be supporting the same Universalising claims we see being played out in theories of humour. To follow some of these theories of comedy and humour would be to understand Goldman's 'failed' joke as either a false joke (Zupančič) or a competing Universalism (Butler). But if we follow the Cynical philosophical tradition, we can read it as a joke that exposes philosophical idealism as false (words and deeds do not coincide) and simultaneously invites us to see how a parallel and embodied life is lived as well as spoken about. How can we come to such a conclusion?

Emma Goldman responds to the newspapermen in a rather stiff manner; without movement, with seriousness, she directs her gaze away from them and towards the camera as she answers their questions. In her excellent book, *Emma Goldman: Political Thinking in the Streets* (2011a) Ferguson points out that Goldman's discomfort at this moment stems from her general dislike of the moving image. Ferguson informs us Goldman, was suspicious of the role of machines in political communication (185). Whether or not she was suspicious of new technologies, Goldman's wit does not appear to be soliciting any laughter or even trying to humour the circus of the press. Dry and strong as the witty comment is, it tells us a fact: Italy is a beautiful country, despite its dictator. Italy is not defined by leaders, even authoritarian ones. Life is more than State politics. We can read Goldman's stiff manner and seriousness as a non-expectation of laughter, a recognition that the anarchist life and the lives of the journalists (part of the State apparatus) are two *parallel* and *different* coordinates of life.

Goldman's answer is uttered in a straightforward manner, as a matter of fact, which reminds us that life can be beautiful, a country like Italy can be beautiful, if it is not held to ransom by the politics of mastery and control, secrecy, surveillance, glorification and caprice, precisely because, like Diogenes the Cynic, anarchists are aware of the problems of idealism and mastery. The story of the witty statement that fails to tickle the newspapermen is not one of exodus (à la Virno) that signals a potential way of life to be lived in some near future, but rather a story that signals a life based on anti-mastery. It simply articulates that a life without control is possible in the present (Italy is a beautiful country) and through restrains (despite Mussolini). Of course, what Goldman's failed joke teaches us is that an anarchist life is not one that is lived after a triumphant victory that exits us from the State formation, but rather one lived in parallel to the dominant one, one that does not, of course, preclude pain. For example, anarchists continued to live their lives during World War II notwithstanding the pains of the war. Jokes may indeed, as Freud taught us, relieve us from pain or discomfort, but in doing so they simultaneously acknowledge the existence of pain and difficultly.

Let's now turn to the use of humour by CIRCA. CIRCA was formed in the UK in 2004 by John Jorday L. M. Bogad, Jen Verson and Matt Treveylan to protest the visit of then US president George W. Bush (Bogad, 2010:547; Jordan, 2012:304). CIRCA is not a real army, rather it is comprised of a battalion of clowns who wear army trousers and jackets decorated with pink feather boas and other colourful paraphernalia. Their faces are painted so they look like any clown at the circus or carnival festivals. On the opening page of CIRCA's website, which is more of an archive than a live site,[17] we find a series of titles that direct us to their writings or a description of who they are or videos about and with CIRCA. The links to the videos do not seem to work anymore, though there are some videos available on YouTube.[18] My discussion draws upon my own experience of the 'army' whilst being a legal observer in Scotland during the anti-G8 demonstrations in July 2005, as well as videos from these actions and activists' writings about them. It is important to note that CIRCA is not *just* a UK-based activist formation. On the contrary, whenever or wherever there are anti-capitalist demonstrations there are usually a battalion of Clowns humouring institutions of power. For example, they can be seen during the Anti-G8 demonstrations in Rostock, Germany in 2017.[19] So, let's see who CIRCA are and what they do.

CIRCA, unlike Goldman – whose humorous comments appear to be spontaneous or at least aren't premeditated – use humour deliberately. At the opening of the UK-based archive website[20] there is the CIRCA manifesto, a call to clown arms, as well an explanation of their acronym. We are told that CIRCA stands for Clandestine, Insurgent, Rebel, Clown, Army. *Clandestine* refers to their refusal of 'the spectacle of celebrity', their claim that they 'are everyone' and their strong belief that 'words, dreams and desires are more important than ... biographies'

17 See CIRCA, 'Home' (No Date).
18 See *Rebel Clown Army Fights Army Recruitment (and Wins)*, *C.I.R.C.A. G8 Road Blockade, 2005.07.04 CIRCA* and *Send in the Clowns*.
19 See *Clandestine Insurgent Rebel Clown Army in Rostock*.
20 CIRCA 'About the Army' (No Date).

(Bogad, 2010:540). Moreover, CIRCA notify us that by covering their faces, giving their faces the clown look, they re-empower themselves. How do this? As they state, we live in society where surveillance is a dominant mode of controlling populations; in painting their faces they make it difficult for the State and its apparatuses to recognise members of the clown army and reclaim their anonymity. They are *Insurgent* they tell us because they don't have an original location from which they emerge nor can they be found everywhere. Additionally, they warn us that by joining the 'army' we will experience an insurgency of the imagination. Clowns move not in straight lines but rather in unpredictable ways, improvising their moves and not believing in any blueprints. They identify themselves as *rebels* because they believe that no 'revolution is ever complete, and rebellions continue forever' and because they will indiscriminately 'desert and disobey those who abuse and accumulate power'. They disguise themselves as *Clowns* because they can use tricks to subvert authority, but more importantly because as clowns they 'embrace ... life's contradiction, creating coherence through confusion'. They form themselves into an *Army*, they tell us, because the world is in a state of constant war. They explain that they 'are an army because [they] are angry and where bombs fall [they] might succeed with mocking laughter. A laughter needs an echo'.

As John Jordan writes, CIRCA is not just a technique of disobedience it is more 'a state of being' (2012:305). When Jorday, Bogad, Verson and Treveyland formed CIRCA in 2003 in an attempt to offer a different welcoming reception to the then President Bush, they collaborated with clowns who helped them develop their specific clown rebellion techniques (304). Whilst, as we have seen, their actions may be improvised, specialised training enabled the clown soldiers to sharpen their techniques and to respond to tense situations. Moreover, Jordan tells us that the training encouraged the activist participants 'to "find their inner clown"', which he identifies as a 'a childlike state of generosity and spontaneity' (305). We can speculate that by finding their inner child clowns are able to act in ways that can diffuse tense situations or attacks from the police or other State organs. It is imagined that the figure of the child shields them from aggression.

My first-hand experiences of CIRCA are drawn from 'The Carnival for Full Enjoyment' that took place on 4 July 2005 during the Anti-G8 activities in Scotland (Bogad, 2010), at which I was present. More precisely, the clowns came to my attention during the 'Carnival of Full Enjoyment', a tactic or a form of resistance that activist in Scotland where using. 'The Carnival for Full Enjoyment' commenced at around 12 o'clock and those interested joined it on Princes Street in Edinburgh (for those who might not know, Princes Street is the main shopping artery of Edinburgh, not dissimilar to Oxford Street in London). The Carnival was made up of disparate groups and people: anti-G8 protesters, local people, black bloc formations, CIRCA, legal observers, activist medics, the Infernal Silver Brigade and many others.

The idea of the carnival as a *tactic* of *resistance* has been very much part of the anti-globalisation movement (Bogad, 2010:537, 542), joyfully protesting against capitalism and authoritarianism. The anti-G8 protests in Scotland where mostly conceptualised as a 'Carnival for Full Enjoyment' (537, 542). As Bogad explains the organisers drew on Bakhtin's concept of the 'carnivalesque' when they were setting up the Carnival as a tactic of resistance (541). Bakhtin developed the concept of the 'carnivalesque' in the chapter 'Rabelais in the History of Laughter' (1984:59–144), found in his book *Rabelais and His World*. In this chapter, Bakhtin unveils how humour and folk culture were represented in Rabelais' writing in the Middle Ages and Renaissance. Laughter features heavily in Rabelais' novels and is very dominant during the carnival. During the carnival period, ordinary people inverted the order of things by turning both social and economic hierarchies and the hierarchy of the mind over the body upside down. For example, during the carnival period, poor people became rich and wise people became fools, mocking hierarchies and dogmatic positions and provoking laughter. Laughter, an embodied act, plays a significant role in inverting these hierarchies. As Bakhtin writes:

> Laughter purifies from dogmatism, from the intolerant and the petrified; it liberates from fanaticism and pedantry, from fear and intimidation, from didacticism, naïvité and illusion, from the single meaning, the single level, from sentimentality. Laughter does not permit seriousness to atrophy and to be torn away from the one being, forever incompleteness.
>
> (Bakhtin, 1984:123)

'The Carnival for Full Enjoyment' was to begin at 12 o'clock from the West End of Princes Street. The satirical and captivating poster 'advertising' the carnival called upon 'Flex, temp, full-time, part-time, casual and contortionist workers, migrants, students, benefit claimers, New Dealers, work refusers, pensioners, dreamers, duckers & divers …' (Bogad, 2010:540) not only to join but also to

> [b]ring drums, music, banners, imagination for action against the G8 that expresses our resistance in work, out of work and wherever we live. Assert our desires for FULL ENJOYMENT with fun in the city – and begin to make capitalism & wage slavery history.
>
> (540)

High aspirations, eh! Perhaps though only as lofty as the aspirations of highbrow intellectuals who, in their eagerness to put down on paper their reflections of their world, even in their eagerness to write something that will transform their socio-political terrain, miss the glaringly obvious. We miss *not just* the ironic gesture of the calling of this occasion, but also the political potential that resides in its *occasion*, in being acted out. The posted invitation to 'The Carnival for Full Enjoyment' ends as follows:

> They say that time is money. Steal some today. Call in sick, go on strike, take an extra-long lunch break! Meet friends from far away and next door to conspire and celebrate; to disrupt the daily grind of the institutions that plunge us into overwork, poverty, and debt. When we claim Job Seekers Allowance, we're told to 'actively seek' work. But we actively seek the end of this system based on profit, and we work towards a global community based on freedom and cooperation.
>
> (540)

The carnival call urges us to bring – via our withdrawal of labour for a day or a few minutes – capital production to a halt. To introduce another day of rest that is *not* the Sunday day of rest (which is, after all, very much part of the capital system of production), but rather one that acts out enjoyment, resists slave waging, acts as the 'leap over' or skipping of time.

Initially its celebratory energetic mood was not suggestive of the trouble to come, of the possibility of energy being brought to a standstill, melancholy and its decomposition. We, as legal observers, just had to follow the Carnival and record any arrests or police harassment, and take note of police tactics. We were walking around Edinburgh when the police directed the Carnival down a narrow alley street, Canning Street. A heavy armoury of police in riot gear, horses and dogs penned the demonstrators and legal observers in for more than several hours, from around 1 o'clock to 5.30 pm. As legal observers, we kept handing 'Bust Cards'– which informed participants of their legal rights and provided them with legal contacts in case of an arrest – and taking notes of the scuffles between police and demonstrators. At some point during this time the music from the Infernal Silver Brigade that was entertaining us whilst we were standing still was interrupted. The police were trying to push the front line of demonstrators back. The front line was predominantly made up of Black Bloc members. I will come back to the make-up of the Black Bloc in a second.

As the police pushed, the demonstrators pushed back. That was a moment of exhilaration, of pure adrenaline. My co-legal observer was at the front line observing what was happening. I, more cowardly and trying to calm my bumping heart, stayed back or rather somewhere in the middle left-hand corner, waiting for the pushing to subside so I could write my notes. Then there was quiet. Everybody decided to sit down. Then the music began. CIRCA was moving between the police and demonstrators, pulling funny faces and drawing flowers and hearts on the police riot shields. The actions of Kolonel Klepto and Major Up Evil, two members of CIRCA present at the carnival, altered the way in which political activism was to be understood, but also our understanding of a way of life:

> By using popular forms of culture in public spaces we attempted to make our ideas and values visible, attractive, and hopefully irresistible! We felt that turning up in the middle of the city with free food, showing films and

putting on performances that glorify civil disobedience, was a strategy that challenges a system which works so hard on demonising us and pushing us to the margins. We created an event that clearly spoke of the pleasure of resistance but somehow fell outside people's expectations of what radical politics looked or felt like.

(Kolonel Klepto and Major Up Evil, 2005:250)

However, the police did not share the same views as Kolonel Klepto and Major Up Evil. At one point, the police announced that if we didn't all leave the pen or enclosed space we would be arrested. One of the legal observers asked my co-observer and me to walk out of the pen and take notes of any arrests, give out witness forms and generally be vigilant of police-demonstrator engagement outside the pen. In getting out of the pen, we were asked for our name and address, required to produce identification, videoed and had our bags searched under section 60 of the Criminal Justice and Public Order Act 1994 (the section designed to search bags, vehicles, etc. for weapons if an inspector or somebody above the rank of an inspector has reasonable suspicion that violence will erupt in an area). While asking for our names and address was within the rights of the police, it was difficult to imagine that violence was going to erupt given that all the 'demonstrators' were in a carnival mood. How could a bunch of clowns with dusting feathers cause any violence? If one asked the police, as I did, on what grounds they were videoing us, they hesitantly threw back at us a section of a Scottish Act that was not even in use – but as we didn't know that at the time there wasn't much that we could do. Any reluctance on our part to argue with the police would have resulted in our arrest. Some 25 protesters were arrested that day, including a 14-year-old.

CIRCA and the 'The Carnival for Full Enjoyment' humoured the streets of Edinburgh. We may have witnessed an occasional smile from a police officer, but the police as an institution, as an apparatus of the State, did not burst into laughter, did not, in other words, join the rhythm of CIRCA and the Carnival. This failure, even refusal, to laugh by the police, to have their body a little out of control, out of uniform, enables us not only to see how the anarchic CIRCA organisation of life is not just diametrically opposed to that of the State, but that their configuration of life exists in parallel to it. We can say CIRCA and the police symbolically represent these two parallel dimensions. But they also represent more. The story of humour and anarchism tells us something about the un-commonalities of life. It tells about the things that we may not find funny. Or it tells us about the things that what we may clumsily call 'the norm' does not find funny. It tells a story of a human existence that lives in a non-common way, without restrains and in parallel to that of the idealised type of life that values Sovereignty, authority, security and surveillance. It tells us the story of lives existing in parallel. It may not be a story that we like or find easy to understand. It may also be a painful story. Some of the CIRCA clowns did get arrested in Edinburgh. Nevertheless, the lack of laughter at the jests and humorous acts of CIRCA, or at Goldman's humorous comments, demonstrate time and time again that it is possible to be and live on this earth without commonalities. When Emma Goldman heard that US president William McKinley had been seriously injured by Czolgosz, a young anarchist, she offered to nurse him (she was a trained nurse) and at the same time she attempted publicly to defend Czolgosz and find him a defence lawyer, as nobody wanted to represent him (Goldman, 1970a:310–17). She had nothing in common with either of them. Life for Goldman was more than commonalities.

Our travels through the practice of humour suggest that the absence of laughter may not necessarily suggest an *absence* of ethics or politics. The absence of laughter may merely transmit a parallel trajectory of life – that which *exists* in the *gap* between those *critiques* that insist on taking over the State via an insurgency, revolution, withdrawal or exit from the State. It may simply be a persistent gesture that waves *wittingly* to certain forms of government, another trajectory of life.

The anarchists' uses of humour and their failure to procure laughter enables us to understand that a new sociality or political formation – an anarchist formation that does not take the State as its focus, that takes account of the lack of commonalities – is not just possible, it is present in our society, if we would just notice the sound of silence at the end of a joke. If only we noticed the parallel lives that currently exist and have been articulated in this chapter by Goldman and CIRCA.

Chapter 6

Mutual aid instead of conclusion

'Who is going to bathe the baby?', a female interlocutor asked me when I presented part of this book at a seminar. I was startled by the question. In her essay 'Anarchism: What it Really stands For' (1969:47–67), Emma Goldman rehearses a variety of common objections to anarchism, the first being that anarchism is not practical although, as she writes, it is 'a beautiful ideal' (49). When this female interlocutor posed the question, although neither her tonality nor her demeanour led me to believe that it was a hostile question, Goldman's 1910 essay and her rehearsal of common objections to anarchism came to mind. Nevertheless, the question startled me. What made my interlocutor think that an anarchist polity would not attend to everyday chores or, as she explained when I pushed her, not be a responsible society? Granted, in my presentation at the working group I was talking about disobedience and Stirner's critique of disobedience, and I may have given the erroneous impression that anarchists are selfish individuals who constantly want to object to the order of things and are indifferent to the idea of creating a common world. Whilst I did say that the chapter on disobedience pertained to providing us with a way of de-tangling our psyche from obedience, and deterring us from living according to norms and institutional and Statist frameworks, I did not suggest that this would lead to anarchists failing to form associations; nor did I intimate that this would lead to irresponsible individualist living. Stirner may be situated as an individualist within the anarchist cannon, but there are others, like Proudhon or Kropotkin, whose idea of anarchism is strictly linked to collective and associative living. So the disentangling of our psyche from the shackles of norms and institutions – blueprinted by capitalism, schooling, law, religion and the State – will enable us to imagine and build a society whereby the State and law are not its backbone, where capitalism and its companion, neoliberalism, cease to exist, and co-operation rather than competition is its organising principle.

Anarchist theory and archives, at least the ones that I have included in this book, reveal that *parrhesia* is *not* just a practice that frees us from the shackles of oppressive societies and leads us to anarchist polities; it is also an essential element of the government of any anarchist polity. Of course, not everyone will

DOI: 10.4324/9780429952692-6

be convinced by the prospering of an anarchist polity; let me remind you that we can only enter an anarchist association through volition, not through coercion. And whilst I don't imagine that I will convince a huge number of readers of the *gift* of anarchism, I do hope that I may entice some to entertain the possibility of a better world than the one that we are currently living in. Given our current condition, where poverty is still a feature of both the developed and developing world, with over 700 million people living on $1.90 dollars a day,[1] where wars are ongoing (the retreat of allied forces from Afghanistan in 2021 may have ended a 20-year war against the Taliban, but it gave rise to gender wars in the country, with women being discriminated against by the Taliban-run government; on 24 February 2022 Russia invaded Ukraine and the war is still going on), where the intense tempo of capitalist societies is depleting our bodies and souls, where the environment is nearing destruction and the Covid-19 pandemic has highlighted the extent of the inequalities, injustices and inefficiencies of our political, economic and legal systems, perhaps an anarchist pre-figurative polity may reveal the virtues of living otherwise.

This chapter addresses the question of my female interlocutor mentioned above. It proposes that the anarchist practice of mutual aid can provide an antidote to neoliberalism and its contemporary perils, which I enumerated in the previous paragraph. The concept and practice of mutual aid, as we will see, draws together the political, economic and ethical aspects of anarchism and anticipates the existence of mutual aid associations in building a non-profit, hierarchical world that addresses both our needs (food, clothing, shelter, water) and our desires (art, music, etc.). I draw specifically on Kropotkin's writings on mutual aid, entertain criticisms from contemporary anarchist thinkers and activists on the functioning and usefulness of mutual aid and offer contemporary examples where mutual aid is practised, or at least has been or is part of the way in which they operate (Occupy, XR, the solidarity of everyday people for refugees, the medical profession, Covid-19 pandemic, etc.). If the dominant mentality of organising life is that of neoliberalism, and if the unequal distribution of material resources, the precarisation of labour, profit for the 1 per cent, as well as mental and physical health aggravations are some of its effects, then discovering that mutual aid is being practised in our contemporary societies provides us with *hope* – hope that there is another way of organising life, despite the cruelty, poverty and devastation that neoliberalism is spreading. Let me be clear, though: in no way am I suggesting that neoliberalism is *generous* to allow mutual aid to exist, rather that not everything has yet been devoured by neoliberalism. I argue that mutual aid operates parallel to these devouring forces, out of the hard work and commitment of people who believe that – to risk repeating a popular cliché – 'another world is possible'.

Before enumerating the characteristics of Kropotkin's concept of mutual aid, I took the decision to present the objections to mutual aid stemming from

1 See Results, 'World Poverty Statistics' (No Date).

contemporary political theorists and philosophers who are sympathetic to the idea of anarchism. It may be a paradoxical way of doing things, presenting the objections before I present the actual characteristics of this practice, but I am doing so because I believe that not only can these objections be neutralised but also that they cannot be countered without full knowledge of Kropotkin's mutual aid. These objections, as you will see, are divided into three main categories: (i) philosophical objections (mutual aid's premises are both essentialist and universalist), (ii) economic (mutual aid does not have a clear concept of value) and (iii) political (mutual aid can be exclusive).

Why doesn't mutual aid work?

Anybody who opens up Kropotkin's *Mutual Aid* (2009) and has been well versed in poststructuralist theory will find his writing at odds with what they have already received from poststructuralism. How can we take seriously a theory of mutual aid that has been built on biology or nature? As the historian Peter Marshall writes, 'By studying human society from the biological point of view, [Kropotkin] believes that it is possible and desirable "to deduce the laws of moral science from social needs and habits of mankind"' (1993:320). This is a point that Kropotkin repeats, as Marshall's quote from Kropotkin's *Ethics* (1992)[2] below shows, throughout his work, even when he refers to ethics:

> Nature has thus to be recognized as the first ethical teacher of man. The social instinct, innate in men as well as in all the social animals – this is the origin of all ethical conceptions and all the subsequent development of morality.
> (Kropotkin, cited in Marshall, 1993:320)

As the preceding quote concretises, and as my discussion of Kropotkin's concept of law in Chapter 2 demonstrates, this Russian polymath anarchist geographer has nature at the core of his anarchist theoretical reflections. This is even more evident in his book *Mutual Aid*, where through careful personal observations and references to contemporary biological and scientific findings of the nineteenth century he reveals that in the animal and human worlds survival of the fittest is not the only instinct. On the contrary, he discovered that mutual aid was a widespread practice in the animal and human worlds. I will talk extensively about Kropotkin's book *Mutual Aid*, as well as drawing on his other writings, to explain his vision of an anarchist mutual aid polity in the next section of this chapter. For the moment, I will turn to the *problem* with his biological or naturalistic basis of mutual aid.

2 Kropotkin's *Ethics: Origin and Development* was published posthumously in 1922 by Kropotkin's friend Nicholas Lebedev. In this book, Kropotkin offers a review of ethical perspectives that have a naturalistic focus. He looks at Epicurus, Bacon, Hobbes, Spinoza, Adam Smith, Comte, Proudhon, Darwin.

In Chapter 2 we encountered Kropotkin's reflections on law. There I indicated how we can understand his concept of nature, including that of human nature, as a technology or *techne*, not a quality that is fixed and determined, but one that is ever changing. My explication of Kropotkin's concept of nature as technology is not one that is present in other contemporary anarchist interlocutors. Saul Newman, for example, has critiqued classical anarchism (including Kropotkin's political theory) for being trapped in the 'Enlightenment narratives of emancipation, progress and rationalism', as well as for its determinism, though never 'as deterministic as Marxism' (Newman, 2016:7). Classical anarchism's naturalism and positioning within the Enlightenment project, with its grand narratives about a rational human subjectivity, freedom and universal truth, as Newman tells us, do not hold true in our postmodern era. Drawing upon the world of the postmodern philosopher Jean-François Lyotard, who was one of the first to alert us to the danger and exclusionary character of grand narratives, Newman writes:

> The universal discourses central to the experience of modernity, the category of a universal objective truth that is or ought to be apparent to everyone, or the idea that the world is becoming more rationally intelligible through advances in science – all these structures of thought and experience have been undergoing a profound process of dissolution due to certain transformations of knowledge in the post-industrial age. Processes of legitimation have become ever more questionable and unstable: the contingency and arbitrariness of knowledge's operation – the fact that it is ultimately based on relations of power and exclusion – is becoming apparent, thus producing a crisis of representation.
>
> (Newman, 2016:7–8)

It is not, however, just our suspicion of grand narratives, as you may have noted from the quote above, that causes Newman to be critical of classical anarchism's naturalism and ultimately universalism. On the contrary, his main concern with classical anarchism stems from it no longer being able to map the present. Newman argues, for example, that one of the problems of classical anarchism lies in the fact that we can no longer hold onto the idea of the universal (unified and autonomous) subject. Philosophically this was witnessed in the early twentieth century with the advance of psychoanalysis, which introduced us to the unconscious, a challenge to this unified rational subject. Indeed, if we take our example the category of woman as our example, we know very well from De Beauvoir to Judith Butler that such an essentialist universal claim does not hold: there is not one unified subject that can be attached to the category of woman. Whilst Newman's observations regarding the philosophical foundations of anarchism and, by extension, mutual aid hold true, whilst we should remain vigilant to universalism and its exclusionary, persecuting and violent acts (far too many to mention) and whilst Kropotkin's use of nature to ground mutual aid at first glance – as we shall see shortly – *lean* towards essentialism and universal claims, the praxis and ethics of anarchism (that is, the practice of mutual aid itself – voluntary free association, decision-making based on extensive discussion, constant revision of initial positions, as well as the understanding of ever-changing nature and anti-authoritarianism) direct us to a non-essentialist anarchism. Furthermore, although we should remain sceptical of grand narratives and we may have managed to 'secure' a general agreement on the idea that they are variations of human subjectivity, we should also not ignore some grand narratives that still co-ordinate our lives, like those of the State, the law, the economy or religion. Newman's observations, thoughtful and thought provoking as they are, may risk merging the critique of our times with the material realities that surround us. The State and its instruments – laws, statutes, the police – are, for example, ever present and provide us with plentiful grand narratives about their need to exist, e.g., for either economic and bureaucratic necessity or security purposes. For example, the UK State insisted on not allowing the existence of gender-neutral passports (Bowcott, 2018) and discriminating against citizens identifying as non-gender on the basis of financial costs; on the basis of bureaucratic complexity or the Immigration Act 2014, the UK State made landlords, amongst others, the guardians of the UK borders, responsible for checking the immigration status of their prospective tenants and only renting to those who are lawfully in the UK, criminalising anybody who fails to do so under the Immigration Act 2016 under the guise of national security. Both examples demonstrate the strength of the grand narrative of the Nation-State and its position as a guardian of citizens' security and well-being.

So, whilst we should be mindful of grand narratives, we should also be mindful of the story that we live in a postmodern world – despite the fact that we may desire to have such a decentralised world – and of the grand narratives and their totalising potential that are with us, such as the claims by the State that its function is to decide how to protect us. As I intimated in Chapters 1 and 2, Newman's work does not see the abolition of the State as necessary for contemporary anarchism to thrive. My argument so far here has been that Newman's critique of Kropotkin's and other nineteenth-century anarchists' so-called biological determinism and attachment to grand narratives is that it falls short. The reference to nature by Kropotkin is neither essentialist nor determinist because nature, as we have discussed in Chapter 2, is understood by Kropotkin to be, like *techne*, ever changing. Moreover, Newman's argument falls short because his description of the world as postmodern fails to see that the State is still with us. The only way that we can understand the existence of anarchist configurations and subjectivities within a predominantly neoliberal world where the State has not withered away is to visualise them as operating in *parallel* with the dominant configurations of power.

However, Newman is not alone in offering a friendly critique of classical anarchism. The philosopher Todd May also offers a critique of classical anarchist theory's naturalist, essentialist and humanist grounds (1994:62–6). For him, the issue is not so much classical anarchism's inability to be mapped onto the present as its moralism or its belief that human beings are endowed with an innate goodness:

> Anarchism, then, is imbued with a type of essentialism or naturalism that forms the foundation of its thought. People are naturally good; if the obstacles to that goodness are removed – specifically, the twin evils of representation and power – then they will realize and express that goodness in their activity. Representation distorts goodness by allowing another or others to tell one who one is and what one wants, rather than allowing those qualities to emerge naturally. Power suppresses one's goodness for the sake of interests that may very well be destructive.
>
> (63)

As we shall see, it is true that anarchists like Kropotkin provide us with a picture of the human, or the animal world for that matter, being constituted by goodness in the state of nature. It is also true that Kropotkin, like so many other anarchists (Stirner, for example), blames the State, the Church and capitalism amongst other things for the demise of this goodness. May's concerns in relation to anarchist naturalism and the creation of the benign – as he calls it – human rest with two issues: first, anarchism is in danger of becoming all ethics and no politics; and second, anarchism prescribes the kind of ethics that wants to see in an anarchist polity without necessarily having to create them through argumentation and disagreement, resulting in anarchism not having 'to articulate what kinds of human activity are good and what kinds are bad' (64). May identifies that the anarchist embrace of naturalism stems from anarchism's deep-rooted suspicion of any form of power and its understanding of power as suppressive (64). However, May cautions that the anarchist aversion to power is not connected in anarchist writings to any form of natural determinism (65). Throughout anarchism's history, May argues, anarchist thinkers have argued that they are offering a sustained critique of power without holding onto universal naturalist beliefs. May turns our attention to anarchist writers who make this point, such as the contemporary anarchist thinker Colin Ward, who argues in *Anarchy in Action* (1996) that anarchism's critique of power is not connected to a naturalist humanist position, championing a type of politics that opens up the diversity of human subjectivity in lieu of a unified one (64). May reminds us that although nineteenth-century anarchists such as Emma Goldman were critical of power, they did not succumb to an idea of universalism. Goldman, May reminds us, was influenced by the philosophy of Friedrich Nietzsche who 'called for "*a fundamental transvaluations of values*"' (64; emphasis in original) and offered critique of any political ideology that was based on a homogenous unified human subject.

Overall, May is sympathetic to the above variations in anarchist thought, especially the denunciations of humanist naturalism; he is nevertheless critical of the a priori anarchist denunciation of power. May understands that although power may impose constraints on action, it is *not* restraining (67). Anarchists should not abandon their strategic politics (by abandoning any claims to power) but instead engage with philosophical perspectives on power, like that of Michel Foucault, for example, who presented power differently, power as productive, rather than restraining, and moreover showed us how nobody is outside power. The failure of anarchism to see or understand power as productive and insist upon resisting power, according to May, retains naturalism and humanism in the guise of power (65). May is right to a certain extent. Classical anarchism does not entertain the possibility of power having any positive aspects, whether they come in the guise of law or political representation. But his explanation of why this is the case is that anarchists want to offer us a horizon without power precisely because they are very aware of the productive and destructive character of power. We do not need to look any further than Kropotkin's account of the distribution of wealth in *The Conquest of Bread* (2015) to recognise the anarchist suspicion of power:

> It is because all that is necessary for production – the land, the mines, the highways, machinery, food, shelter, education, knowledge – all have been seized by the few in the course of that long story of robbery, enforced migration and wars, of ignorance and oppression, which has been the life of the human race before it had learned to subdue the forces of Nature. It is because, taking advantage of alleged rights acquired in the past, these few appropriate today two-thirds of the products of human labour, and then squander them in the most stupid and shameful way. It is because, having reduced the masses to a point at which they have not the means of subsistence for a month, or even a week in advance, the few can allow the many to work, only on the condition of themselves having the lion share.
> (Kropotkin, 2015:11)

Kropotkin is fully aware that economic rights and power benefit those who came upon them either through birth or some other arrangement and this is to the detriment of wage slaves and other populations, who live from hand to mouth and day to day. The description of power relations in the quote above leaves no doubt that power cannot be productive all the time; power is oppressive, and this makes it easier for us to understand why anarchists deem power to be the root of all our misfortunes. So whilst May is correct to note the failure of anarchism to consider different modalities of power and consider the potentialities of, for example, productive power, and whilst he is correct to note that this failure may reproduce within anarchism humanism and naturalism, he fails to notice that the relationship that anarchists have to power is one that does not challenge power for the purpose of usurping it, but rather for the purposes of doing away with it altogether and replacing it with a totally different mode of governing. I have already demonstrated in Chapter 2 in relation to law how if your strategy of emancipation relies on the contestation of the very structures that oppress you then the struggle and end goal becomes colonised by the very lexicon of the structure that oppresses you. I would like to suggest that the very potentiality of anarchism lies in insisting *not* on succumbing to the charms of power, but in wanting to deliver a very different modality of associating, that of mutual aid. Mutual aid is a mode of governing that demands not only that we form non-hierarchical associations to govern without authority, but also that we do so without structures and commands that will keep an association static. May's critique of anarchism's failure to embrace power, and its holding onto a humanist and naturalist discourse, is only a valid operative if anarchism does not offer a different mode of governing, and it does. It offers that of mutual aid. In addition, as anarchism is offering mutual aid as a model of governing, a model that does not understand subjects, communities or life as being static, it cannot be criticised for holding onto a naturalistic and essentialist concept of life.

Mutual aid has been criticised not only for its foundational claims, but also for its economic efficacy. Anarchist thinkers engaging with economics offered their own criticisms of mutual aid. In the 'Introduction: Anarchist Economics: A Holistic View' of the edited collection *The Accumulation of Freedom: Writings on Anarchist Economics* (2012), Shannon, Nocella and Asimakopoulos not only make us aware of the existence of anarchist economics, they also acknowledge the limitations of classical anarchist economics and offer an array of anarchist alternatives. Anarchism, as I have argued throughout the book, is an anti-capitalist, anti-authoritarian, anti-oppression practice and way of thinking that demonstrates an art of living without the aforementioned features and *without* law. Shannon and colleagues identify three major strands of anarchist economics – 'mutualism, collectivism, and communism' (25) – that aspire to provide us with an art of living without capitalism, authoritarianism, oppression and law. The whole collection can be seen as a critique of these traditions and an attempt to develop through the critique a contemporary anarchist economics, one that will allow us 'to analyze capitalism contemporarily, historicize aspects of its development, and speculate about its future' (Shannon, Nocella and Asimakopoulos, 2012:17). Shannon and colleagues avoid providing us with a definitive list of features of contemporary capitalism – unlike, for example, David Harvey, who has done so by telling us that neoliberal policies are being driven by 'accumulation by dispossession' (2004). Instead, they focus on five features – 'wage/labor exploitation, private property, markets, class society and states' (Shannon et al., 2012:17). These six non-exhaustive features enable Shannon et al. to frame the collection but also to familiarise us with the distinctive aspects of anarchist economics. They engage critically with Kropotkin's *The Conquest of Bread* (2015). As it is well known that in this book Kropotkin provides us with a history of mutual aid societies (ancient, medieval and nineteenth-century), an explanation of how needs and desires will be managed in an anarcho-communist polity, an economic theory that calls for the usurpation of wealth, the 'communization of supplies' (Shannon et al., 2012:31) and the organisation and redistribution of wealth based not on production but on need. Kropotkin calls this economic model or way of life anarcho-communist. Although Shannon and colleagues sympathising with Kropotkin's ideas of anarcho-communist economics they also raise a series of objections to his proposed vision of anarcho-communism. For example, they argue that Kropotkin presents anarcho-communism as an uncontested and uniform concept and practice whereas in reality the meaning of anarcho-communism is far from settled. As they write, '[t]here are those who believe that formal anarchist organisations are crucial to social struggle and those who think those kinds of organizations become ends unto themselves and get in the way of struggle ...' (Shannon et al., 2012: 32). I will return to this particular objection later. At the moment I will turn my attention to one of the contributions in this edited collection that explicitly engages with Kropotkin's mutual aid.

In 'Examining the History of Anarchist Economics to See the Future' (2012:42–63) Chris Spannos provides us with an eloquent and thoughtful account of the history of anarchist economics, including those of anarcho-communism. I will focus mainly on his critique of anarcho-communism and his corrective perspective. Anarchist economics, Spanos succinctly writes, 'have traditionally rejected inequalities of power and privilege arising from private ownership of the means of production' (43). The anarchist rejection of the capitalist organisation of property, resources, productive and social life comes with plans to create associations bereft of the privilege and hierarchies that capitalism creates. Drawing on the words and writings of classical anarchists such as Bakunin, Proudhon and Goldman amongst others, Spannos identifies two orientations within anarchist thought that gesture towards a life without capitalism. These are:

> (1) The concept of ownership over productive assets is abolished so that ownership becomes a non-issue, meaning that no one owns productive property. ...
> (2) Society as a whole owns all productive property but again ownership conveys no special rights or privileges.
> In either orientation class rule due to ownership of productive property is abolished and the way is cleared to also establish anarchist self-managed decision-making.
>
> (46)

The orientations are clear and Spannos's summing up makes it explicit that in order to have an anarchist polity, a series of associations into which people have entered freely, we need first to bring about the abolition of private productive property and secondly to redistribute property in a way in which not the individual but society as a whole owns property. In other words, we need to convert private productive property into communal property, thus creating an anarcho-communist society. One of the most difficult things that we may encounter, according to Spannos, is the redistribution of productive property which, in Kropotkin's opinion, entails the redistribution of usurped productive property according to need. He thus turns to Kropotkin, and especially his insights in *The Conquest of Bread*, as a way of assessing possible ways of achieving anarcho-communism. He writes:

> Another method based on the communist principle of remuneration according to need is proposed by Kropotkin in his anarcho-communist work, *The Conquest of Bread* (1892). For Kropotkin if private ownership of productive property in capitalism produces scarcity of goods for those at the bottom, then the new economy, based on the abolition of private ownership of productive assets combined with the introduction of mutual aid and voluntary cooperation, should distribute the abundant fruits of society's productivity to all based on what they need.
>
> (51)

During Spanish Civil War the idea of redistribution of property and goods based on one's needs, and not on profit or according to one's ability, was put into practice successfully. Spannos explains how this was achieved by drawing upon the writings of Gaston Leval,[3] a Spanish anarcho-syndicalist active during the Spanish Civil War. During the war we are told that families were paid for their labour according to their family needs and not their production; families where one parent worked and had numerous dependents were paid more than those where both parents worked but didn't have any dependents (52). Although Spannos is excited by the success of this model during the Spanish Civil War, he is sceptical about the possibility of being able to put such a model into practice outside the circumstances of war or conflict (52). What are the limits that he foresees of the model of 'redistribution according to one's needs'? The premise of remuneration according to one's needs operates on the presumption that 'it is amending remuneration for hours work with a need component' and not merely rewarding need irrespective of whether somebody worked or not (52). The problem with this is that it fails to consider 'how much income and how much labor are responsible and fair?' (53) for this exchange to take place. In other words, we may be able to calculate the needs of an individual and a family, but if we don't have clear standards for the value of labour one gives, this makes it an economic model that is almost impossible to implement in Spannos's opinion. He suggests that the idea is great but its failure to consider how it will be executed in practice turns this into a model that is not only utopian but also dysfunctional. It avoids thinking about the

---

3   Gaston Leval was a Spanish anarcho-syndicalist who took part in the Spanish Civil War and wrote historical accounts of the period. Most notable is his book *Collectives in the Spanish Revolution* (1975).

possible disparities in people's understanding of value. It even presupposes 'a morally good society' (52). He anticipates the possibility of conflicts arising over discussions about the value of different types of work (should a doctor be paid more than an artist?), the value of the intensity of a type of work, the hours spent in work and how we account for our inability to work (52–3).

For mutual aid and its redistributive aspect to work, Spannos assesses that we need to account for the question of value. He criticises Kropotkin's idea of mutual aid (remuneration according to one's needs) for its failure to become politically effective, at least not without an update. In sum, in Spannos's opinion anarcho-communist economics are theoretical, have no political efficacy, are presumptive of the kind of society in which they will be exercised (a morally good one) and are unable to address questions of fairness and productivity in advance. Spannos's criticisms allude to the criticisms of mutual aid that we have seen were made by Todd May, namely that the problem with Kropotkin's mutual aid is that it is essentialist, it prefigures the moral values that a society should have and, more importantly, it has very little political efficacy. This is not explicitly stated by Spannos but his remarks on the ethical orientation of Kropotkin's anarcho-economics, as well as the reference to the presumption of a morally good society in which the redistribution of wealth according to needs will take place, betrays Spannos's concern about the foundations of Kropotkin's ideas and their practicality or politics. If my critique of Todd May is that he fails to address the spirit of mutual aid and Kropotkin's anarchism – namely that the forms that it will take will be addressed by people who enter freely into associations, that he fails to understand the interconnectedness of ethics and politics in general and in anarchism in particular – my critique of Spannos is that he fails to see that once a society declares itself as anarcho-communist it will be able in due course to redistribute productive capital in accordance with the needs of that society. The ethical dimension of this society – as a society that does not value individual wealth and profit – will guide the decisions of its associates, not in advance but in its duration. Therefore, I cannot see the jump from theory (ethics) to practice (politics) hindering the kind of economics that will be practised in an anarcho-communist association. The problem arises when we want to provide a blueprint, as Spannos seems to tacitly suggest, before the constitution of a polity that will share mutual aid principles.

In *Communal Luxury: The Political Imaginary of the Paris Commune* (2016), Kristin Ross suggests that Kropotkin's use of Darwinian theory (that there is a natural associative as well as competitive instinct) is indicative of nothing more than 'mutual aid [being] an objective factor in human sociability' (133).[4] I will follow her suggestion here and view Kropotkin's use of biologism as a way of

---

4   For the concept of nature not being teleological in Kropotkin's writings on mutual aid, see Catherine Malabou's lecture 'Teleology: Conceptual Corpse or Plastic Concept' at the Centre for Research in Modern European Philosophy, Kingston University, 9 June 2017 at https://backdoorbroadcasting.net/2017/06/catherine-malabou-teleologi%E2%). 92%B6. Accessed 18 June 2019.

revealing a world where mutual aid becomes a way of life, as well as recognising that it is not merely a theory but also a practice. If we begin addressing mutual aid from this vantage point, we will be able to appreciate the potentiality of the concept and practice of mutual aid and perhaps find it in more places than Kropotkin did.

One such potentiality was excavated by the Professor of Afro-American Literature and History Saidiya Hartman. It is not clear to me from what I have read whether Saidiya Hartman is critical of Kropotkin's biology, but she was certainly able to see mutual aid being practised in 1915 in Harlem, New York. In her essay 'The Anarchy of Colored Girls Assembled in a Riotous Manner' (2018:465–90), Hartman tells the story of Esther Brown and her friends who lived in 1915 Harlem and engaged in mutual support to survive in a city and country that was overtly racist and made it hard for black people, especially women, to survive. Hartman points to the fact that Kropotkin failed to report in his writing that mutual aid was practised amongst black women although he went into great detail about mutual aid in the animal kingdom and other social groups:

> Kropotkin never described black women's mutual aid societies or the chorus in *Mutual Aid*, although he imagined animal sociality in its rich varieties and the forms of co-operation and mutuality found among ants, monkeys and ruminants. Impossible, recalcitrant domestics weren't yet on his radar or anyone else's. (It would be another decade and a half before Marvel Cooke and Ella Baker wrote their essay 'The Bronx Slave Market' and two decades before Claudia Jones's 'An End to the Neglect of the Problems of the Negro Woman'.)
> (Hartman, 2018:466)

Hartman is of course pointing to the third type of criticism that is levied on mutual aid: that it has been exclusionary, and to that effect racist, not identifying mutual aid practices in racialised groups. However, Kropotkin was clear that mutual aid was practised by families and other kin relations, and I assume this would include Esther Brown and her kin. In addition, Kropotkin thought that mutual aid practised in communes was an extensive and inclusive practice that aimed to produce equality for all:

> It is by free groupings that the social Commune will be organized, and these groupings will overthrow walls and frontiers. There will be millions of communes, no longer territorial, but extending their hands across rivers, mountain chains and oceans, uniting individuals and peoples in the four corners of the earth into the same single family of equals.
> (Kropotkin, 1992:89)

If I was to guess how he would have felt reading Hartman's essay, I would say that Kropotkin would have been delighted to find out about mutual aid being practised amongst Black girls in Harlem. So, let's now turn to Hartman and what she tells us about the practice of mutual aid in 1915 Harlem. Hartman tracks the mutual aid practices of Esther Brown in 'social clubs, tenements, taverns, dance halls, disorderly houses, and the streets' (2018:471), spaces where Esther and her friends dreamt of different worlds, conversed about their daily travails, strategised, laughed and generally helped each other to unburden themselves of the claws of racist capitalism. In refusing household-related jobs, the most available jobs for Black women at the time, which paid very little and exploited young Black women, Esther Brown and her friends found solidarity in the streets and practised mutual aid by supporting each other, through child rearing, providing accommodation for each other and having fun. Hartman identifies mutual-aid practices that take place outside the factory or the work environment and sometimes outside the family structure. These arrangements are private but take place publicly and are done to enable people to live their lives free from State control and normativity. The resistance of Emma and her friends to labour, housework and taking up sex work were ways of freeing themselves from what I call responsive capitalism – that is, a way of organising one's life in response to the demands and desires of those that have the control over the means of production. Hartman, along with Esther Brown, teaches us an invaluable lesson: mutual aid is a huge weapon against the organising force of capitalism as it can free us from the capitalist organisation of time and life. There is no indication that Esther Brown was an anarchist, though Hartman alludes to the fact that she did attend Emma Goldman's lecture at Renaissance Casino in 1914 on 'Marriage and Love' (465). However, Esther Brown's way of practising mutual support, outside the work economy, counteracts criticism (like that of Spannos) that put work at the centre of redistribution according to need. What Hartman alerts us to via Esther Brown is the potentiality of mutual aid to value practices that are not captured by productivity, such as emotional support or pleasure, as well as work. Kropotkin was very much aware of the importance of leisure, relaxation and creativity in building mutual-aid associations, communes and worlds. With this in mind, I will return to Kropotkin's writings on mutual aid and, like an archaeologist, excavate the promises, practices and orientations that guide us towards a future that values communal property, work and emotional labour, as well as leisure and creativity.

Mutual aid revisited

Peter Kropotkin's economic and social re-conceptualisation of our polities, organised around the principle of mutual aid, provides us with the prospect of a world where access to pleasure and work will not be commanded by profit, prejudice and tradition, but rather made possible by mutual aid, the abolition of private property, the distribution of wealth of all according to their need, and space for leisure or luxury time.

Kropotkin develops his anarcho-communist concept of mutual aid in numerous writings including, *Mutual Aid*, first published in 1902, and *The Conquest of Bread*, first published in 1892. I will first turn to his book *Mutual Aid*. Mutual aid underpins Kropotkin's call for anarcho-communist polity. In this book, he records the widespread instances of mutual aid within the animal and human kingdom. Kropotkin points out that in *The Descent of Man*, Darwin also talks about how the co-operation instinct – present in animals and humans – plays a pivotal role in our survival. Darwin discovered that the instinct of co-operation or mutual aid overrides that of competition. As Kropotkin suggests, following their own interests, Darwin's followers decided to focus instead on the narrow interpretation of Darwin's theory of evolution and bracketed out references to mutual support. In *Mutual Aid*, Kropotkin therefore sets out to restore mutual aid to its pivotal position as a contributor to our survival, explaining how mutual aid is present within family structures (animal/human) and non-family-based associations. Even predatory animals, like the Brazilian kites, he writes, practise mutual aid by sharing food and are supportive of different species like the percnopters. Without disguising the fact that animals are predatory, he tells the story of how they share their food and co-operate with each other regardless of biological ties; bees and ants are some of the examples that he uses to demonstrate mutual aid outside the family realm. The example that struck me was the example of Brazilian kites. This is what Kropotkin says about them:

> The Brazilian kite, one the most 'impudent' robbers, is nevertheless a most sociable bird. Its hunting associations have been described by Darwin and other naturalists, and it is a fact that when it has seized upon a prey which is too big, it calls together five or six friends to carry it away. After a busy day, when these kites retire for their night-rest to a tree or to the bushes, they always gather in bands, sometimes coming together from distances from ten or more miles, and they often are joined by several other vultures especially the percnopters, 'their true friends,' D'Orbigny says. In another continent, in the Transcaspian deserts, they have, according to Zarudhnyi, the same habit of nesting together.
> (Kropotkin, 2009:43–4)

Moreover, Kropotkin tracks the practice of mutual aid in humans in villages and farming associations, entertainment clubs, unions and guilds. In human societies, he observes, there is an undoubtedly strong tendency towards mutual support, especially when people are striving to bring about transformations in their living, working, economic and social conditions.

The propensity towards mutual aid is not restricted to the animal world. Humans also practise mutual aid. Apart from mutual support witnessed in family environments, Kropotkin traces mutual aid in villages and farming associations, entertainment clubs, unions and guilds. Consider what he says regarding the organisation of apprentices in medieval times throughout Europe:

> In the medieval cities, when the distinction between masters and apprentices or journeymen became more and more apparent in the fifteenth century, union of apprentices ... occasionally assuming an international character, were opposed to unions of masters and merchants.
> (Kropotkin, 2009:209)

Apprentices or journeymen formed associations to challenge master and merchant unions' pricing of their labour. Although the State intervened to regulate wage pricing in England, it would not have been achieved without apprentice and journeymen unions (Kropotkin, 2009:209). By the eighteenth century apprentices and journeymen unions in Europe had been destroyed through legal statutes and instruments; however 'workers' unions where continually reconstituted' (209), a sign of the strength of the belief in mutual support. In human societies, Kropotkin observes, there is an undoubtedly strong tendency towards mutual support, especially when people are striving to bring about transformations in their living, working, economic and social conditions.

Mutual aid is, if we follow Kropotkin, a very established way of doing things in our world. Capitalism and neoliberal mentalities have valorised competition or the survival of the fittest; but this does not mean, and this is Kropotkin's valuable contribution, that this is the only way of doing things.

One will be excused at this point for wondering whether Kropotkin had a vision regarding mutual aid beyond pointing to its existence. How do we transform our living worlds into ones where mutual aid, not capitalism, not legalism, nor the State are the dominant ways of organising life? In his book *The Conquest of Bread* (2015) Kropotkin explains how this may happen. As Marshall suggests, Kropotkin was confident that the dispossessed would destroy the State and re-establish a way of life that would be guided by mutual aid (Marshall, 1993:325). In the place of the State, Kropotkin imagines that voluntary associations will emerge. *Conquest of Bread* offers multiple examples of such associations, from housing to work associations, bringing together consumers and producers. These associations are envisaged as being of various sizes, small and big, international and local, and governed by customs and free agreement. What he imagined as being an anarcho-communist society. As Marshall puts it:

> It meant politically a society without government, that is anarchy, and economically, the complete negation of the wage system and the ownership of the means of production in common 'everybody contributing for the common well-being to the full extent of his capacities, shall enjoy from the common stock of society to the fullest possible extent of his needs'.
> (Marshall, 1993:323)

As the quote from Marshall suggests, Kropotkin thought that an anarcho-communist society, a mutual aid society, requires the abolition of private property for a start. The abolition of private property will come about when the dispossessed, factory workers, farmers, artisans, etc., arise up against the capitalist system. This will inevitably happen, as capitalism will make the lives of workers, farmers, artisans, etc. more and more difficult. Once the State is abolished through revolutionary means, Kropotkin says, the members of the association will decide amongst themselves first how to address the needs of the associations or, as he writes, from the very 'first day of the revolution the worker shall know ... that henceforward none need crouch under the bridges, while palaces are hard by ... none a perish with cold near shops full of furs ...' (27). In addition, post the revolution, association members will first attend to the needs of their members 'before schooling them in their duties' (27). And in making sure that this will happen, possession of every private property will be taken over and turned into common property. Once private property is abolished, Kropotkin suggests, there will be no need to establish a better wage system in which workers will be paid more fairly and in accordance with the hours they work. Such a collectivist system, as he argues, is untenable (30). Why is it untenable? Because it discards that, in an anarcho-communist society where property and 'the instruments of labour [are considered] common inheritance' (Kropotkin, 2015:30) there will be no need for a wage system. The wage system, as he explains below, is strictly associated with capitalist production:

> The wage system arises out of the individual ownership of the land and the instruments of labour. It was the necessary condition for the development of capitalist production, and will perish with it, in spite of the attempt to disguise it as 'profit sharing'. The common possession of the instruments of labour must necessarily bring with it the enjoyment in common of the fruits of common labour.
>
> (Kropotkin, 2015:30)

So the abolition of a wage system and consequently the remuneration of all according to their needs are the two anchors of Kropotkin's anarcho-communist society. Such a society is possible in Kropotkin's opinion as he identifies anarcho-communist tendencies even within our existing capitalist society. He uses multiple examples to demonstrate that the capitalist society of the nineteenth century was moving towards communism. One of his examples was the season ticket introduced by trams and railways in the UK. This season ticket allowed passengers to travel unlimited and multiple times without restrictions. This was, according to Kropotkin, a good indication that individual consumption was of no interest to the railway or tram companies (32). Perhaps Kropotkin could not foresee how a capitalist society and private companies would operate in ways to maximise their profits to the extent that travelling by train within the UK has become a luxury. With this example Kropotkin wanted to show that a communistic ethos was present even within capitalism, that rail companies were willing to accommodate the needs of their customers at the expense of profit by introducing season tickets. But his example holds little validity today. Perhaps we can think of non-profit organisations as entities that are not interested in consumption patterns or profitability, but rather in helping communities to get out of poverty and have good living conditions, as examples of organisations that exemplify a more communistic ethos today, even within a neoliberal society. Oxfam is not of course an anarchist association; it does not wish for the abolition of the State, as it relies partially on State tax breaks for its survival. But it is embedded in a non-profit ethos that exemplifies the communistic ethos that Kropotkin saw even within capitalism.

There are other more successful examples that Kropotkin identifies as having a communistic attitude within capitalist societies. The British National Boat Institute is one such example. Kropotkin writes excitingly about it:

> In the same way, those who man the lifeboat do not ask credentials from the crew of a sinking ship; they launch their boat, risk their lives in the raging waves, and somewhat perish, all to save men whom they do not even know. And need to know them? 'They are human beings, and they need our aid – that is enough, that establishes their right – To the rescue!'
> (Kropotkin, 2015:33)

When there is a boat sinking, the rescue boats do not care about who they are saving as long as they are saved. The rescuers work closely with each other to save the passengers of boats that have capsized. This is a familiar scenario for us. Refugee Rescue, a non-profit organisation and its boat *Mo Chara* have been rescuing refugees since 2015 in the Mediterranean and surrounding seas. The boat operates around the island of Lesvos (Refugee Rescue). On 29 June 2019 Carola Rackete, captain of Sea Watch's *Sea-Watch 3* of, a German non-governmental organisation, defied Italian laws that criminalise rescue operations, saved 42 migrants and took them to Lampedusa. Carola Rackete was arrested on the same day but released on 2 July by an Italian judge (African Times Editor, 2019). Médecins Sans Frontières (MSF) or Doctors without Borders, a non-profit self-governed organisation made up of health carers and administrators that provide medical assistance in war zones, disaster zones and for refugees rescued by boats like *Mo Chara* and *Sea Watch 3*, are another contemporary example of mutual aid organisations that run on a non-profit basis within our neoliberal world. It is not only organisations that run to the rescue of refugees. In 2015 when hundreds of refugees were arriving on the shores of Lesvos ordinary people ran to their rescue and offered them food and shelter. They were even nominated for the Nobel Peace Prize in 2016 (Schoenbauer, 2016). More recently, and because of the Covid-19 pandemic, local mutual aid groups were created across the world offering support to vulnerable individuals, well before any State support was offered. In the UK we have seen the creation of more than 4,000 mutual aid groups (O'Dwyer, 2020). Kropotkin was not wrong in identifying a strong mutual aid and communistic attitude within early capitalistic societies and this also applies to contemporary societies.[5] This same

---

5 For example, the Black Panther Party in the 1960s and 1970s ran free breakfast clubs for all schoolchildren in need (Hilliard 2007: 7; Spade 2020: 9–10); Housing Works, which was founded in 1990 by four ACT UP (AIDS Coalition To Unleash Power) activists and is still active, reaches out to homeless HIV-positive New

attitude is present even in today's so-called neoliberal societies, as the aforementioned examples record.

Whilst a communistic attitude may be present today, it may be more difficult to convert this attitude into a way of life where there all private property is abolished and remuneration is given according to one's needs. Even in social movements where self-governance or democratic citizens' assemblies are constitutive parts of their ideological structure, like XR) – the environmental organisation that succeeded in forcing both the UK government and Parliament to declare a climate emergency – are not necessarily anarchist groups. XR does not demand the abolition of the State, nor the abolition of private property. They are deeply mutualist in the sense that they believe that all our actions are interconnected and if we do not refrain from consuming the way we do in five years we will succeed in destroying the Earth; but they rely on the State to bring this about. Let's turn to XR and their 'politics' to understand better how even the most visible social movement of the twenty-first century, one that is recognised as radical, is at some distance from what Kropotkin may have understood as the organising principles of a mutual aid society or anarcho-communism.

On 31 October 2018 a group of UK-based environmental activists that answer to the name of XR gathered in Parliament Square, London to read out a Declaration of Rebellion against the UK government. XR, as it has come to be known, is a non-horizontal assemblage of environmental activists that put on civil acts of disobedience with the aim not just of publicising the 'unprecedented global emergency' that we are facing but also of forcing governments to act to stop the catastrophe that is about to engulf the globe. The need to act is urgent. As they write on their Facebook page:

> [T]he planet is in crisis and we are in the midst of a mass extinction bigger and faster than the one that killed the dinosaurs. Scientists believe we have entered a period of abrupt climate breakdown. The Earth's atmosphere is already over 1°C warmer than pre-industrial levels and the chance of staying below the 1.5°C limit set in the Paris Agreement is tiny. Projections show we are on course for 3 degrees of warming and probably higher.
>
> We and our children will face unimaginable horrors as a result of floods, wildfires, extreme weather, crop failures and the inevitable breakdown of

---

Yorkers and provides them with job training programmes and primary care clinics in order to help them rebuild their lives. The organisation funds its mutual-aid activities through a bookshop café, a bar and a chain of thrift shops, not through State funds (Shepard 2002:351–9). In the twenty-first century one of the most notable examples of territories run on principles of direct democracy and mutual aid is the Autonomous Administration of North and East Syria (AANES). AANES is run by street communes that make sure that nobody will be deprived of shelter, food, education or employment and, more importantly, that nothing is left at the mercy of capitalism (Sahin and Khabat 2020:3–17).

society when the pressures are so great. We are unprepared for the danger our future holds.

(XR, 2018)

At their first public action on 31 October 2018 XR were expecting a few hundred people to turn up and support them. To their surprise 1,500 joined to voice their discontent and amplify the need to act (XR, 2018). Their 15 April 2019 day of action at Parliament Square turned into almost two weeks of direct actions and occupations. The group occupied four central spots in central London: Oxford Circus, Marble Arch, Waterloo Bridge and Parliament Square. Their civil disobedience actions saw over a 1,000 XR members being arrested. They attracted the attention of the media, people and politicians all over the world. XR groups now exist in Australia, the Solomon Islands, the US, Spain, India, South Africa and many more countries. The demands of the group are threefold: (a) governments must 'tell the truth', 'declare climate and ecological emergency' and co-operate with other institutions to publicise this truth; (b) governments must act immediately to stop any biodiversity destruction and 'reduce greenhouse gas emissions to net zero by 2025'; and (c) the curious demand that all this should be organised and take place under the mantra of 'beyond politics'(XR, No Date a). The third demand refers to the necessity to bring about environmental and ecological justice outside established partypolitical frameworks, to organise and decide on these changes via a citizens' assembly. Their demand 'beyond politics' is, on the one hand, a plea for *another* way of doing *politics*, one that puts at its core the ideals of participatory democracy captured in the guise of the citizens' assembly, and, on the other hand, a call for precisely no politics (in the sense of no partisan politics), as the issue of the environment is beyond such old structures. The message they want to amplify with this striking caption, 'beyond politics', is simple: the ecological disaster is only five years away, and if we don't act now as citizens regardless of our ideological positions, sexuality, race, ethnicity, ability, age, etc., we will not have a planet on which to act out our politics. Indeed, during the period of direct actions in mid-April 2019 we witnessed a disparate assemblage of peoples and groups supporting XR and joining their actions, events, entertainment and, especially, citizens' assembly. Even the UK Parliament voted and declared that there is a climate emergency on 1 May 2019 (BBC News, 2019). This was just a symbolic vote, but although Parliament recognises that something urgent needs to be done, it does not legally compel the government to act. Consequently we can say that their message 'beyond politics' works to embrace crosspolitical positions, peoples and parties from a variety of ideological stances. We can only hope so. XR is a movement and a process, and this message 'beyond politics' may hold this possibility. It would however be somewhat naive if we allowed the euphoria that the success of this movement inspired to obfuscate the limits of the call 'beyond politics', limits that show that this beyond holds within it the very politics that they would like to by-pass.

Let's consider how XR frames this call. 'Government', they write, 'must create and be led by the decisions of a Citizens' Assembly on climate and ecological justice' (XR, No Date b). For a demand highlighted by the desire to act 'beyond politics' the sentence above betrays a certain attachment to elected and representative governments. It is the government that is imagined to call into being the citizens' assembly, and once it has created it will follow its decisions. In other words, XR does not want to have a completely different politics, but rather a politics where the existing political status quo and civil society institutions accommodate their demands for ecological justice. This becomes even more apparent when we consider their views on the police. More recently, social movements like BLM have repeatedly pointed out police brutality and institutional racism, and offer a powerful critique of institutional racism and the police. As Punk Academic reminds us in his contribution to the *Critical Legal Thinking* blog, the police have a long history of brutality against Black and ethnic minority communities, working-class people and disobedient subjects (Punk Academic, 2019). However, in their attempt to show that they are 'beyond politics', XR declared their love for the police (Taylor and Gayle, 2019). I am not saying this just to point out that XR are uncritical of the history of policing and police culture in general, but rather to point out once more that XR are not a movement that will open us up to a completely different politics.[6] On the contrary, it is a social movement that is deeply invested in sustaining the current status quo in an attempt to bring ecological justice. But as the Wretched of the Earth (2019),[7] an assemblage of activists in support of XR, reminded them in an open letter published in *Red Pepper* magazine on 3 May 2019, no environmental justice will be enough without a total transformation of the social, political and economic structures that produce the inequalities and threats to extinction locally and globally.

Perhaps the only movement that came close to imagining a total transformation of the social, political and economic structures and operating in an anarchistic fashion was the Occupy movement. On 17 September 2011 a group of left-wing activists, mostly anarchists or with anarchist tendencies (Bray, 2013), occupied Zuccotti Park in New York to protest against economic inequality. They stayed there until 15 November 2011. They set up a tent city (which included food kitchens, well-being tents, information points) and operated through a general assembly where decisions had to be unanimous. In fact, political theorists such as Jodi Dean cite the political organisation of the movement and its decision-making practices as the reason for its demise (Dean, 2016). This may be true, but we should not underestimate the force of the law in bringing down Occupy Wall Street and subsequently all the Occupy movements. I am not concerned here though with the failure of Occupy, but rather with the anarcho-communist spirit that they demonstrated and their

6 For an extensive critique of XR, see Loizidou (2020:99–113).
7 Wretched of the Earth, (2019).

strong anti-capitalist intentions. At the core of its politics Occupy Wall Street had economic inequality and demands for achieving equal distribution of wealth, better working conditions, bank regulation and the abolition of corporate influence on government (Taylor and Gessen, 2011). Whilst not calling for the abolition of private property explicitly, Occupy Wall Street pointed to the effects of private property and the destitution caused to ordinary citizens through the uncontrolled loans of banks for private property purchases. If Kropotkin was writing a contemporary version of *The Conquest of Bread,* perhaps the Occupy Wall Street movement would have featured high up as an example of an association of people that were self-governed, practising mutual aid and working towards the abolition of private property and wage slavery.

So far we have seen how Kropotkin's understanding of mutual aid, his call for the end of private property and remuneration according to the needs of each one resonates partially with a lot of contemporary movements and organisations. My aim here is not to conclude by offering an anarchist economic theory that updates that of Kropotkin. I am not an economist. My aim here is to try to offer some understanding of the characteristics that we may need to build an anarcho-communist society or, rather, societies. If mutual aid is present even in capitalist societies, if movements can wage the anti-capitalist idea and demonstrate possible ways of materialising it, if Kropotkin's suggestions for a five-hour working day for four or five days is increasingly desirable[8] (Kropotkin, 2015:95), if there are provisions for luxury (art, theatre, etc.) after the production of basics (food and clothing) (99–112), what stops us from desiring and bringing about anarcho-communism? Or rather, what do we need to cultivate to bring about a mutual self-governed society?

Throughout this book I have spoken of *parrhesia*, humour and love that embraces ambivalence as characteristics of an anarchist art of living. In this concluding chapter we have observed that mutual assistance, voluntarism, abolition of private property and distribution according to one's need are the necessary ingredients for such a world. We can see that Kropotkin imagined that a society that organises itself away from the law, that has mutual aid, negation of wages and ownership of the means of production is possible. Some aspects of this society exist; like Kropotkin, I argue that we practise mutual aid despite the asphyxiation that neoliberalism forces upon our ability to organise together for a common good. But to achieve it, to have a life that it is not just *parallel* to the dominant neoliberal one, we may need to shed our attachment to concepts such as politics, Sovereignty, State – to have, in other words, a radical break from what we know and embrace the possibility that to live well requires imagination, trust and dreaming. It requires the undoing of private property,

---

8   Iceland has trialled with success a 4-day-a-week programme to address and reduce the issue of burnout. Productivity remained the same. See BBC Business (2019) 'Four-day week "an overwhelming success" in Iceland', *BBC*, 6 July 2019. https://www.bbc.co.uk/news/business-57724779. Accessed 6 July 2021.

with its worries about having enough money to pay our rents or mortgages or being able to put food on the table, without the worries of medical care and care in general. Above all, we need to trust that we are not an 'I' but a 'We', and we need to imagine that 'We' can breathe together in a different world. A world in which we dare to say 'We' without fearing that in doing so the 'I' will disappear. We need to trust that our imagination may take us there. In other words, we need to take a break from whatever returns us to the insular 'I': law, capital, State. *Anarchism: An Art of Living Without Law* is an invitation to join me in thinking of the possibility of being a 'We'.

Bibliography

African Times Editor (2019) 'Judge Releases Sea Watch Captain Who Landed Migrants at Italian Port', *African Times*, 2 July. https://africatimes.com/2019/07/02/judge-releases-sea-watch-captain-who-landed-migrants-at-italian-port. Accessed 5 August 2019.

Agamben, G (1998) *Homo SacerL Svoereign Power and Bare Life*, Heller-Roazen, Daniel (trans), Stanford, CA: University of California Press.

Agamben, G (1999) *The Man without Content*, Albert, G(trans), Stanford, CA: Stanford University Press.

Agamben, G (2005) *State of Exception*, Attell, K (trans), Chicago, IL and London: University of Chicago Press.

Agamben, G (2013) *The Highest Poverty: Monastic Rules and Form-of-Life*, Kotsko, A (trans) Stanford, CA: Stanford University Press.

Ahmed, S (2014) *Wilful Subjects*, Durham, NC: Duke University Press.

Althusser, L (2001) *Lenin and Philosophy and Other Essays*, New York: Monthly Review Press.

Arendt, H (1990) *On Revolution*, London and New York: Penguin Books.

Aristodemou, M (2000) *Law & Literature: Journeys from Her to Eternity*, Oxford: Oxford University Press.

Aristodemou, M (2014) *Law, Psychoanalysis, Society: Taking the Unconscious Seriously*, Abingdon: Routledge-Glasshouse.

Aristotle (1934) *Nicomachean Ethics*, Rackham, H (trans), Henderson, J (ed), Cambridge, MA and London: Harvard University Press.

Aristotle (1961) *Parts of Animals*, Peck, L.A (trans), Henderson, J (ed), Cambridge, MA and London: Harvard University Press.

Aristotle (2000) *Art of Rhetoric*, Freese, H.J (trans), Henderson, J (ed), Cambridge, MA and London: Harvard University Press.

Aristotle (2005) *Poetics*, Halliwell, S (trans and ed), Cambridge, MA and London: Harvard University Press.

Associazione Ya Basta (No Date) www.yabasta.it. Accessed 20 October 2021.

Audi, R (2001) *The Cambridge Dictionary of Philosophy* (second edition), Cambridge: Cambridge University Press.

Baars, G (2011) '"Reform or Revolution?" Polanyian v Marxian Perspectives on the Regulation of the Economic', *Northern Ireland Legal Quarterly*, 62, 415–431.

Badiou, A and Truong, N (2012) *In Praise of Love*, Bush, T (trans), London: Serpent's Tail.

Bibliography 171

Bakhtin, M (1984) *Rabelais and His World*, Iswolsky, H (trans), Bloomington and Indianapolis: Indiana University Press.

Barthes, R (2002) *A Lover's Discourse: Fragments*, Howard, R (trans), London: Vintage Books.

Bataille, G (2000) 'Laughter', in Botting, F and Wilson, S (eds) *The Bataille Reader*, Oxford: Blackwell Publishers. https://www.bbc.co.uk/news/uk-politics-48126677. Accessed 1 May 2019.

BBC Business (2019) 'Four-Day Week "an Overwhelming Success" in Iceland', 6 July. https://www.bbc.co.uk/news/business-57724779. Accessed 6 July 2021.

BBC News (2019) 'UK Parliament Declares Climate Change Emergency', 1 May, https://www.bbc.co.uk/news/uk-politics-48126677. Accessed 6 July 2021.

Beever, A (2013) *Forgotten Justice: The Forms of Justice in the History of Legal and Political Theory*, Oxford: Oxford University Press.

Bergson, H (2008) *Laughter: An Essay on the Meaning of Comic*, Marston Gate, Staffs: Wildside Press.

Berkman, A (1989) *What is Communist Anarchism?*, London: Phoenix Press.

Berkman, A and Goldman, E (2005) *Trial and Speeches of Alexander Berkman and Emma Goldman in the United States District Court, in the City of New York, July, 1917: Anarchism on Trial*, New York: Elibron Classics.

Berlant, L and Ngai, S (2017) 'Comedy Has Issues', *Critical Inquiry*, 43 (2), 233–249.

Bhandar, B (2018) *Colonial Lives of Property: Law, Land and Racial Regimes of Property*, Durham, NC: Duke University Press.

Black Lives Matter (BLM) 'About'. http://blacklivesmatter.com/about. Accessed 7 August 2016.

Black Lives Matter (BLM) 'What We Believe'. https://uca.edu/training/files/2020/09/black-Lives-Matter-Handout.pdf. Accessed 2 December 2021.

Blumenfeld, J, Bottici, C and Critchley, S (eds) (2013) *The Anarchist Turn*, London: Pluto Press.

Bogad, M.L (2010) 'Carnivals Against Capital: Radical Clowning and the Social Justice Movement', *Social Identities*, 16 (4), 537–557.

Bookchin, M (1980) *Toward an Ecological Society*, New York: Black Rose Books.

Bookchin, M (1996) *Social Anarchism or Lifestyle Anarchism: An Unbridgeable Chasm*, Oakland, CA and Edinburgh: AK Press.

Bookchin, M (2004) *Post-Scarcity Anarchism*, Oakland, CA and Edinburgh: AK Press.

Bookchin, M (2005) *The Ecology of Freedom: The Emergence and Dissolution of Hierarchy*, Oakland, CA and Edinburgh: AK Press.

Borovoy, A (2011), 'Anarchism and Law', *The Anarchist Library*, 15 January. https://theanarchistlibrary.org/library/alexei-borovoy-anarchism-and-law. Accessed 17 July 2016.

Bottici, C (2013) 'Black and Red: Freedom of Equals', in Blumfeld, J, Bottici, C and Critchley, S (eds) *The Anarchist Turn*, London: Pluto Press.

Bowcott, O (2018) 'High Court Backs UK Refusal to Issue Gender Neutral Passports', *The Guardian*, 22 June. https://www.theguardian.com/world/2018/jun/22/high-court-backs-uk-refusal-to-issue-gender-neutral-passports. Accessed 8 March 2019.

Braidotti, R (2006) '*The Ethics of Becoming Imperceptible*', in Boundas, C (ed) *Deleuze and Philosophy*, Edinburgh: Edinburgh University Press.

Bratich, Z.J (2009) 'Book Review: Virno Paolo. (2008) *Multitude Between Innovation and Negations*. Los Angeles: Semiotext(e)', *Journal of Communication Inquiry*, 33 (1), 71–85.

Bray, M (2013) *Translating Anarchy: The Anarchism of Occupy Wall Street*, London: Zero Books.
Brown, W (2015) *Undoing the Demos: Neoliberalism's Stealth Revolution*, New York: Zone Books.
Butler, J (1990) *Gender Trouble: Feminism and the Subversion of Identity*, New York and London: Routledge.
Butler, J (1993) *Bodies that Matter: On the Discursive Limits of 'Sex'*, New York and London: Routledge.
Butler, J (2000) 'Restaging the Universal: Hegemony and the Limits of Formalism', in Butler, J, Laclau, E and Zizek, S (eds) *Contingency, Hegemony Universality: Contemporary Dialogues on the Left*, London and New York: Verso.
Butler, J (2004) *Precarious Life: The Powers of Mourning and Violence*, London and New York: Verso.
Butler, P (2019) 'Welfare Failures and Cuts Fuelling Extreme Poverty, MPs Say', *The Guardian*, 11 July. https://www.theguardian.com/society/2019/jul/11/welfare-failures-and-cuts-fuelling-extreme-poverty-mps-say. Accessed 25 February 2020.
Call, L (2008) 'A is for Anarchy, V is for Vendetta: Images of Guy Fawkes and the Creation of Postmodern Anarchism', *Anarchist Studies*, 16 (2), 154–172.
Carson, A (1998) *Eros the Bittersweet*, Champaign, IL and London: Dalkey Archive Press.
Chomsky, N (2005) *Chomsky on Anarchism*, Oakland, CA and Edinburgh: AK Press.
Clandestine Insurgent Rebel Clown Army (CIRCA) (No Date) 'About the Army', *Internet Archive: WayBack Machine*. https://web.archive.org/web/20050717014556/http://www.clownarmy.org:80/about/about.html. Accessed 20 October 2021.
Clandestine Insurgent Rebel Clown Army (CIRCA) (No Date) 'Home', *Internet Archive: WayBack Machine*. https://web.archive.org/web/20060217121449if_/http://www.clownarmy.org/index.html. Accessed 20 October 2021.
Clark, P.J (1976) *Max Stirner's Egoism*, London: Freedom Press.
Conaghan, J and Chudleigh, L (1987) 'Women in Confinement: Can Labour Law Deliver the Goods?', *Journal of Law and Society*, 14 (1), 133–147.
Critchley, S (1999) 'Comedy and Finitude: Displacing the Tragic-Heroic Paradigm in Philosophy and Psychoanalysis', *Constellations*, 6 (1), 108–122.
Critchley, S (2007) *Infinitely Demanding: Ethics of Commitment, Politics of Resistance*, London and New York: Verso.
Critchley, S (2015) *Notes on Suicide*, London: Fitzcarraldo Editions.
Çubukçu, A (2021) 'After Seeing Like a State: The Imperialism of Epistemic Claims', *Polity*, 53 (3), 492–499.
Cunningham, M (2009) *The Dancer and the Dance*, London and New York: Marion Boyars.
Dean, J. (2016) *Crowds and Party*. London and New York: Verso Books.
De la Boétie, É (2007) 'The Discourse of Voluntary Servitude', in a De la Boétie, É and Bonnefon, P *The Politics of Obedience*, Montreal, New York and London: Black Rose Books.
De la Boétie, É and Bonnefon, P (2007) *The Politics of Obedience and Étienne De La Boétie*, Montreal, New York and London: Black Rose Books.
Deleuze, G and Guattari, F (1999) *A Thousand Plateaus: Capitalism & Schizophrenia*, London: Athlone Press.

Derrida, J (1992) 'Force of Law: The "Mystical Foundation of Authority"', in Cornell, D, Rossenfeld, M and Garlson, G.D (eds) *Deconstruction and the Possibility of Justice*, New York and London: Routledge.

Diamantides, M (2000) *The Ethics of Suffering: Modern Law, Philosophy and Medicine*, Aldershot: Ashgate.

Diogenes Laertius (2005) *Lives of Eminent Philosophers*, Books VI–X, Hicks, D.R (trans), Henderson, J (ed), Cambridge, MA and London: Harvard University Press.

Douzinas, C (2013) *Philosophy and Resistance in the Crisis: Greece and the Future of Europe*, Cambridge: Polity Press.

Douzinas, C and Warrington, R (1991) '"A Well-Founded Fear of Justice": Law and Ethics in Postmodernity', *Law and Critique*, 2, 115–147.

Douzinas, C and Warrington, R (1996) *Justice Miscarried: Ethics, Aesthetics and the Law*, London and New York: Harvester Wheatsheaf.

Douzinas, C and Warrington, R with McVeigh, S (1991) *Postmodern Jurisprudence: The Law of Text in the Text of Law*, London and New York: Routledge.

Duffy, N (2019) 'Transgender Hate Crimes Rocketed by 81% in the UK', *Pink News*, 27 June. https://www.pinknews.co.uk/2019/06/27/transgender-hate-crimes-rocket-81-uk. Accessed 21 May 2020.

El-Enany, N (2020) *(B)ordering Britain: Law, Race and Empire*, Manchester: Manchester University Press.

Extinction Rebellion (XR) (No Date a) 'About Us'. https://rebellion.earth/the-truth/about-us. Accessed 1 May 2019.

Extinction Rebellion (XR) (No Date b) 'Our Demands'. https://rebellion.earth/the-truth/demands. Accessed 1 May 2019.

Extinction Rebellion (XR) (2018) 'About Us', Facebook, 31 October.https://www.facebook.com/pg/ExtinctionRebellion/about/?ref=page_internal. Accessed 1 May 2019.

Fairbairn, C, Gheera, M, Pyper, D and Loft, P (2020) 'Gender Recognition and the Rights of Transgender People', *House of Commons Library*, 22 July. https://researchbriefings.files.parliament.uk/documents/CBP-8969/CBP-8969.pdf. Accessed 1 December 2021.

Falk, C (No Date) 'Emma Goldman: A Guide to Her Life and Documentary Sources: Chronology 1901–1919'. www.lib.berkeley.edu/goldman/pdfs/EG-AGuideToHerLife_Chronology1901-1919.pdf p.10. Accessed 16 December 2021.

Falk, C (1999) *Love, Anarchy and Emma Goldman*, New Brunswick, NJ and London: Rutgers University Press.

Fanon, F (2004) *The Wretched of the Earth*, New York: Grove Press.

Ferguson, K.E (2011a) *Emma Goldman: Political Thinking in the Streets*, Plymouth: Rowan & Littlefield Publishers.

Ferguson, K.E (2011b) 'Why Anarchists Need Stirner', in Newman, S (ed), *Max Stirner*, Basingstoke and New York: Palgrave Macmillan.

Fitzpatrick, P (1987) 'Racism and the Innocence of Law', *Journal of Law and Society*, 14 (1), 119–132.

Fitzpatrick, P (2004) 'Juris-Fiction: Literature and the Law of the Law', *ARIEL: A Review of International English Literature*, 35 (1–2), 215–229.

Fitzpatrick, P (2010) *Modernism and the Grounds of Law*, Cambridge: Cambridge University Press.

Foucault, M (1991) 'Truth and Power', in Rabinow, P (ed), *The Foucault Reader: An Introduction to Foucault's Thought*, London: Penguin Books.

Foucault, M (1994) 'The Subject and Power', in Fabion, D.J (ed), Hurley, R *et al.* (trans), *Michel Foucault Power: Essential Works of Michel Foucault 1954–1984, Volume* Three, London: Penguin Books.

Foucault, M (1997) 'Friendship as a Way of Life', in Rabinow, P (ed), Hurley, R *et al.* (trans), *Michel Foucault Ethics, Subjectivity and Truth: Essential Works of Michel Foucault 1954–1984, Volume* One, New York: The New York Press.

Foucault, M (2001) 'Fearless Speech', in Pearson, J (ed), *Fearless Speech*, Los Angeles: Semiotext(e).

Foucault, M (2003) *Abnormal: Lectures at the Collège de France 1974–5*, Marchetti, V and Salomoni, A (eds), Burchell, G (trans), New York: Picador.

Foucault, M (2004) *Society Must Be Defended: Lectures at the Collège de France 1975–6*, Bertani, M and Fontana A (eds), Macey, D (trans), London: Allen Lane-Penguin Books.

Foucault, M(2005) *The Hermeneutics of the Subject, Lectures at the Collège de France, 1981–82*, Burchell, G (trans), New York: Palgrave Macmillan.

Foucault, M (2007) 'Friendship as a Way of Life', in Rabinow, P (ed), Hurley, R *et al.* (trans), *Ethics, Subjectivity and Truth: Essential Works of Michel Foucault 1954–84, Volume* 1, New York: The New York Press.

Foucault, M (2008) *Psychiatric Power: Lectures at the Collège de France 1973–1974*, Burchell, G (trans), Davidson, A (ed), Basingstoke and New York: Palgrave Macmillan.

Foucault, M. (2010) *The Government of Self and Others: Lectures at the Collège de France 1982–83*, Burchell, G (trans), Gros, F (ed), Basingstoke and New York: Palgrave Macmillan.

Foucault, M (2011) *The Courage of Truth*, Burchell, G (trans), Gros, F (ed), Basingstoke and New York: Palgrave Macmillan.

Franks, B (2008) 'Postanarchism and Meta-Ethics', *Anarchist Studies*, 16 (2), 135–153.

Freud, S (1928) 'Humour', *International Journal of Psycho-Analysis*, 9, 1–6.

Freud, S (1905 [2001]) *Jokes and Their Relation to the Unconscious, Volume* 13, London: Vintage.

Gearey, A (2004) 'Love and Death in American Jurisprudence: Myth, Aesthetics, Law', *Studies in Law Politics and Society*, 33, 3–23.

Gearey, A (2018) *Poverty Law and Legal Activism: Lives that Slide Out of View*, Abingdon and New York: Routledge-Cavendish.

Gelderloos, P (2010) 'The Justice Trap: Law and the Disempowerment of Society', *The Anarchist Library*. https://theanarchistlibrary.org/library/peter-gelderloos-the-justice-trap-law-and-the-disempowerment-of-society. Accessed 11 February 2022.

Gilman-Opalsky, R (2020) *The Communism of Love: An Inquiry into the Poverty of Exchange Value*, Chico, CA and Edinburgh: AK Press.

Gimson, A (2016) *Boris: The Making of the Prime Minister*, London: Simon & Schuster.

Golder, B and Fitzpatrick P (2009) *Foucault's Law*, Abingdon: Routledge-Cavendish.

Goldman, E (1933) 'An Anarchist Look at Life'. *Berkeley Library*, 1 March. https://www.lib.berkeley.edu/goldman/pdfs/Speeches-AnAnarchistLooksatLife.pdf. Accessed 10 August 2020.

Goldman, E (1934) 'Was My Life Worth Living?', *Harper's Magazine*, December. https://harpers.org/archive/1934/12/was-my-life-worth-living. Accessed 15 February 2021.

Goldman, E (1969a) 'Anarchism: What It Really Stands For', in Goldman, E, *Anarchism and Other Essays*, New York: Dover Publications, Inc.

Goldman, E (1969b) 'Prisons: A Social Crime and Failure', in Goldman, E, *Anarchism and Other Essays*, New York: Dover Publications, Inc.
Goldman, E (1969c) 'The Psychology of Political Violence', in Goldman, E, *Anarchism and Other Essays*, New York: Dover Publications, Inc.
Goldman, E (1969d) 'Marriage and Love', in Goldman, E, *Anarchism and Other Essays*, New York: Dover Publications, Inc.
Goldman, E (1970a) *Living My Life, Volume* 1, New York: Dover Publications, Inc.
Goldman, E (1970b) *Living My Life, Volume* 2, New York: Dover Publications, Inc.
Goldman, E (2000) 'The No Conscription League', in Glassgold, P (ed), *Anarchy! An Anthology of Emma Goldman's Mother Earth*, New York: Counterpoint.
Goodrich, P (1990) *Languages of Law: From Logics of Memory to Nomadic Masks*, London: Weidenfeld & Nicolson.
Goodrich, P (1992) 'Critical Legal Studies in England: Prospective Histories', *Oxford Journal of Legal Studies*, 12 (2), 195–236.
Goodrich, P (1996) *Law in the Courts of Law: Literature and Other Minor Jurisprudences*, London: Routledge.
Goodrich, P (1999) 'The Critique Love of the Law: Intimate Observations on an Insular Jurisprudence', *Law and Critique*, 10, 343–360.
Goodrich, P (2016) 'Proboscations: Excavations in Comedy and Law', *Critical Inquiry*, 43 (2), 361–388.
Gornick, V (2011) *Emma Goldman: Revolution as a Way of Life*, New Haven, CT: Yale University Press.
Gov UK (2021) 'Deaths in the United Kingdom', *Gov UK: Coronavirus (Covid19) in the UK*, 26 August. https://coronavirus.data.gov.uk/details/deaths. Accessed 26 August 2021.
Graber, D and Wengrow, D (2021) *The Dawn of Everything: A New History of Humanity*, Milton Keynes: Allen Lane.
Gros, F (2010) 'Course Context', in Burchell, G (trans), Gros, F (ed), *Michel Foucault: The Government of Self and Others: Lectures at the Collège de France 1982–83*, Basingstoke and New York: Palgrave Macmillan.
Gruening, M (2000) 'Speaking of Democracy', in Glassgold, P (ed), *Anarchy! An Anthology of Emma Goldman's Mother Earth*, New York: Counterpoint.
Guérin, D (1970) *Anarchism*, New York: Monthly Review Press.
Hadot, P (2006) *The Veil of Isis: An Essay on the History of the Idea of Nature*, Cambridge, MA and London: The Belknap Press.
Haldar, P (2007) *Law, Orientalism and Postcolonialism: The Jurisdiction of the Lotus Eaters*, Abingdon and New York: Routledge-Glasshouse.
Harbold, W (1969) 'Justice in the Work of Pierre-Joseph Proudhon', *The Western Political Quarterly*, 22 (4), 723–741.
Hartman, S (2018) 'The Anarchy of Colored Girls Assembled in a Riotous Manner', *South Atlantic Quarterly*, 17 (3), 465–490.
Harvey, D (2004) 'The "New Imperialism": Accumulation by Dispossession', *Socialist Register*, 40, 63–87.
Harvey, D (2007) *A Brief History of Neoliberalism*, Oxford: Oxford University Press.
Heidegger, M (2004) *What is called Thinking?*, Gray, G.J (trans), New York: Harper Perennial.
Hemmings, C (2018) *Considering Emma Goldman: Feminist Politics of Ambivalence and the Historical Imagination*, Durham, NC: Duke University Press.

Hilliard, D (ed) (2007) *The Black Panther: Intercommunal News Service 1967–1980*, New York, London, Toronto and Sydney: ATRIA Books.
Hobbes, T (1985) *Leviathan*, London: Penguin Classics.
Hobbes, T (1999) *Human Nature and De Corpore Politico*, Oxford: Oxford University Press.
Hochschild, R.A (2003) *The Commercialization of Intimate Life: Notes from Home and Work*, Berkeley, CA, Los Angeles and London: University of California Press.
Horvat, S (2016) *The Radicality of Love*, Cambridge: Polity Press.
Hughes, D (2018) 'Conservatives Rule Boris Johnson Comparing Muslim Women in Veils to Letter Boxes and Bank Robbers was "Respectful"', *The Independent*, 21 December. https://www.independent.co.uk/news/uk/politics/boris-johnson-cleared-burka-niqab-bank-robber-letterboxes-conservative-party-a8693761.html. Accessed 26 August 2021.
Irigaray, L (1993) *An Ethics of Sexual Difference*, Burke, C and Gill, G.G (trans), Ithaca, NY: Cornell University Press.
Jordan, J (2005) 'Notes Whilst Walking on "How to Break the Heart of Empire"', *transversal texts*, August 2005. https://transversal.at/transversal/1007/jordan/en. Accessed 20 October 2021.
Jordan, J (2012) 'Clandestine Insurgent Rebel Clown Army', in Boyd, A and Oswald Mitchel, D (eds), *Beautiful Trouble: A Toolbox for Revolution*, New York and London: OR Books.
Kahn, P (2000) *Law & Love*, New Haven, CT: Yale University Press.
Kant, I (1987) *Critique of Judgment*, Pluhar, S.W (trans), Indianapolis, IN and Cambridge: Hackett Publishing Company, Inc.
Kant, I (1993) *Grounding for the Metaphysics of Morals: On a Supposed Right to Lie because of Philanthropic Concerns*, Ellington, J.W (trans), Indianapolis and Cambridge: Hackett Publishing Company, Inc.
Kierkergaard, S (2013) *Concluding Unscientific Postscript*, Hannay, A (ed), Cambridge: Cambridge University Press.
Kinna, R. (2019) *The Government of No One: The Theory and Practice of Anarchism*, Milton Keynes: Pelican Books.
Kisselgoff, A. (1992) 'DANCE; Merce Cunningham, Explorer and Anarchist', *The New York Times*, 15 March. https://www.nytimes.com/1992/03./15/arts/dance-merce-cunningham-explorer-and-anarchist.html. Accessed 20 August 2019.
Kolonel Klepto and Major Up Evil (2006) 'The Clandestine Insurgent Rebel Clown Army Goes to Scotland via Few Other Places', in Harvie, D, Milburn, K, Trott, B and Watts, D (eds), *Shut Them Down! The G8, Gleneagles 2005 and the Movement of Movements*. Yorkshire and Brooklyn, NY: Dissent! Automedia.
Kropotkin, P (1992) *Ethics: Origin and Development*, Montreal and New York: Black Rose Books.
Kropotkin, P (2002) 'Law and Authority', in Baldwin, N.R (ed), *Anarchism: A Collection of Revolutionary Writings*, Mineola, TX and New York: Dover Publications Inc.
Kropotkin, P (2009) *Mutual Aid: A Factor of Evolution*, London: Freedom Press.
Kropotkin, P (2015) *The Conquest of Bread*, Milton Keynes: Penguin Books.
Leopold, D (2006) 'Introduction', in Leopold, D (ed), *The Ego and Its Own*, Cambridge: Cambridge University Press.
Leval, G (1975) *Collectives in the Spanish Revolution*, London: Freedom Press.
Lever, K (1956) *Art of Greek Comedy*, Edinburgh: Edinburgh University Press.

Locke, J (1988) *Two Treatises of Government*, Cambridge: Cambridge University Press.
Loizidou, E (2007) *Judith Butler: Ethics, Law, Politics*. Abingdon and New York: Routledge-Glasshouse.
Loizidou, E (2011) 'This is What Democracy Looks Like', in Klausen, C.J and Martel, J (eds), *How not to Be Governed: Readings from a Critical Anarchist Left*, Plymouth, MA: Lexington Books.
Loizidou, E (2013) 'Disobedience Subjectively Speaking', in Lozidou, E (ed), *Disobedience: Concept and Practice*, Abingdon: Routledge-Glasshouse.
Loizidou, E (2016) 'Dreams and the Political Subject', in Butler, J, Gambetti, Z and Sabsay, L (eds), *Vulnerability in Resistance*, Durham, DC and London: Duke University Press.
Loizidou, E (2020) 'A Parallel Art of Living', in Hesselberth, P and de Bloois, J (eds), *Politics of Withdrawal: Media, Arts, Theory*, London: Rowman & Littlefield.
Loizidou, E (2021) 'Planetary Confinement: Bio-Politics and Mutual Aid', *Law and Critique*, 33, 133–138.
Malabou, C (2017) 'Teleology: Conceptual Corpse or Plastic Concept', Centre for Research in Modern European Philosophy, Kingston University, 9 June.https://backdoorbroadcasting.net/2017/06/catherine-malabou-teleologi%E2%). 92%B6. Accessed 18 June 2019.
Marneros, C (2021) 'Human Rights After Deleuze: Towards an An-archic Jurisprudence', PhD, University of Kent.
Marshall, P (1993) *Demanding the Impossible: A History of Anarchism*, London: Fontana Press.
Marx, K and Engels. F (1998) *The German Ideology*, Amherst, MA and New York: Prometheus Books.
May, T (1994) *The Political Philosophy of Poststructuralist Anarchism*, University Park, PA: The Pennsylvania State University Press.
May, T (2008) 'Equality Among the Refugees: A Rancièrean View of Montreal's Sans-Status Algerians', *Anarchist Studies*, 16 (2): 121–134.
McDonald, A (2012) 'To Destroy the Idea of Divinity: Anarchism as Practical Program and as Utopia', *Griffith Law Review*, 21 (2), 349–368.
Meyer, R.L (2006) 'Law like Love?', *Law and Literature*, 18 (3), 431–447.
Moran, J.L (1996) *The Homosexual(ity) of Law*, London and New York: Routledge.
Morreall, J (1987) *The Philosophy of Laughter and Humor*, New York: SUNNY.
Motha, S (2018) *Archiving Sovereignty: Law, History, Violence*, Ann Arbor: University of Michigan Press.
Murphy, T (1999) 'Brit Crits: Subversion and Submission, Past, Present and Future', *Law and Critique*, 10, 237–278.
Newman, S (2001) *From Bakunin to Lacan: Anti-Authoritarianism and the Dislocation of Power*, New York and Toronto: Lexington Books.
Newman, S (2008) 'Editorial: Postanarchism', *Anarchy Studies*, 16 (2), 101–105.
Newman, S (ed) (2011a) *Max Stirner*, Basingstoke and New York: Palgrave Macmillan.
Newman, S (2011b) 'Max Stirner's Ethics of Involuntary Servitude', in Newman, S (ed), *Max Stirner*, Basingstoke and New York: Palgrave Macmillan.
Newman, S (2012) 'Anarchism and Law: Towards a Post-Anarchist Ethics of Disobedience', *Griffith Law Review*, 21 (2), 307–329.
Newman, S (2016) *Post Anarchism*, Cambridge: Polity Press.
No Author (1908a) 'Denaturalization of Jacob Kersner', 24 September, Emma Goldman Archive, International Institute of Social History, Amsterdam (on file with author).

No Author (1908b) 'Emma Goldman before Board of Special Inquiry', 6 April, Emma Goldman Archive at the International Institute of Social History, Amsterdam. Document 830214126 (on file with author).

No Author (2011) 'Judge Praises Fortnum and Mason Protesters for "Common Sense of Decency"', *The Telegraph*, 17 November. https://www.telegraph.co.uk/news/uknews/law-and-order/8896852/Judge-praises-Fortnum-and-Mason-protesters-for-common-sense-of-decency.html. Accessed 16 December 2021.

No Author (2014) 'The Strange Death of Lazarus Averbuch', *Mysterious Chicago Tours*, 8 December. https://mysteriouschicago.com/the-strange-death-of-lazarus-averbuch. Accessed 16 April 2021.

O'Dwyer, E (2020) 'Covid-19 Mutual Aid Groups Have the Potential to Increase Intergroup Solidarity – but Can They Actually Do So?', *LSE Blogs*, 23 June. https://blogs.lse.ac.uk/politicsandpolicy/covid19-mutual-aid-solidarity. Accessed 1 February 2021.

Office of National Statistics (2021) 'Crime in England and Wales', June. https://www.ons.gov.uk/peoplepopulationandcommunity/crimeandjustice/datasets/crimeinenglandandwalesappendixtables. Accessed 1 December 2021.

Phillipopulos-Mihalopoulos, A (2015) *Spacial Justice: Body, Lawscape, Atmosphere*, Abingdon and New York: Routledge-Glasshouse.

Phillips, A (2015) *Unforbidden Pleasures*, Milton Keynes: Hamish Hamilton.

Plato (1925) *Symposium*, Henderson, G (ed), Lamb, M.R.W (trans), Cambridge, MA and London: Harvard University Press (Loeb).

Plato (2006) *The Republic, Books* VI–X, Shorey, P (trans), Cambridge, MA and London: Harvard University Press.

Porter, D (ed) (2006) *Vision on Fire: Emma Goldman on the Spanish Revolution*, Oakland, CA and Edinburgh: AK Press.

Porton, R (1999) *Film and the Anarchist Imagination*, London and New York: Verso.

Precarious Workers Brigade (No Date). 'About'. https://precariousworkersbrigade.tumblr.com/about. Accessed 20 October 2021.

Prichard, A (2007) 'Justice, Order and Anarchy: The International Political Theory of Pierre-Joseph Proudhon (1809–1865)', *Millennium: Journal of International Studies*, 35 (3), 623–645.

Proudhon, J.P (2005) 'The Authority Principle', in Guérin, D (ed), *No Gods No Masters: An Anthology of Anarchism*. Edinburgh, Oakland, CA and London: AK Press.

Proudhon, J.P (2011a) 'General Idea of the Revolution in the Nineteenth Century', in Mckay, I (ed), *Property is Theft: Pierre-Joseph Proudhon Anthology*, Edinburgh, Oakland, CA and London: AK Press.

Proudhon, J.P (2011b) 'What is Property?', in Mckay, I (ed), *Property is Theft!: Pierre-Joseph Proudhon Anthology*, Edinburgh, Oakland, CA and London: AK Press.

Punk Academic (2019) 'Extinction Rebellion: Credit, Criticism & Cops', *Critical Legal Thinking*, 29 April. http://criticallegalthinking.com/2019/04/29/extinction-rebellion-credit-criticism-cops. Accessed 29 April 2019.

Refugee Rescue (No Date) www.refugeerescue.org. Accessed 24 February 2021.

Results (No Date) 'World Poverty Statistics'. https://results.org/world-poverty. Accessed 2 January 2022.

Roberts, J.C (2016) *The Terms of Order: Political Science and the Myth of Leadership*, Chapel Hill: University of North Carolina Press.

Ross, K (2016) *Communal Luxury: The Political Imaginary of the Paris Commune*, London and New York: Verso.
Rossdale, C (2014) 'Dancing Ourselves to Death: The Subject of Emma Goldman's Nietzschean Anarchism', *Globalizations*, 12 (1), 116–133.
Rossdale, C (2019) *Resisting Militarism Direct Action and the Politics of Subversion*, Edinburgh: Edinburgh University Press.
Sahin, E and Khabat, A (2020) 'Communal Lifeboat: Direct Democracy in Rojava (NE Syria)', in Sitrin, M and Colectiva Sembrar (eds), *Pandemic Solidarity: Mutual Aid during the Covid-19 Crisis*, London: Pluto Press.
Schmitt, C (2005) *Political Theology: Four Chapters on the Concept of Sovereignty*, Schwab, G (trans), Chicago and London: Chicago University Press.
Schmitt, C (2008) *Constitutional Theory*, Seitzer, J (trans), Durham, NC and London: Duke University Press.
Schoenbauer, R (2016) 'Volunteers Who Saved Lives on Lesvos Nominated for Nobel Peace Prize', UNHCR, 7 October. https://www.unhcr.org/uk/news/latest/2016/10/57f7732d4/volunteers-saved-lives-lesvos-nominated-nobel-peace-prize.html. Accessed 5 August 2019.
Schultz, J (1998) *Reviving the Fourth Estate: Democracy, Accountability and the Media*, Cambridge: Cambridge University Press.
Schürmann, R (1990) *Heidegger: On Being and Acting: From Principles to Anarchy*, Bloomington: Indiana University Press.
Scott, J.C (1998) *Seeing Like a State: How Certain Schemes to Improve the Human Condition Have Failed*, New Haven, CT and London: Yale University Press.
Scott, J.C (2012) *Two Cheers for Anarchism: Six Easy Pieces on Autonomy, Dignity and Meaningful Work and Play*, Princeton, NJ: Princeton University Press.
Shannon, D, Nocella, J.A and Asımakopoulos, J (2012) 'Introduction: Anarchist Economics: A Holistic View', in Shannon, D, Nocella, J.A and Asimakopoulos, J (eds), *The Accumulation of Freedom: Writings on Anarchist Economics*. Edinburgh, Oakland, CA and Baltimore, MD: AK Press.
Sharpe, A (2002) *Transgender Jurisprudence: Dysphoric Bodies of Law*, Abingdon: Cavendish.
Sharpe, A (2010) *Foucault's Monsters and the Challenge of Law*, Abingdon and New York: Routledge-Glasshouse.
Shepard, B (2002) 'Building a Healing Community from ACT UP to Housing Works', in Shepard, B and Hayduk, R (eds), *From ACT UP to the WTO: Urban Protest And Community Building in the Era of Globalisation*, London and New York: Verso.
Shulman, A (1971) *To the Barricades: The Anarchist Life of Emma Goldman*, New York: Thomas Y. Crowell Company.
Skinner, Q (2009) *Visions of Politics: Hobbes and Civil Science, Volume* II, Cambridge and New York: Cambridge University Press.
Sloterdijk, P (1987) *Critique of Cynical Reason*, Minneapolis, MN and London: University of Minnesota Press.
Soble, A (1989) *Eros, Agape and Philia. Readings in the Philosophy of Love*, St. Paul, MN: Paragon House.
Sophocles (1984) *The Three Theban Plays: Antigone, Oedipus the King, Oedipus at Colonus*, Fagles, R (trans), London: Penguin Books.
Sophocles (1998) *Antigone*, Lloyd-Jones, H (trans), Cambridge, MA and London: Harvard University Press.
Spade, D (2020) *Mutual Aid*, London and New York: Verso.

Spannos, C (2012) 'Examining the History of Anarchist Economics to See the Future', in Shannon, D, Nocella, J.A and Asimakopoulos, J (eds), *The Accumulation of Freedom: Writings on Anarchist Economics*, Edinburgh, Oakland, CA and Baltimore, MD: AK Press.

Stirner, M (2006) *The Ego and Its Own*, Leopold, D (ed), Cambridge: Cambridge University Press.

Stone, M (2011) 'Law, Ethics and Levinas's Concept of Anarchy', *Australian Feminist Law Journal*, 35 (1), 89–105.

Stone, M, Wall, I, Douzinas, C (eds) (2012) *New Critical Legal Thinking: Law and the Political*, Abingdon: Routledge.

Taylor, A and Gessen, K (2011) *Occupy!: Scenes from Occupied America*, Brooklyn, NY: Verso.

Taylor, M and Gayle, D (2019) 'Extinction Rebellion Targets Heathrow as Activists Held in Jail', *The Guardian*, 18 April. https://www.theguardian.com/environment/2019/apr/18/climate-activists-target-heathrow-airport-as-protests-continue. Accessed 18 April 2019.

The Emma Goldman Papers (No Date) 'Birth Control Pioneer'. https://www.lib.berkeley.edu/goldman/MeetEmmaGoldman/birthcontrolpioneer.html. Accessed 15 August 2013.

Tuitt, P (2004) *Race, Law, Resistance*, Abingdon: Glasshouse Press.

Virno, P (2008) *Multitude: Between Innovation and Negation*, Los Angeles: Semiotext(e).

Wall, R.I (2012) *Human Rights and Constituent Power*, Abingdon and New York: Routledge-Glasshouse.

Wall, R.I (2021) *Law and Disorder: Sovereignty, Protest, Atmosphere*, Abingdon and New York: Routledge-Glasshouse.

Ward, C (1996) *Anarchy in Action*, London: Freedom Press.

Watson, W (2015) *The Lost Second Book of Aristotle's Poetics*, Chicago and London: The University of Chicago Press.

Williams, P (1991) *The Alchemy of Race and Rights*, Cambridge, MA: Harvard University Press.

Woodcock, G (1983) *Anarchism: A History of Libertarian Ideas and Movements*, Middlesex and New York: Penguin Books Ltd.

Wretched of the Earth (2019) 'An Open Letter to Extinction Rebellion', *Red Pepper*, 3 May. https://www.redpepper.org.uk/an-open-letter-to-extinction-rebellion. Accessed 4 May 2019.

Zupančič, A (2008) *The Odd One In: On Comedy*, Cambridge, MA and London: MIT Press.

Cases, Statutes, Filmography and YouTube videos

Case

Goldman [&] Berkman v United States; Transcript of Record 1917 Sept. 25 Supreme Court of the United States.

Statutes

Gender Recognition Act 2004.
The Marriage (Same Sex Couples) Act 2013.
Immigration Act 2014.

Films

Anarchism in America, Steven Fischler and Joel Sucher, USA, 1981.
Love Actually, Richard Curtis, UK, USA, France, 2003.
The Deserted, Tsai Ming Liang, Taiwan, 2017.

YouTube Films

2005.07.04 CIRCA, No Creator, YouTube, https://www.youtube.com/watch?v=r2f_US4Pvd8 Accessed 20 October 2021.
C.I.R.C.A. G8 Road Blockade, No Creator, YouTube, https://www.youtube.com/watch?v=MX0aQU9x0Z4. Accessed 20 October 2021.
Clandestine Insurgent Rebel Clown Army in Rostock 2007, No Creator, YouTube, https://youtu.be/3h1CH0Vchv8. Accessed 9 September 2021.
Rebel Clown Army Fights Army Recruitment (and Wins), No Creator, YouTube, https://www.youtube.com/watch?v=bOOLLk9xlkY. Accessed 20 October 2021.
Send in the Clowns, No Creator, YouTube, https://www.youtube.com/watch?v=2R3dmu9uZXo. Accessed 20 October 2021.

Index

abortion 67–68
accumulation 10, 155
Accumulation of Freedom: Writings of Anarchist Economics, The 155
'active nihilism' 120
aesthetics 20, 122
Afghanistan 149
African Americans 62
Agamben, G. 71, 137
Ahmed, Sara 35
alienation 63
Al-Qaeda 120
Al-Sira 21
Althusser, Louis 25
ambivalence: of emotions 93; of law 94; of love 94, 96, 111–112
anarchization 9, 12, 13, 55, 78
Anarchism in America 113–115
'anarchist calisthenics' 53, 57
anarcho-communism 25, 155–158, 160, 162–163, 167, 168
anarchy 2
Anarchy in Action 153
Ancient Greece 14, 73, 77, 94–95, 125
Ancient Rome 73
animals 34, 35, 160–161
Anonymous 7
anti-G8 demonstrations 17, 50, 66, 114, 142–144
anti-globalisation demonstrations 66
anti-globalisation movement 143
Antigone 120–121
appropriation 21, 72
Arendt, Hannah 60
Aristodemou, Maria 90, 95, 97–99
Aristotle 121, 126–130, 134
art of life 14
Asimakopoulos, J. 155–156

asylum seekers 42–43
attachments 5
austerity 15, 77, 84
authority 1, 77; juridical 14–15; legitimacy of 1–2
autonomy 26, 50, 51

Badiou, Alain 89, 91
Bakhtin, M. 144
Barthes, Ronald 87
Bedouins 21
Bergson, Henri 118, 119, 122
Berkman, Alexander 39–42, 82, 101, 103, 110
Berlant, Lauren 116
Bhandar, Brenna 20–22
biologism 158–159
birth control 40
Black Lives Matter (BLM) 50, 55, 167
Black people 8, 12, 159–160
Blast, The 39, 41, 82, 104
bodies 57
Bodies that Matter 34
Boétie, Etienne de la 16, 55–57, 59, 60, 61
Bogad, M. 142–144
Bookchin, Murray 113
Book of the Courtier, The 130
Boots 84
Bottici, C. 51
bourgeois values 88–89
Boyer, John 109
Brasília 8
Bratich, Z.J. 138
Brazil 8, 11
Brazilian kites 161
Breitbart New Network 83
British National Boat Institute 164

Brown, Esther 159–160
Brown, Wendy 46
Buddhism 6
Bush, George W. 142, 143
Butler, Judith 23, 34, 123–124, 130, 136
Butler, Patrick 10

Cage, John 5
capitalism 1, 13, 156–157, 162–163; and individualism 72–73; and love 89, 100; and property law 21; and the State 13, 46; racial 21
'Carnival for Full Enjoyment' 143–146
Carson, Anne 90–95, 111
cartoons 116
Castiglione, B 130
censorship 75
chance dance 5
Charlie Hebdo 116
children 10; and obedience 56, 59–60
Chomski, Noam 10–11, 13, 136
choreography 5–7
Christianity 67–68
CIRCA *see* Clandestine Insurgent Rebel Clown Army
civil disobedience 9, 84, 146, 166
civil society 26, 29, 167
civil unrest 46
Clandestine Insurgent Rebel Clown Army (CIRCA) 15, 17, 114, 117, 118, 139, 142–147
Clark, P.J. 72
classical anarchism 8, 11, 15, 16, 22, 24, 44–45, 47–51, 151–156
cleromancy 5
Cleyre, Voltairine de 100
co-existence 35
collective conscience 28
collective subjectivity 57
Colonial Lives of Property 20
colonisation 12–13; complicity of law in 22; and property 20–21, 71
comedy: conservative 125; definition of 127–128; false 125; origins of 128; as relational 133; role of 118; theories of 122–135; true 126; universality of 114–115, 121, 125; as a weapon 116
commonwealth 64
communal justice 28
Communal Luxury: The Political Imaginary of the Paris Commune 158
communism 155, 163

Communism of Love, The 89
Comstock Law of 1873 40
Concluding Unscientific Postscript 133
Conquest of Bread, The 154, 155, 157, 160, 162, 168
conscience 28
conscription 39–42, 103
Constitutional Theory 137
contracts: legal definition 31–32; zero-hour 10; *see also* social contract
Courage of Truth, The 74
Court of Queen Eleanor of France 97
Court of the Countess of Champagne 96, 97
Covid-19 pandemic 9, 14, 18, 119, 149, 164
cowardice 56
creativity 1–14
crime 36
criminal actions 13
criminal law 36
Critchley, Simon 91, 97, 114, 117–121
Critical Inquiry 116
Critical Legal Studies 90, 95
criticism 64–67
critique 1, 6
Critique of Cynical Reason 140
Critique of Judgment 132
cultural norms 57
cultural practices 57
cultural stereotyping 1
Cunningham, Merce 1, 2, 5–7
customs 34
Cynics 140–141
Czolgosz, Leon 13, 65–66, 147

dancing 1, 5–7
Darwin, Charles 161
Dean, Jodi 167
decency 69
decolonisation 21–22
Deleuze, Gilles 93
democracy 33, 46, 66, 83
democratic citizenship 45
demonisation 13
Derrida, Jacques 1
Descent of Man, The 161
Deserted, The 4
destruction 1–2; as a creative force 2–4
Diogenes Laertius 140
Diogenes the Cynic 139–141
disobedience 16, 53–55, 57, 61–74, 85; civil 9, 84; everyday acts of 53–54, 57; and personal growth 61; and pleasure 59

dispossession 10, 21, 155
Douzinas, Costas 42
draft 39–42
Duffy, Nick 24

economic adjustments 26
economic inequality 4, 36, 46
economic insecurity 12
economics 156–158
Edinburgh 143–146
Ego and Its Own, The 61–63
elite 44
Emma Goldman: Political Thinking in the Streets 141
Emma Goldman: Revolution as a Way of Life 105
emoticons 3
emotions 93
Engels, Frederick 61, 71–72
England 36, 42, 162
environmental activism 7, 165–167
environmental justice 4
equality 29–30, 47, 49–51; and democracy 46; as justice 30, 33; and law 19–20, 26; moral 26; relative 46; and the State 25–27, 46–47, 50–51
Eros the Bittersweet 92, 94
erotic love 16–17, 87, 89–90, 92–93, 99, 105
ethical subjects 120–121
ethics 20, 120–121
Ethics 150
Exchange 5
exclusion 33
Extinction Rebellion (XR) 4, 7, 9, 14, 50, 55, 165–167

Falk, Candase 104, 106
Fanon, Franz 12, 22
fear 5
fearless speech *see* parrhesia
Fearless Speech 74, 76
feminism 34
Ferguson, K.E. 141
Film and the Anarchist Imagination 114
Fischler, Steven 113, 114
Fitzpatrick, Peter 45, 94
Floyd, George 46
food banks 10
Fortnum and Mason 84

Foucault, Michel 1; on art of life 14; on parrhesia 73–77, 82–83; on power 45, 51, 154
foundations 3–5
France 46–47, 55, 116
freedom 47–49; sexual 88; social versus individual 67–68; and the State 46–47; *see also* freedoms
freedoms 26
free speech 74, 75
French Revolution 45
Freud, Sigmund 122–123, 131–133, 135, 142
friendship 98

Garnier, Eric 46
gender 34
gender-neutral passports 152
Gender Recognition Act 2004 23, 30
Gender Recognition Certificate (GRC) 23–24
Gender Trouble 34
German Ideology, The 61, 71
Germany 53
Gilman-Opalsky, Richard 89, 90, 99–100
global environmental crisis 9
Golder, Ben 45
Goldman and Sachs 85
Goldman, Emma 1, 13, 15–17, 24, 61, 65–66, 100–104, 147; on African Americans 62; on freedom 48–49; on law 22, 23, 36–44, 49; on love 89–90, 104–111; on parrhesia 77–83, 85–86; use of humour 113–118, 139, 141–142
Goodrich, Peter 20, 43; on love 90, 95–99
Gornick, Vivian 105–106
Government of No One, The 1, 8
Government of Self and Others, The 74
governments: and parrhesia 73–74; tyrannical 55–56
grammar 3
Greece 4
Gros, Frederick 73
Guevara, Che 88

habits 34
Harbold, W. 29
Hartman, Sadiya 159–160
Harvey, David 10, 155
hate crimes 24
healthcare systems 11–12
Hegel, G.W.F. 123–125

Heidegger, M. 2–3
Heidegger on Being and Acting: From Principles to Anarchy 2
Heraclitus 34
Her Majesty's Revenues and Customs Office (HRMC) 85–86
Hess, Karl 114
hierarchies 1
High Court of Love 96
Hobbes, T. 26, 35, 130–131, 135–137
Horvat, Srećko 88–90, 99–100
human development 61–62
humanism 63
Human Nature and De Corpore Politico 130, 131
human rights 124
Human Rights Act 1998 124
humour 17, 113–147; distinction between wit and 123; theories of 122–135
hypocrisy 41

I Ching (Book of Changes) 5–6
idealism 73
Immigration Act 2014 152
inauthenticity 121
Indigenous populations 21
Indigenous practices 21
Indignados 4, 55
individual conscience 28
individualism 46, 49, 61; and capitalism 72–73; liberal 63; possessive 72; unique 62–63, 72
individual justice 28–29
Infinitely Demanding: Ethics of Commitment, Politics and Resistance 117, 119, 120
infrapolitics 46
instinct 34–35
institutional law 23, 35, 37–39, 44

Johnson, Boris 118–119, 125
jokes 135–139; *see also* joking
Jokes and Their Relation to the Unconscious 122
joking 131–132; *see also* jokes
Jorday, John L. 142, 143
juridical authority 14–15
justice: communal 28; commutative 30–31, 33, 44; distributive 30; equality as 30, 33; as immanent 27–28; individual 28–29; and law 19–20, 29, 95; Proudhon on 27–31, 33; and the State 25–26, 50–51; universal 48–49

Kant, Immanuel 73, 123–124, 132–133, 135
Kershner, Jacob A. 78–79
Kierkegaard, S. 132–135
Kinna, Ruth 1–2, 4, 6, 8–9, 12, 13, 14, 55, 78, 83
Kisselgoff, Anna 1, 2, 5, 6, 7
knowledge 75
Kropotkin, Peter 16, 17, 24, 149–164, 168; on freedom 48; on law 22, 23, 32–36, 44, 54

Lacan, Jacques-Marie-Émile 99, 121
language 3, 137–138; and obedience 58–59
Languages of Law 43
laughter: absence of 114–118, 121–122, 125, 135, 141; Bakhtin on 144; incongruity theory 121, 130, 132–134; and pleasure 132–134; and political life 119; production of 127–128, 131, 133; role of 118; and superiority 121, 130–131; and tension release 121, 130; theories of 17, 121–135
L'Avare 130
law 16, 19–52; as an aid 25–33; alternative 16; ambivalence of 94; and colonisation 12–13, 22; contemporary anarchist thinkers on 44–52; corrupt 44; criminal 36; critique of 16, 19–20, 36–37, 43; Goldman on 36–44; history of 33–34; and hypocrisy 41; inconsistencies and paradoxes of 42–43; institutional 23, 35, 37–39, 44; juridical 16; Kropotkin on 32–36, 44, 54; limits of 19n1, 32; and love 95–100; man-made 37, 38, 39, 41; natural 37–39; prohibitive character of 58–59; Proudhon on 22–23, 25, 27, 44; and the State 13–14; and tradition 43; and Western democratic governments 19; *see also* property law
Law in the Courts of Love 96
Law, Psychoanalysis, Society 97
Ledru-Rollin, Alexandre August 31
legal justice 29, 95
legitimacy 1–2
Leopold 61, 62
Leval, Gaston 157
Leviathan 26, 131, 136
LGBTQ citizens 119
liberalism 61–63

libertarian movements 10, 11
Living My Life 90, 105n13, 106, 117
Locke, John 26–27, 29
love 16, 87–112; ambivalence of 94, 96, 111–112; and anarchism 100–111; and capitalism 89, 100; Carson on 90–95, 111; description of 87; erotic 16–17, 87, 89–90, 92–93, 99, 105; free 17, 88, 91; Goldman on 89–90, 104–111; as an illusion 98; and law 95–100; and marriage 97; as a movement 94–95, 97, 99–100; non-possessive 90; Platonic ideal of 91; radical 88, 90; same sex 94
Love Actually 98
Lover Discourse: Fragments, A 87
Lyotard, Jean-Francois 151

marginalised groups 19n1, 20
marriage 17, 97; same-sex 124
Marriage (Same Sex Couples) Act 2013 124
Marshall, Peter 150, 162
Marx, Karl 61, 71–72
May, Todd 47, 51, 152–155, 158
McDonald, Angus 23n2
McKinley, William 13, 65–66, 147
middle class 44
militarism 42
mimetic arts 134
Molière 130
Moore, Sir Thomas 14
moral actions 123
moral equality 26
Morreall, John 130, 131, 133
Mother Earth 39, 41, 62n3, 83, 101, 110
mothers 10
Multitude: Between Innovation and Negation 136
music 5
Muslims 119, 137
mutual aid 9, 10, 14, 17–18, 25, 46, 148–169
Mutual Aid 34, 150, 160–161

nationalism 42
naturalism 152–153
natural law 37–39
nature 34; *see also* state of nature
neoliberalism 10, 139, 155
Nettlau, Max 61
Neubrandenburg 53
Newman, Saul 7–10, 13, 14, 35, 47–52, 83, 151–152; on law 22, 23n2; on Max Stirner 62–63

newness 3–4
Ngai, Sianne 116
Nietzsche, Friedrich 153
Nocella, J.A. 155–156
non-hierarchical techniques 9, 51, 96
norms 23–24, 62, 72; cultural 57

obedience 54–61; and language 58–59; as a learned practice 56; limits of 60; linked to the body 57; and pleasure 59; political 55; psychological reasons of 55, 57–60; *see also* disobedience
Occupy movement 7–8, 14, 50, 167
Occupy Wall Street 15, 55, 167–168
Odd One In, The 125
On Jokes and Their Relation to the Unconscious 131
Ortellando, Pablo 10, 11
ownership 21; *see also* property

parrhesia (fearless speech) 16, 55, 77–84; and democracy 83; Foucault on 73–77
'passive nihilism' 120
Pausanias 94
pedestrian crossings 53
penal system 13
performative speech acts 74
performativity 34
persecution 42–43
personal growth 61
phallic songs 127, 128
Philips, Adam 16, 55, 57–61, 69
Philosophical Investigations 137
Philosophy of Laughter and Humour, The 130
physis 93
platform economies 10
Plato 83, 91, 130, 140
pleasure 59, 132–134
Poetics 121, 126–127, 134
poetry 127, 129
poikilos nomos 94
police 38, 39; brutality 7, 8, 46, 167
political actions 50
political cartoons 116
political efficacy 15
political obedience 55
Political Philosophy of Poststructuralist Anarchism, The 51
political power 44–45
Political Theology 137
politics 8, 166; poststructuralist perspective 49; radical 88–90; recognition 8

Porton, Richard 114
possessiveness 17
Post Anarchism 47
postanarchism 47, 51
postcolonial narratives 20
postmodern philosophy 48
poststructuralist philosophy 48, 49
poverty 10, 149
power 153–155; forms of 51; Foucault on 45, 51, 154; political 44–45
Power of a Lie, The 109
Precarious Life 136
Precarious Workers Brigade 117
pre-formulated pathways 53–54
principles 123
prisons 36, 38, 62n3
Pritchard, Alex 27
private ownership 21; *see also* private property; property ownership
private property 18, 69, 71, 101, 156–157; abolition of 18, 36, 102, 156–157, 160, 162, 168
privatisation 10–12
profit 10
profiteering 18
prohibitions 58–59
property: colonisation of 71; communal 156–157; destruction of 1; inward 68–69, 71; liberal conception of 69–70, 72; outward 68, 69, 72; Proudhon on 70–71, 100–101; redistribution 13, 14, 156–157; relational aspect of 71–72; in Roman law 71; as a social good 70–71; Stirner on 68–71; types of 68, 71; usurpation of 71; *see also* private property; property law; property ownership
property law: and capitalism 21; and colonisation 20–21; decolonisation of 21–22
property ownership 38, 70–71; and inequality 38, 70; as legal fiction 71; *see also* private property
prophesy 75
Prophet Muhammed 116
Proudhon, Pierre-Joseph 16, 24, 101–102; on justice 27–31, 33; on law 22–23, 25, 27, 44; on property 70–71, 100–101; on social contract 32–33
public services 10–12
public speaking 74
punishment 36, 38

questions 101–104
quotidian concerns 72

Rabelais, François 144
Rabelais and His World 144
racial capitalism 21
racial inequalities 21
racism 61–62, 167
Rackete, Carola 164
Radicality of Love, The 88
radical love 88, 90
radical politics 88–90
reason 2–3, 123
rebellions 46, 56–57, 60
rebels 60
recession 100–101
recognition politics 8
Red Brigades 120
Refugee Rescue 164
refugees 8, 18, 42, 164
Reitman, Ben 101, 104–111
religion 61, 62, 63, 69
remuneration 18, 157, 163, 165, 168
Republic, The 83
resistance 1–2
revolution 46
rhetoric 74–75
Roberts, Cedric J. 67
Rocker, Rudolph 61
Roman law 71
romantic comedies 98
Ross, Kristin 158
Rossdale, Chris 57
Rousseau, J.-J 31–32
rule of law 16, 27
ruling class 35, 36
Russia 149
Russian Revolution 88–89
Ryoki, André 10, 11

sage 75
Sappho 92–93
Schmitt, Carl 136, 137
Schopenhauer, Arthur 132
Schürmann, Reiner 2–4, 6–7
Scott, James C. 8–10, 13, 14, 16; on disobedience 53–54, 57; on law 45–47
season tickets 163
security 12
Seeing Like a State 8
Selective Draft Act 1917 39, 42
Selective Service Act 1917 41, 82, 103

self-creation 69
self-government 11, 14, 47–48
self-interest 26, 28, 30
self-love 98
self-mastery 14, 16
servitude 59, 60
sex 34; and radical politics 88–89
sexual freedom 88
sexual permissiveness 88
Shannon, D. 155–156
Shulman, A. 40
Sisters Uncut 50
Skinner, Quentin 130, 131
slavery 33
Sloterdijk, P. 140
social cohesion 35
social conflicts 26
social contract 31–33
Social Contract 31–32
social contractarians 26, 31
social media 3
social rights 26
social settlements 10
social war 31
Society Must be Defended 51
Socrates 87
Sophocles 120
Sovereignty 136–137
Spain 4
Spanish Civil War 157
Spannos, Chris 156–158
Spencer, Herbert 131
spontaneity 59
Starbucks 84
State: abolition of 8, 10–11; and capitalism 13, 46; as driver for change 7; and enslavement 61; and equality 25–27, 46–47, 50–51; exodus from 136; and freedom 46–47; and humour 17, 117; as an illegitimate institution 10, 12; and justice 25–26, 50–51; and law 13–14; neoliberal 10, 13; role of 8–9, 45–46
state of nature 26–28, 34–35, 45–46, 153
Steimer, Mollie 113
Stirner, Max 12, 16, 24, 55, 60–73; on property 68–71
Sucher, Joel 113, 114
suffrage 45
superiority 121, 130–131
Symposium 87

Taliban 149
Taoism 6
tax evasion 84–85
techne 75, 77, 151, 152
Terms to Order, The 67
text messages 3
three-pronged method 21
Top Shop 84
Torse 6
tradition 43
tragedy 125
transgender people 23–24, 30
Treveylan, Matt 142, 143
Trump, Donald 83
Truong, N. 89
truth 55, 66–68, 73–77, 140; duty to speak 77; right to tell 83
Tsai Ming Liang 4
Tudor, David 5
Two Cheers for Anarchism 8, 45, 53
Two Treatises of Government 26

Ukraine 149
UK Uncut 15, 16, 77–78, 83–86, 117
Unforbidden Pleasures 58, 59
Universality 48–50, 123–130, 134–136; of comedy 114–115, 121, 125; Kant's principle of 123; types of 124
universal justice 48–49
universal society 101
usages 33–34
USSR 88
utopia 14

values 123; bourgeois 87–88; fundamental transvaluations of 155; moral 158; new 110; Universal 130
Verson, Jen 142, 143
violence 1–14, 113
Virno, Paulo 128, 136–139
virtual reality (VR) 4
Visons of Politics: Hobbes and Civil Science 131
Vodaphone 84

wage system 162, 163, 168
war 42
Ward, Colin 153
Warrington, Ronnie 42
Watson, W. 127
Weinberg, Harry 100
welfare cuts 10
welfare system 10

What is Communist Anarchism?
    100–101
Wilde, Oscar 60, 61
Wilful Subjects 35
wisdom 75
wit 121–135, 139–147
Wittgenstein, Ludwig 136
women: Black 159–160; Muslim 119
World Trade Organization (WTO) 66
World War I 39, 103

World War II 142
Wretched of the Earth, The 22
WTO *see* World Trade Organization

XR *see* Extinction Rebellion

Ya Basta Association 117

zero-hour contracts 10
Zupančič, A. 125, 128, 130

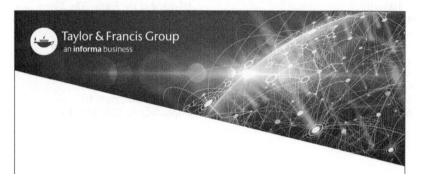